W9-CZL-316

750

320

D

The North American Idea

Other Books by Robert A. Pastor

Democracy and Elections in North America: What Can We Learn From Our Neighbors? (Editor, 2004)

Not Condemned to Repetition: The United States and Nicaragua (2002). Revised edition of *Condemned to Repetition* (1987)

Toward a North American Community: Lessons from the Old World for the New (2001)

Exiting the Whirlpool: U.S. Foreign Policy Toward Latin America and the Caribbean (2001). Revised edition of *Whirlpool* (1993)

A Century's Journey: How The Great Powers Shape the World (Editor, 1999)

The Controversial Pivot: The U.S. Congress and North America (Editor with Rafael Fernandez de Castro, 1998)

Collective Responses to Regional Problems: The Case of Latin America and the Caribbean (Editor with Carl Kaysen and Laura Reed, 1994)

Democracy in the Caribbean: Political, Economic, and Social Perspectives (Editor with Jorge Dominguez and Delisle Worrell, 1993)

Integration with Mexico: Options for U.S. Policy (1993)

Democracy in the Americas: Stopping the Pendulum (Editor, 1989)

Limits to Friendship: The United States and Mexico (with Jorge Castañeda, 1988)

Latin America's Debt Crisis: Adjusting to the Past or Planning for the Future? (Editor, 1987)

Migration and Development in the Caribbean: The Unexplored Connection (Editor, 1985)

Congress and the Politics of U.S. Foreign Economic Policy (1980)

THE
NORTH AMERICAN
IDEA

A Vision of a Continental Future

ROBERT A. PASTOR

OXFORD
UNIVERSITY PRESS

OXFORD
UNIVERSITY PRESS

Oxford University Press is a department of the University of Oxford.
It furthers the University's objective of excellence in research, scholarship,
and education by publishing worldwide.

Oxford   New York
Auckland   Cape Town   Dar es Salaam   Hong Kong   Karachi
Kuala Lumpur   Madrid   Melbourne   Mexico City   Nairobi
New Delhi   Shanghai   Taipei   Toronto

With offices in
Argentina   Austria   Brazil   Chile   Czech Republic   France   Greece
Guatemala   Hungary   Italy   Japan   Poland   Portugal   Singapore
South Korea   Switzerland   Thailand   Turkey   Ukraine   Vietnam

Oxford is a registered trade mark of Oxford University Press
in the UK and certain other countries.

Published in the United States of America by
Oxford University Press
198 Madison Avenue, New York, NY 10016

© Robert A. Pastor 2011

First issued as an Oxford University Press paperback, 2012.

All rights reserved. No part of this publication may be reproduced, stored in a retrieval system, or transmitted,
in any form or by any means, without the prior permission in writing of Oxford University Press, or as expressly
permitted by law, by license, or under terms agreed with the appropriate reproduction rights organization.
Inquiries concerning reproduction outside the scope of the above should be sent to the Rights Department,
Oxford University Press, at the address above.

You must not circulate this work in any other form
and you must impose this same condition on any acquirer.

Library of Congress Cataloging-in-Publication Data
Pastor, Robert A.
The North American idea : a vision of a continental future / Robert Pastor.
    p.   cm.
Includes bibliographical references and index.
ISBN 978-0-19-978241-3 (hardcover); 978-0-19-993402-7 (paperback)
1. Free trade—North America. 2. Canada. Treaties, etc. 1992 Oct. 7.
3. North America—Economic integration. I. Title.
HF1746.P373   2011
382.'917—dc22   2011006036

9 8 7 6 5 4 3 2 1

Printed in the United States of America
on acid-free paper

To my brothers Bruce and Donald Pastor

for their friendship and constant support,

And to the Next Generation of North Americans

Contents

Part II: Trespassing

Part III: The North American Advantage

Figures and Tables

Preface:
Memoir of a North Americanist

Every man takes the limits of his own field of vision for the limits of the world.

—Arthur Schopenhauer

Pat Buchanan, speechwriter for Richard Nixon, TV commentator, and erstwhile candidate for the Republican presidential nomination, marshals words and sends them into combat. This time I was the target, and Lou Dobbs, the former CNN anchor, was his ally in the assault. Buchanan commented on an outburst by Dobbs and asked: "What had detonated the mild-mannered CNN anchor?" Only Buchanan would call Dobbs mild or mannered, but the answer to his question was me. Dobbs called me "the architect of this North American Union." Buchanan agreed it was "a mind-boggling concept" and berated me for testifying before the Senate Committee on Foreign Relations that "U.S. borders should be erased and the three countries merged."[1]

Never mind that his accusations were untrue. Each time this dynamic duo let loose on TV or radio, my e-mail inbox filled with the most scurrilous attacks. "It's true you are a treasonness [*sic*] wretch, and you should be deported to Mexico or even Canada," wrote Philip DiNardo of Wilmington, North Carolina. Others were less polite: "You are an ENEMY of USA and should be hung for treason," wrote Tom Neighbors, who concluded with a graphic expletive. Some neighbor.

The idea that the strongest nation in the world would permit its two weaker neighbors to undermine its sovereignty is so absurd that one needs to ask why Dobbs and Buchanan fear such a scenario, or why they hold me responsible.[2]

Let me state my views clearly: I believe that the future of the United States, Canada, and Mexico depends on our constructing a very different relationship than we have contemplated. It will be a community of three sovereign states, not a union, and it would not erase the borders. This book will explain why we need to embark on this journey and what the destination will look like.

My journey began where I was born, in Newark, New Jersey. I had no idea that I was also born in North America, but during the course of a career that has taken me around the world many times, and through most of the states and provinces of Mexico, Canada, and the United States, I came to see myself as both an American and a North American.

I am writing this book for all three North American nations, but particularly for my fellow Americans because we do not see the problems facing our continent as clearly as our neighbors. That is because all of the world's crises are deposited at our door, and we are unaware that decisions made by our leaders have unintended and often hugely adverse effects on our neighbors. We continue to approach transnational problems as if our neighbors are responsible when in fact, we share the responsibility, and solutions are only possible with closer cooperation. We have forgotten the point of our nation's first foreign policy—the Monroe Doctrine—that our security depends first on our relationship with our neighbors.

Today, the capability of the United States to lead is impeded by too much power and too limited vision. As a nation, we cannot see ourselves the way the world sees us, and until we do, we cannot lead the world through the new challenges that await us. The path toward that new style of leadership runs first through Ottawa and Mexico City. We need to find new ways to relate to our neighbors if we are to discover a new way to exercise global leadership.

Franklin Roosevelt's "Good Neighbor Policy" to Latin America in the 1930s proved to be the experiment that permitted us to design the architecture for a new world system of international institutions in the 1940s. We are at a similar moment in the twenty-first century, and by incorporating the "North American idea" into our consciousness, we can begin to explore new designs for our region and eventually for the world. The "North American Idea" is both simple and consequential: It means that all three nations take into account the interests of the others as each conducts its domestic and foreign policies. It means that all three countries undertake together the task of designing a continental future and a genuine partnership that goes beyond rhetoric to a clear definition of a community in North America.

As a young national security advisor for Latin America during the late 1970s, I visited Mexico for discussions with a middle-level official in Mexico's budget department. We were friends since we did post-graduate degrees at Harvard. I asked whether he thought the U.S.-Canadian Automotive Agreement of 1965 should include Mexico. He rejected the idea, but when he ascended to the presidency of his country a decade later, in December 1988, he—Carlos Salinas de Gortari—reversed 160 years of protectionism and anti-Americanism and proposed a much bolder idea, the North American Free Trade Agreement (NAFTA).

That agreement unleashed forces that accelerated the integration of the economies and societies of the three countries of North America and also democratized Mexico. By 2000, however, NAFTA ran out of steam, and countervailing forces emerged to halt and reverse integration. Groups from the Left feared job loss due to trade; from the Right, they feared waves of migrants and a loss of sovereignty.

Added to these fears was the terrifying attacks of 9/11, which introduced new restrictions on the borders. The open door of America began to close. Our welcome was transformed into a warning: "Stop, or I'll shoot!" From the Second World War to 9/11, the United States was a leader in tearing down walls—of imperialism, trade and investment barriers, immigration, travel. All of this changed after 9/11, and no nations have felt the impact more directly than Canada and Mexico.

That is why we need to re-think our role in the world, starting in North America, and aim to build a community. Only that will make us secure and competitive. Only then will we have enhanced our capacity to lead. This book defines such a community, explains why it is needed and what it would do, and proposes a strategy to reach that goal.

Robert A. Pastor
Washington, D.C.

Acknowledgments

Like North America, this book has been a long time in the making.

My intellectual path to North America began in Mexico in the mid-1980s when I was a Fulbright Professor at El Colegio de Mexico. Since then, thousands of people and dozens of institutions in Mexico and Canada helped me to understand the many sides of the "North American Idea." Like Mexico during its debt crises, I owe more than I can repay to many people.

As the national security advisor for Latin America from 1977–81, I was puzzled at the difficulty of U.S.-Mexican relations, and I used my time as a professor to learn from my students, colleagues, and many others. I am particularly grateful to my friend and collaborator Jorge Castañeda, who would later become foreign minister, for helping me understand why there were *Limits to Friendship*, the title of our book. Just as the book was published, Mexico emerged from its cocoon and began its transition toward freer trade and democracy. I worked on both issues. As director of the election-monitoring program at The Carter Center, I was the first to be invited by Mexico to monitor elections in 1992, and returned in 1997, 2000, and 2006. As an advisor to then-Governor Bill Clinton's campaign in 1992, I discussed with Mexican President Carlos Salinas the parameters of what became the side-agreements to NAFTA.

With the support of the Brookings Institution, Rafael Fernandez de Castro, a Mexican scholar who served as national security advisor to President Calderon, and I edited *The United States Congress and North America*, about why Congress is as important as the presidents of the United States and Mexico and the prime minister of Canada in shaping the continent's future. C. Fred Bergsten and the International Institute for Economics provided support for me to study Europe's experience in integration in order to avoid its mistakes and adapt its success for North America, and the result was *Toward a North American Community: Lessons from the Old World for the New*. After completing that book, I moved to American University and founded the Center for

North American Studies, where thirty-six faculty and hundreds of students from all three countries taught and learned about the policy challenges faced by North America.

My appreciation for the Canadian perspective grew as I travelled in Canada giving lectures at a dozen universities, and as I worked with distinguished senior fellows to AU's Center for North American Studies from Canada, including former Prime Minister Joe Clark, legal scholar Maureen McTeer, trade negotiator Michael Hart, and economist James Dean. We also benefited from senior fellows from Mexico, including Marcela Celorio, Raul Benitez, Isidro Morales, and Daniel Hernandez.

The Council on Foreign Relations in New York and counterparts in Mexico and Canada invited me to co-chair a tri-national panel that produced in the spring of 2005, *Building a North American Community*. The experience of working with senior statesmen and women from the three countries persuaded me that a North American approach was far more likely to succeed in improving relations than the traditional dual-bilateral approach. The three governments appropriated some of the language from the report but, regrettably, little of the substance.

Among the many other colleagues who advised me on the issues, read drafts, or developed ideas that were building blocks to the North American Idea, let me mention Jason Ackerman, Sergio Aguayo, Greg Anderson, Robert Ayres, Miguel Basañez, Stephen Blank, Robert Blecker, Philip Brenner, Jorge Castañeda, Jack Citrin, Stephen Clarkson, Thomas D'Aquino, James Dean, Anthony DePalma, Michelle Egan, Joseph Eldridge, Dan Erikson, Christine Frechette, Gordon Giffin, Frank Graves, Michael Hart, Carla Hills, Randy Henning, Gary Hufbauer, Roberta Jacobson, Jennifer Jeffs, Stephen Kull, Abraham Lowenthal, Laura MacDonald, James McHugh, R. Craig McNamara, Shoon Murray, Neil Nevitte, Carlos Pascual, Tony Quainton, Colin Robertson, Andres Rozental, Christopher Sands, Jeffrey Schott, Isabel Studer, and Sidney Weintraub. I am grateful to American University—and especially, Benjamin Ladner, former President, Louis Goodman, Dean of the School of International Service, and Neil Kerwin, current President—for helping to establish and support the Center for North American Studies.

I have been blessed by numerous superb research assistants over the years, including Nicole Byrd, Anthony Elmo, John Henderson, Joanna Mantello, Helen McClure, Emily Phillips, Ingrid Specht, Vassia Stoilov, Anne Swanson, Chris Wilson, and Aimel Rios Wong. I am especially appreciative of the extraordinary effort and skills of Tom Long, a doctoral candidate at American

University, who helped with research, editing, data collection, and construction of the many tables and figures in the book.

Many officials from Mexico, Canada, and the United States shared with me their views confidentially, and so I will not mention them here, but the good news is that the number of officials who understand the logic of the North American Idea is growing.

Despite all of this advice, and in part because some may disagree with parts of this book, I alone assume full responsibility.

John Wright, my resourceful agent, and David McBride, the meticulous senior editor at Oxford University Press, were initially skeptical of the North American Idea. Their probing questions forced me to do more research and refine my arguments. Despite their reservations, they never lost faith in the enterprise, and my reward came when they told me that the book had persuaded them that the logic of the North American Idea was so compelling that they believed it would change the minds of the skeptics.

I cannot conclude a book without thanking my wife, Margy, not only for putting up with me as I slogged through my seventeenth book, but also for her helpful editorial suggestions. And thanks to my son Kip who did the first design for the cover with the creativity and devotion that he brings to all of his work.

In mid-March 2010, as I was editing the third of what would be six drafts, my doctors informed me that I had an advanced case of cancer that had metastasized. The statistics on survival rates helped concentrate my mind on how I wanted to spend my remaining time on this planet. I set my highest priority to spend time with my family, and while we were always close, we drew even closer. Margy, my daughter Tiffin and her husband Mike Eisenberg, my son Kip, and my two brothers, Bruce and Donald, who put aside their work to advise me on medical matters—to all of them, I am eternally grateful for their love and support.

Naturally, I had to reduce my workload, but I decided that this book and the North American Idea merited priority. If this book could help the people of our three countries see more clearly the problems and the promise of our continent, then the idea could become a reality. And if Canadians, Mexicans, and Americans stopped seeing each other as "foreigners," then I will rest peacefully, knowing that the future for my children and their children will improve on the past.

Robert A. Pastor

The North American Idea

Part I: Should We Fear North America?

A great thought begins by seeing something differently, with a shift of the mind's eye.
—Albert Einstein

1

A Piñata for Pandering
Pundits and Politicians

The key to our own future security may lie in both Mexico and Canada becoming much stronger countries than they are today . . . It is time we stopped thinking of our nearest neighbors as foreigners.[1]

—Ronald Reagan

As the first decade of the twenty-first century drew to a close, news reports of ghastly murders on the U.S.-Mexican border terrified both Mexicans and Americans and transformed the image of Mexico from a modernizing democracy to a killing field. There were massacres at birthday parties, hand grenades tossed into crowds, car bombs, a face peeled off and stitched to a soccer ball.[2] At the same time, the U.S. Department of Homeland Security struggled to prevent terrorists, drug traffickers, and migrants from finding holes in America's porous borders, while the Centers for Disease Control in Atlanta tried to keep Canadian mad cow disease and Mexico's H1N1 "swine" flu from spreading into America's schools and homes.

Each report demanded attention, but no one connected the dots and saw the underlying crisis in North America. That is because the very idea of "North America" has not penetrated our consciousness. As a result, the governments of the United States, Mexico, and Canada react to one crisis at a time, one country at a time, and the problems often grow worse.

At the end of the George W. Bush administration and the beginning of Barack Obama's, the issue of the moment was drug-related violence in Mexico. President Bush committed $1.2 billion to assist Mexico, and Obama reaffirmed and increased the pledge. While Obama recognized the "shared responsibility" with Mexico for a crisis fueled by U.S. demand for drugs and supply of weapons, no one discussed how the violence might relate to the development gap separating the countries or to the financial crisis or to the many other challenges that confronted the two countries and Canada.

The failure to address these issues in a comprehensive way is not due to a lack of attention. The three leaders of Canada, Mexico, and the United States meet more often with each other than with other leaders. The problem is that each meeting has a formulaic quality: the leaders pretend that relations are better than they are. They pretend because they know how much is at stake, but at the same time, they are unwilling to invest the political or financial capital to confront their shared challenges in a more effective way.

Let me draw a few pictures.

On January 19, 2009, on the eve of the inauguration of Barack Obama as president, the U.S. intelligence community received credible reports that Somali terrorists were crossing the border from Canada to bomb the inauguration.[3] The incoming national security team debated possible scenarios—a bomb at the Capitol or on the mall, sniper attacks, chemical weapons. They worked through multiple scenarios without knowing which were plausible or probable. Inexperienced and nervous, the Obama team proceeded with the inauguration, but also with additional security precautions, crossed fingers, and prayers. Fortunately, the report was a false alarm.

Now imagine if there were an attack, and that some in the intelligence community concluded that their Canadian counterparts were either asleep at the switch or penetrated by terrorist cells. Canadians have imagined that scenario, and it led them to try to make their airports much more secure than those in the United States. Visitors who fly to the United States from Ottawa or Toronto face more harassment than from any other destination in the world—even Tel Aviv. I know because I fly from all three airports.

Why is Canada tougher on air travelers than Israel or, for that matter, the United States? "Canada," in the words of two scholars, "cannot afford even one breach of security, not one."[4] If one attack occurs, the United States might unilaterally shut the border—as it did on 9/11 with Canada, and as it did in 1969 and 1985 with Mexico over drug issues. With nearly half of its economy dependent on trade with the United States, the closing of the border would throw Canada "into crisis," according to a report by the Canadian International Council.[5] Of course, zero risk is a standard that can never be met.

One year later, on March 27, 2010, a prominent Arizona rancher was killed soon after he complained that drug traffickers were crossing into his property near the Mexican border. Before any suspect was identified, pressures in the state to stop undocumented migration passed the boiling point, and a new law was approved giving Arizona police the powers to arrest anyone who didn't have an immigrant visa and looked like an illegal migrant. The law ignited a backlash and harsh comments by President Obama and by Mexican President Felipe Calderon in an address before a Joint Session of the U.S. Congress. In that speech on May 20, 2010, Calderon also blamed Congress for its failure to renew the ban on assault weapons. As a result, Calderon charged, American gun shops near the border sold these and other weapons to Mexican drug cartels.

Calderon's speech elicited angry reactions from some congressmen, and within a week of the visit, President Obama ordered 1,200 National Guard troops to the Arizona border, asked Congress to provide $500 million to support their efforts, and sent "drones"—pilot-less planes—to monitor border traffic.

It used to be that the three nations of North America took great pride in having the longest undefended borders in the world. No longer.

Just two decades ago, in 1992, the three nations of North America pledged to move in a very different direction. They set aside two centuries of distrust and signed an agreement to construct a continental market. By the year 2001, trade had tripled, foreign investment rose twice as fast as trade, and the outline of a North America that was more than just a geographical expression was visible. But the terror of 9/11 and the failure of the three governments to build on the NAFTA foundation allowed old problems to fester and new problems to multiply. The fears that accompanied these problems made it hard to see that each crisis was connected, and that a solution would only become possible with a deeper level of cooperation.

There are other more subtle signs of the neighborhood's deterioration. Since 9/11, the three governments have announced new border initiatives that are reported as "smart" and fast, and yet the border remains dumb and slow by almost any standard. One of those initiatives was a pre-clearance facility for Canadian customs officials in Buffalo, New York and one for U.S. customs officials in Fort Erie, Ontario. After five years of negotiations on issues that would appear trivial to a detached observer, both sides gave up trying. A second case: the leaders of the three countries set up a "North American Competitiveness Council" to harmonize regulations and they began with two innocuous ones: harmonizing regulations on jelly beans—a favorite of the Canadian prime minister—and on Cheerios—a favorite of President Bush's Secretary of Commerce Carlos Gutierrez, who had been CEO of Kellogg Company. Not only did the three governments fail to make any progress at establishing a framework for harmonizing regulations, they didn't even solve the jelly bean and Cheerios problems. They couldn't even agree on the size of the labels. So, in brief, big problems are hard to solve, but so too are small ones.

Does it matter? One does not need to explain the importance of the United States to Mexicans and Canadians. They feel the weight of their neighbor every day. It took them nearly two centuries to reduce their national anxieties of U.S. power to the point that they could contemplate a free trade agreement. The choice of moving closer to the United States was a difficult one because it meant they could become more dependent on a country with a long history of either bullying or ignoring them.

As their economies grew closer to the United States, small decisions made by the United States for domestic—sometimes protectionist—reasons had a very large effect on them. The U.S. Congress, for example, passed new rules on labeling products, including pork, and the rules were implemented in a way that discriminated against Canada's producers. Up to that time, about 7 percent of the pork consumed in the United States had come from Canada, but these new rules reduced Canada's pork exports by one-third, with a devastating effect on the industry.[6]

Although Canada and Mexico pursued very responsible fiscal policies, neither country could escape the effects of the U.S. financial crisis. Mexico's economy suffered the most. Its exports to the United States declined by 17 percent while the overall economy deteriorated by 6.5 percent. Canadian exports to the United States fell even further—by 38 percent—in 2009, though the overall effect on the economy was not as severe as Mexico's.[7] When the United States tightens its borders for security reasons, or shuts them down to make a point regarding drugs, or has a recession, our two neighbors feel as if we have grabbed their jugular vein.

Given the imbalance in power, it is not surprising that the United States takes its neighbors for granted, but there are two things wrong with this attitude. First, Canada and Mexico are very important to the United States economically (our two largest markets), socially (largest source of immigrants and tourists), and for national security. If Mexico and Canada chose to be uncooperative on security issues, the United States would face a far more serious challenge than it initially confronted in Afghanistan or Iraq.

Secondly, our transnational problems—like drugs, energy, immigration—cannot be solved unilaterally. Each requires more and better cooperation, not less. So the United States has a compelling—if little-noticed—stake in working with its neighbors and contributing to their success just as they have a stake in the prosperity and security of the United States.

So these issues matter a great deal. Why then have our governments not solved them? There are several reasons. First, the issues are not easy, and some like drugs and immigration cannot be solved, although they can be managed better. Secondly, the three governments are badly organized to address transnational problems. The three legislatures view transnational issues as domestic issues, and as a rule, legislators look inside their country not outside for guidance. Third, some—perhaps most—U.S. leaders prefer to divide its two neighbors, believing this maximizes its influence, even though a North American approach might be more effective. Canadians prefer to work directly with the United States, and Mexicans, logically, feel excluded. Fourth, many American leaders believe that the public is negative or ambivalent about NAFTA and uninterested in North America. Finally, some Americans fear "integration"— which is interpreted as more immigrants, drugs, or unfair competition. There are two dimensions to these fears—trade that jeopardizes jobs and integration that undermines sovereignty. Let us assess NAFTA and the hopes and fears that have surrounded it and then probe the issue of sovereignty.

➤ The Hopes and Fears of NAFTA

Christopher Columbus is usually credited with "discovering" America even though millions of people were there before he arrived. Five centuries later, in 1992, North America was "rediscovered" when Mexico, Canada, and the United States signed the North American Free Trade Agreement.

NAFTA generated a sunny set of hopes and a thunderstorm of fears. Mexicans hoped that their country would rise to the first world; Canadians hoped that the agreement would compel the United States to stop imposing duties on soft-wood lumber and comply with decisions of a dispute-settlement mechanism; and the United States hoped that NAFTA would put an end to undocumented migration from Mexico. Alas, none of these hopes came true.

Mexico and Canada feared that U.S. investors would purchase their country's assets, but despite substantial additional foreign investment in both countries, the percentage of total foreign investment in both countries by U.S.-owned firms declined. (See chapter 4, figure 4.4) The United States feared that its jobs would march south to Mexico, and its labor and environmental standards would be undercut by weaker policies in Mexico. Actually, labor and environmental standards improved substantially in Mexico, and the period of most rapid growth in U.S. trade—1993–2001—coincided with the largest expansion of job-creation in U.S. history. Jobs were lost after 2002 when the rate of trade growth declined. So those fears also didn't come true.

Leaving aside hopes and fears, if one judges NAFTA by the specific goals written in the agreement, it was successful. NAFTA aimed to dismantle trade and investment barriers, and it accomplished that. As a result, trade tripled, and foreign direct investment increased by six times in North America since 1994. In an econometric analysis, World Bank economists estimated that by 2002, Mexico's GDP per capita was 4–5 percent higher, its exports 50 percent higher, and its foreign direct investment 40 percent higher than they would have been without NAFTA.[8]

NAFTA had a much smaller effect on the United States because of the larger size of its economy. Still, the first seven years of NAFTA—from 1994–2001—were a period of trade expansion and unprecedented job creation in the United States. NAFTA certainly does not deserve credit for all or even much of this job growth, but it surely cannot be blamed for serious job losses. If one focuses only on jobs, U.S. employment grew from 110 million jobs in 1993 to 137 million in 2006—before the recession; and in Canada, from 13 million to 16 million. The United States benefited also from increasing competition in product and resource markets and by lower prices of many commodities. Canada was least effected by NAFTA because its trade with Mexico was low and the major effect of freer trade with the United States was already absorbed with the Canada-U.S. Free Trade Agreement implemented in 1988.[9]

Still, in the period leading up to the 2008 presidential election, NAFTA became a veritable piñata for pandering pundits and politicians. Everyone took a whack at it. In the presidential debate in Ohio in March 2008, both Barack Obama and Hillary Clinton denounced NAFTA and pledged to re-open NAFTA to incorporate enforceable sanctions if labor or environmental standards were violated. They went further by threatening to repeal NAFTA if Canada and Mexico did not accede to their demands.[10] What explains the harsh criticism?

The short answer is the downturn in the U.S. economy beginning in the fall of 2007 and continuing through the presidential campaign that led people to search for scapegoats, and the easiest targets were foreigners and trade. Public opinion tends to sour on trade policy when the economy contracts, and during the period from the fall of 2007 to March 2009, a plurality of the American public opposed free trade and NAFTA, and this was disproportionately the case for Democratic voters in Ohio. By March 2009, public opinion changed, and a plurality returned to be supporters of freer trade and NAFTA. (See Chapter 3, Figure 3.1) The new president and secretary of state followed public opinion and abandoned their criticism, and in April 2009, the administration announced that it would not reopen NAFTA.[11]

The reason for the disquiet about NAFTA is that many blamed it for all of North America's problems. But NAFTA's mandate was deliberately narrow—to reduce trade barriers—not to deal with all the issues on the North American agenda. The real problem was that governance did not keep pace with the integration process. Indeed, the three governments have been asleep at the switch, awakening only *after* an accident, and then returning to sleep before solving the problem. After stumbling badly, the United States helped Mexico after the peso crisis of 1994–95 when capital fled and the country staggered on a precipice of bankruptcy. Despite this near-death experience, neither the United States nor Mexico developed an adequate fund or consultative mechanism for preventing or alleviating the next macroeconomic crisis. In the financial crisis of 2007–09, Mexico turned primarily to the International Monetary Fund.

The countries also chose not to develop trilateral institutions to deal with terrorism after 9/11, or to address chronic problems, like drug trafficking or trade disputes that arise from government involvement with natural resources. The failure to build on NAFTA's foundation to address the next generation of integration challenges meant that when the comparative advantage of the agreement was exhausted, integration stalled and then reversed. From 1990 to 2001, trade among the three countries grew much faster than with the rest of the world, almost reaching the levels of integration that Europe achieved after five decades. But from 2001 to 2010, intraregional trade slowed, and in the United States the number of manufacturing jobs shrunk from over 17 million to 11.6 million.[12]

Similarly, North America's share of world gross product in 1994 was par with that of the European Union, but by 2001, it overshadowed the EU. In the next eight years, however, Europe caught up. In 2003, China passed Mexico as the second largest source of U.S. imports, and in 2007, China passed Canada. In brief, North America passed through two stages since NAFTA came into effect. The first stage—1994–2000—saw accelerated growth and integration. The second—2001–2010—saw a decline.

Ross Perot, the Texan entrepreneur who ran for president in 1992, warned Americans of a "sucking sound" of jobs moving to Mexico if the United States approved NAFTA. He got it backward. When trade grew, jobs were plentiful in the United States, and when NAFTA declined, so too did jobs. In the first decade of the twenty-first century, North America's leaders were still debating an agreement that was a decade old while Europe and Asia, with their eyes on the future, overtook us.

The fears that former CNN anchor Lou Dobbs, Perot, Congressman Ron Paul and others exploit are real. They cannot be denied, and should not be ignored. The question, however, is not whether the fears are legitimate, but rather how the United States as a nation will address them.

We ought to be concerned about job loss, but we should not assume that trade is the problem, and protectionism is the solution. In fact, almost every economist who has researched the question believes advances in technology—automation—and education are far more influential in reducing manufacturing jobs than trade. Because of technological innovation, fewer workers can produce more goods at less cost. The United States remains the largest manufacturer in the world, producing 25 percent of the world's product, but by 2007, because of automation, 75 U.S. workers could produce as much as 100 could in 2000.[13] Technology and trade transformed the economy, reducing manufacturing jobs but increasing jobs in services and information. The answer to job loss is not protection; it is more education, training, and assistance for those who lose their jobs because their firms cannot compete.

Free trade should be viewed as expanding the market and thus enlarging the area of competition. When Wal-Mart moves into a rural area, it often takes a toll. Small retail shops either close or find niches in the market that Wal-Mart does not fill. Is this progress? Not for the shops that close or the workers who lose their jobs, but other people in the community are better off because they can buy more goods for less.

By enlarging the arena of competition to include all of North America, the pace of change accelerated. More competition meant that some firms and workers were hurt; others benefited, but consumers—and we are all consumers—won. Moreover, an expanding market means that there are more people with higher incomes who are purchasing our goods. In the case of North America, in 2007, on average, each Canadian purchased $8,974 of U.S. goods and each Mexican $1,533. On a per capita basis, Canadians and Mexicans purchase twelve times more from the United States than the Chinese and Japanese do. What this means is that the U.S. economy depends far more on its North American partners than on any other two countries. The converse is even truer: Canada and Mexico are much more dependent on the U.S. economy. And that was why neither Canada nor Mexico could escape the effects of the U.S. financial crisis, though both had more effective regulation of financial services.

➤ Is Sovereignty at Risk?

"The leaders of Mexico, Canada, and the United States have been working to create a so-called North American Union," Lou Dobbs told his CNN audience on September 29, 2006. "And they've done so rather stealthily . . . [but]

the plan [is] an outright attack on our sovereignty."[14] Given the relative size of the United States, it is understandable why Canada and Mexico would be reluctant to draw closer to Washington with a free trade agreement or a deeper arrangement, but as incongruous as it appears, the most fervent opposition to a closer relationship has come from within the United States.

In *The Late Great USA: The Coming Merger with Mexico and Canada*, Jerome Corsi makes a conspiratorial case that George W. Bush, Dick Cheney, the Council on Foreign Relations, and others, including me, were secretly conspiring to create a North American Union in the same way that Jean Monnet and others established the European Union—step-by-step. "Our national sovereignty is in danger," he warned.[15]

The proximate cause of this conspiracy theory was the formation of the Security and Prosperity Partnership (SPP) at a summit of the three leaders of North America at Waco, Texas in March 2005. It followed the publication of a report by a Council of Foreign Relations task force of thirty-one leaders from Canada, Mexico, and the United States. The report, *Building a North American Community*, articulated a vision of a community and included specific proposals. The chairs of the task force were John P. Manley, former deputy prime minister of Canada; Pedro Aspe, former finance minister of Mexico; and William Weld, former governor of Massachusetts. I served as vice chair together with Thomas P. D'Aquino, then CEO of the Canadian Council of Chief Executives, and Andres Rozental, former deputy foreign minister of Mexico.

Corsi, who wrote a book impugning John Kerry's service in Vietnam and another attacking Barack Obama, developed arguments that the John Birch Society and Phyllis Schlafly's Eagle Forum used to try to show that the SPP was a first step toward a North American Union (NAU).[16] Together, they persuaded conservative legislators to introduce bills in twenty-three states that condemned the NAU and also a nonexistent NAFTA superhighway.

At a scholarly level, Samuel P. Huntington, former Professor at Harvard, wrote that the influx of Mexican immigrants threatened the very core of the American "Anglo-Protestant culture." The Mexicans, according to Huntington, are different from previous immigrant groups because of their numbers, contiguity, illegality, concentration in several regions in the United States, historical presence (the only group to claim territory), and continued high level of migration. The danger, he writes, is that they "could change America into a culturally bifurcated Anglo-Hispanic society with two national languages."[17]

These two arguments—that the sovereignty of the United States was in jeopardy by deepening collaboration with our neighbors and that the unifying culture of the United States was endangered by the wave of Mexican migrants—have influenced the debate in the government and among the public, and slowed or halted any proposal aimed at promoting the further integration of North America.

Let us address the sovereignty issue first. "Sovereignty" is one of those words that is used often but rarely defined. Webster's dictionary defines it as "supreme political power or authority" over a territory or nation, but this definition begs several questions. Does "supreme" power refer to formal or actual power? Almost every prosperous country has a formal law to prevent illegal immigration, but that does not prevent it from occurring. Most countries address this as a policy problem not a sovereignty one. A second question is how to define a nation. If a nation is defined by its values as well as by its borders, if it is defined by its trade with the world as well as by the products it makes, if it is defined by its alliances abroad as well as by its national institutions, then the "nation" extends considerably beyond its borders.

The ultimate question is how does one defend sovereignty? Building walls at the border will not defend against nuclear weapons. Nor can the United States rely solely on border inspections to defend against terrorism. The United States needs to reach beyond borders and share intelligence with allies. Indeed, if the United States waited for a bomb in a computer sent to Chicago by UPS to ignite when it reached its destination, or for a passenger from Europe to blow himself up as his plane descends into Detroit airport, it would be too late. In the twentieth and twenty-first centuries, international agreements and partnerships are far more effective instruments in defending democratic values, advancing economic interests, and especially, protecting against sub-national threats than stationing the National Guard at the borders.

Mexican President Carlos Salinas understood the power of this truth when he proposed a new arrangement with Mexico's two northern neighbors. "Historically," he said to Mexicans, "nationalism has been the answer to any external challenge. Now the big challenge is not being left out of the great integrationist efforts and the great exchange of resources."[18]

The significance of this paradigm shift by Mexico should not be underestimated. No country was as zealous in building walls to keep a neighbor away as Mexico was toward the United States. The reason is obvious. In the middle of the nineteenth century, the United States annexed more than one-third of Mexico's territory and the growing power of the United States combined with the continued weakness of Mexico filled the latter with profound anxiety. Yet once Salinas made the decision to reverse course and open Mexico to the United States, there was hardly a debate.

This may have been because migration had made Mexicans more comfortable with the United States. It may have been because the authoritarian nature of the Mexican regime controlled the debate and limited criticism. It may have been due to the Mexican public's satisfaction with the initial results of trade liberalization, which provided them with more, better, and cheaper goods.

Eventually, an opposition emerged in Mexico against free trade, and it found its voice through the major leftist party, Partido de la Revolucion Democratica (PRD), led by Andres Manuel Lopez Obrador, former mayor of Mexico City, and the party's 2006 candidate for president. The PRD remains the most suspicious of both the United States and freer trade and continues to oppose initiatives that would, for example, change the Mexican constitution to permit competition and foreign investment in the energy sector.

Canada's most zealous defenders of sovereignty also come from the left side of the political spectrum. Maude Barlow, an activist opposed to globalization, has played a pivotal role in protesting both NAFTA and any initiative that would integrate the economies. Barlow is now trying to prevent Canada from exporting any water to the United States or Mexico, though Canada has more fresh water than any other nation in the world, and fresh water, unlike oil, is renewable.

No country is immune to an argument that its sovereignty is in danger, but few realize that these arguments are often just a defense of the status quo. Few also realize that a nation's definition of sovereignty changes over time. Mexico insisted for many decades that no one would be permitted to monitor its elections as that would constitute a violation of its sovereignty. In 1990, Salinas said that "The nationalism of the Mexican people precluded an invitation to international observers."[19] Yet, just two years later, and in every election since then, Mexico invited monitors, and its elections became among the most free and fair in the Americas.

Canada had closed its oil industry to foreigners, arguing that foreign investment would diminish its sovereignty. Then, Canada opened its oil resources to foreign investment, and today, the Canadian energy industry is among the most productive in the world.

Ronald Reagan claimed that the United States had sovereign control over the Panama Canal and surrendering it would do untold damage to America's economic and strategic interests. The Canal Treaty that transferred jurisdiction to a sovereign Panama, however, improved America's standing in Latin America, and the Canal has been managed by Panama more efficiently, securely, and profitably with fewer accidents than under U.S. control.

In all three cases, the definition of sovereignty changed, doors were opened to the wider world, and the outcome was that human rights, prosperity, and security were all enhanced. The desperate need to defend "sovereignty" often emanates from fears that one is losing control or one's culture is at risk. This is where the Huntington thesis merges with the conspiracy theorists. Huntington acknowledges that his thesis stems from a deep concern "about the unity and strength of my country as a society based on liberty, equality, law, and individual rights." As a scholar, and one of our nation's best, he warned the reader that this concern might have influenced the way he presented his evidence.[20] He was right to warn us. His thesis that Mexican immigrants are dangerous and different from previous waves is not borne out by the evidence.

Huntington is correct about the dramatic increase in the numbers of Mexican-American immigrants, and that they come from next door. He is right that the magnitude of illegal entries is relatively new and more serious than ever before, but he is wrong that the pattern of assimilation by Mexican-Americans is different from previous waves. Surveys show that nine of ten Latinos who are new to the United States believe that it is important to change so that they can fit into American society, and only 10 percent of their American-born children rely mainly on Spanish. By the third generation, the number falls to 1 percent.[21] The problem with Huntington's data on the increasing numbers of Spanish-speaking people in the United States is that he fails to disaggregate by generation. Recent studies suggest that Mexican-Americans acquire English faster than previous waves, and according to Robert Putnam, a Harvard professor, and Jeb Bush: "Today's immigrants are, on average, assimilating socially even more rapidly than earlier waves."[22]

The opening of each country to each other and the world represents an enhancement of rights not their restriction. Sometimes, sovereignty can be defended better by eliminating barriers not raising them, by working closely with each other not by distancing ourselves. The "North American Idea" represents an expansion of choice for the three countries, not an erosion of the state.

The most serious flaw in the prism through which the sovereignty-defenders look at the world is that they look at our neighbors as "problems." To them, Mexico is *the problem* in regards to drugs, violence, corruption, and illegal migration. Canada is not viewed in the same way, but there are moments—such as accusing it as the source of mad cow disease; the "millennium bomber"; and some even suggested, incorrectly, the 9/11 bombers—when Canadians feel as if they are treated like Mexicans. Viewing either neighbor as the problem leads us in a dangerous direction because it is impossible to manage, let alone solve, any of these problems without their cooperation.

If, on the other hand, we incorporate the North American Idea into our collective consciousness, recognizing the interconnectedness of our economies and societies, we should then ask ourselves: "Is the United States also a part—perhaps even a substantial *cause*—of these problems? Is it possible that Mexico and Canada suffer *the effects* of these problems as much or more than the United States?"

Regarding drugs, the United States is the source of the demand, and the profits earned from the United States are used by the cartels to corrupt many officials. On the violence in Mexico, the Calderon administration seized about 80,000 guns from the cartels in its first four years in power. It sent the serial numbers of most of these guns to the U.S. government, and 80 percent of them were traced to gun shops in the United States. There are 6,700 U.S. gun sellers within a few miles of the border, averaging one shop every third of a mile across the 1,933 mile border.[23] On illegal migration, America's demand for cheap, hardworking labor is the other side of the Mexican supply chain.

These problems need to be defined correctly if they are to be managed effectively. They do not fit comfortably into the separate compartments of "domestic" or "foreign" policy. They share both compartments. "Supply" and "demand" are inextricably linked across borders. Blaming the supplier or the demander, which is the modus operandi for nationalists, is like blaming all divorces on one spouse.

Transnational problems are not unique to Mexico and the United States; they also can be found on the northern border, which covers 5,525 miles.[24] U.S. politicians continue to blame Canada for "porous" borders that allow terrorists to come to the United States, although only one such person—Ahmed Ressam, the "millennium bomber"—was arrested in 1999 in a routine way with cooperation from both sides. There are always two sides to transnational issues, but in the absence of a sense of community, it is always easier to blame the other side.

The imbalance in power between the United States and its neighbors means that the United States sometimes insists on its one-sided perception of a problem to the consternation of its neighbors. If, on the other hand, Americans absorb the North American Idea and accept that they are part of the problem and that collaboration with Mexico and Canada are essential for a solution, then the three countries can find more creative paths to address chronic problems like drugs, violence, illegal immigration, and trade, and new transnational issues like pandemics or the crisis of the auto industry.

Fortunately, in the first months of the Obama administration, the president and Secretary Clinton announced that the United States shared the problem of illicit drug trafficking with Mexico, and it shared the responsibility to stop it. Unfortunately, they did not take the next steps of incorporating Canada into the project, defining a North American approach to that issue, and relating it to the other issues on the agenda.

➤ The Emergence of North America

Despite fears by some of a loss of sovereignty as a result of NAFTA and globalization, the nation-state remains the most potent unit of governance in this century, as it has been since the seventeenth, and it has not grown weaker. Nonetheless, to prosper, assure security, and adapt to cultural differences, states need to devise new forms of relating to each other. The answer may come in regional compartments, but much will depend on how the states structure their regions and how they relate to one another. Charles Meier, a Harvard historian, has written that "the over-riding question for international politics in the decades to come" is how the world makes the transition to "a comity of regions."[25]

North America does not yet reside in our political imaginations. It is, at best, an expression of geography, but NAFTA is the economic platform of a new region. The idea of "North America" is like the idea of Social Security in the 1920s or Medicare in the 1950s. It is an idea whose time has not yet arrived.

NAFTA occurred at a moment when nations were seeking regional trading partners. Regional trade regimes were founded in the 1950s, but since 1990 there has been a proliferation, with 202 coming into force since then and more than 200 others having been announced.[26] Only two of those represent coherent and formidable entities—the European Union and North America—although East Asia seems to be moving toward greater integration on trade issues. (See Figure 1.1) Compared to the EU, North America was the largest in territory, gross product, and per capita GDP. It was also the most populous until the European Union expanded to 27 nations in 2004. From the onset of NAFTA in 1994, North America outpaced any regional entity, expanding its share of the world's product from 30 to 36 percent in 2001.

Although frequently compared to the European Union, North America is quite different in its origin, objectives, composition, political philosophy, and institutionalization. The European effort to unite was born of centuries of conflict, a fear of Soviet expansion, a concern about economic decline and increased competition from the United States, and a romantic hope that Europe could once again be a global leader, this time by transcending sovereignty.

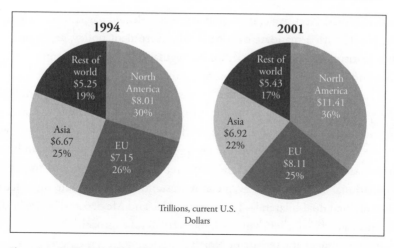

Figure 1.1: **Regional Shares of World Product, 1994 and 2001**

Note: The European Union expanded from 12 to 15 countries in 1995, to 25 in 2004, and 27 in 2007. Asia includes Japan, China, South Korea, Taiwan, Hong Kong, and the ten countries of ASEAN.

Source: UN Stats Division, *National Accounts Estimates of Main Aggregates*, and World Bank, *World Databank*, 1994 and 2001. Data for Taiwan from IndexMundi. Accessed in 2010.

In contrast, North America originated from a desire to dismantle trade and investment barriers among the three governments and to do so in a framework of predictable rules. Thus, in the preamble of the Treaty of Rome, in 1957, six European nations declared their determination "to lay the foundations for an ever closer union among the peoples of Europe."[27] In comparison, NAFTA's preamble reads as if it were drafted by Lilly Tomlin, the Canadian comedienne, who once said: "Together, we are in this alone." NAFTA is a business contract among three governments that seemed more intent on affirming their separate sovereignties than in finding areas of common interest.

Over fifty years, Europe expanded from six to twenty-seven members and from a coal and steel community to a free trade area, a customs union (common external tariff), a common market (free movement of labor), and an economic and monetary union (a unified currency). The disparity in the size, wealth, and power of its members was small compared to the gap separating the United States from Mexico and Canada. Despite the narrower range, the EU defined as a central goal the narrowing of income disparities between its rich and poor members. It appropriated substantial resources—about € 650 billion (roughly $850 billion) since 1961—to that end, and it accomplished its goals.[28] Ireland went from the second poorest to the second richest country in the EU, although the 2009 financial crisis set it back. The EU established a supranational executive commission, a directly elected parliament, independent courts with a mandate over national government policy, and a host of other institutions aimed to harmonize regulations, enforce common standards, and implement common external policies.

In contrast, NAFTA established a few symbolic institutions but none with the capability to be effective in any area, and instead of forging a common approach, the three governments agreed that each would enforce its own laws—a standard that surely didn't need repeating. North America, in brief, affirmed the independence of each nation, relied on the market, and distrusted supranational institutions or even common standards. As a result, most activities remained dual-bilateral—between the U.S. and Mexico and between the U.S. and Canada—rather than a common, trilateral approach.

The defining characteristic of North America, however, especially as contrasted with the EU, is asymmetry. The United States accounts for 97 percent of North America's military spending, 84 percent of its gross product, and 68 percent of its population.[29]

As Canada and Mexico reduced their tariffs, the gravitational pull of the United States gradually created a regional market. In 1901, with high imperial tariffs, Canada's trade with Great Britain was essentially the same in value as its trade with the United States. By 1952, with the end of the British preference system, Britain declined to 13 percent of Canada's trade and the United States accounted for 63 percent.[30]

Since NAFTA, Canada's trade with the United States averaged about 75 percent of its total trade with the world and about 45 percent of its gross product while Mexico's trade with the United States averaged about 70 percent of its total trade and about 35 percent of its GDP. In contrast, the United States trade with its two neighbors amounted to about 30 percent of its total trade but only about 6 percent of its gross product. (See Table 11 in Appendix) Canada's trade with Mexico expanded by almost five times, albeit from a low level of $4.1 billion.[31] (See Table 6 in Appendix) In brief, these numbers reflect the imbalance in trade and economic power in North America.

The conventional wisdom in the United States is that Mexico and Canada are not important. A cursory reading of the newspapers in the last decade would lead one to conclude that Iraq or Afghanistan were the most important countries to U.S. national security, China was its dominant trading partner, and Saudi Arabia was its main source of energy imports. All three propositions are false.

U.S. national security depends more on cooperative neighbors and secure borders than it did on defeating militias in Basra or Taliban in Kandahar. Canada and Mexico have been the first and second largest markets for U.S.

exports, and they are also the first and second largest sources of energy imports for most of the past decade. In terms of trade, energy, immigration, travel, and security, there are no two countries that matter more to the United States than its proximate neighbors.

China has been expanding its trade rapidly, but as of 2009, the two largest markets for U.S. goods and services remain Canada and Mexico. (See Figure 1.2) The United States exported nearly three times more to Canada and twice as much to Mexico than to China. Many economists have waxed enthusiasm about the growing power of Brazil and India, but U.S. trade with Mexico in 2009 was more than six times larger than with either of these emerging markets.

Still, regional integration cannot be measured only by the size or growth of trade. A region's economy is integrating when trade among its members grows faster than its trade with the world. Figure 1.3 shows that the three countries of North America experienced very rapid growth in intraregional trade from 1980–2000, with intraregional exports reaching 56 percent of their total exports in 2000. It is worth noting that at that point, North America was almost as integrated as Europe was after fifty years.

Stephen Blank and Martin Coiteux, who have studied the integration process, argue that North America is actually more integrated than Europe. Using a "trade intensity index" that accounts for the size and dependence of member states, the authors found that the North American countries trade among themselves three to five times more than the countries in the EU.[32]

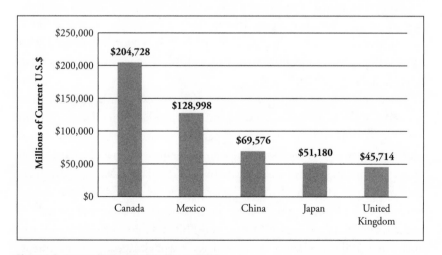

Figure 1.2: Largest Markets for U.S. Exports, 2009

Sources: TradeStats Express, National Trade Data, Foreign Trade Division, U.S. Census Bureau, accessed in 2010.

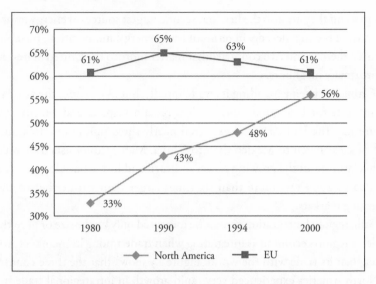

Figure 1.3: Intraregional Exports as % of Total Exports for NA and EU, 1980–2000
Source: World Trade Organization, *Statistics Database*, accessed in 2010.

Another sign of an increasingly integrated region is the growth of foreign direct investment. Businesses in all three countries increased their investments in each other by six times: from $90 billion in 1987 to $557 billion in 2008. (See Figure 1.7) The accelerated growth began with NAFTA.

The increasing cross-investment has strengthened North American firms. A study of 348 of the largest multinational corporations in the world found that almost none were truly global. Nearly half were North American with 75 percent of all their sales in North America. About one-third were based in Europe, and one-fifth in Asia.[33]

Since the first oil embargo in 1973, virtually every U.S. president has insisted that the United States should end its dependence on oil imports from unstable or unfriendly nations. Few apparently realize that the two principal sources have been its neighbors—providing about one-third of total U.S. oil imports. From an energy security standpoint, Canada and Mexico have guaranteed under NAFTA to share their energy with the United States in case of an emergency. During the debates by the Democratic presidential candidates in the spring of 2008, Barack Obama and Hillary Clinton threatened to re-open NAFTA if Canada and Mexico did not accept changes in the agreement. The Canadian prime minister warned that Canada might seek to change the oil provision, and that quieted the criticism.

Trade and energy underscore the economic importance of Canada and Mexico to the United States, but people remain the most important link connecting the three countries. Canada and the United States are immigrant nations with citizens who have come from virtually every nation in the world, but especially from each other. The first large wave of immigrants to Canada was American "loyalists," who opposed the revolution against Great Britain, and Canadians were among the largest sources of immigration to the United States until the last quarter century. While the numbers of Canadian immigrants remained at the same level, the percentage of total immigrants declined from 6 percent to 2 percent, and Canada fell below four poorer countries— Mexico, the Philippines, China, and India. The most significant migration in the last three decades were Mexicans coming to the United States, but large numbers of Americans—about one million—now reside permanently in Mexico,[34] and Canada has about 50,000 residents in Mexico and sends more than one million tourists there each year.

Mexicans have been living in the United States since the latter seized the northern third of Mexico following the war in the middle of the nineteenth century, but the numbers were quite small. Indeed, during the Congressional debate on immigration in the 1920s, Congress exempted Mexican immigrants from the restrictions because of our "special relationship" and the low numbers. "Remember," Senator Alva Adams of Colorado told his colleagues, "Mexico is not a populous country."[35] During the Second World War, when labor was scarce, the United States arranged for Mexicans to work temporarily in the United States in a *bracero* program that lasted until 1964. From then until the 1980s, Mexicans would come north to Texas, California, and other border states, but most would stay for a short period and return home. This pattern changed in the last quarter century.

More than 80 percent of the total Mexican-origin population in the United States has arrived or been born in the United States since 1970, rising from 6.1 million to 30.6 million in 2010. Of that total, only 5.1 million were legal immigrants, representing one-third of the total foreign-born legal resident population in the United States; 6.4 million are undocumented migrants; and the largest number—19.4 million—represent U.S.-born children of Mexican heritage.[36] Put another way, there were almost as many Mexicans and Mexican-origin Americans living in the United States in 2010 as there were Canadians living in Canada. Moreover, the U.S. Census Bureau projects a doubling to 66 million Mexicans in the United States by 2050. By then, one out of every four Americans will be Hispanic and two-thirds of them will be from Mexico.

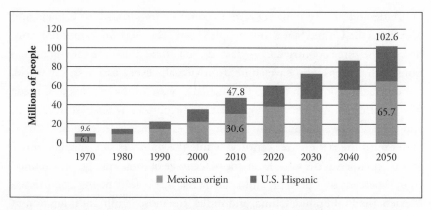

Figure 1.4: Mexican-Origin and Hispanic Population in the U.S., 1970–2050

Source: U.S. Census Bureau, "Hispanics in the U.S.," p. 3, including estimated population from 2010–2050. Mexican population estimate based on 64 percent of total Hispanic population, as measured in the 2006 American Community Survey.

Since 1990, as the numbers began to soar, Mexicans also dispersed, finding jobs in North Carolina, Wyoming, Georgia, and almost every state.

The immigrants are not only connecting the societies but also the economies with a hardworking labor force in the United States and about $20–25 billion in remittances—the second largest source of foreign exchange—received by Mexico on average each year.

North American society has always been enhanced by immigrants, but the magnitude of the Mexican migration to the United States is raising hopes in Mexico and fears in the United States. In the long term, that migration will inevitably connect the countries as it has done with every previous ethnic migration, but since the numbers from Mexico are far larger than any in the past, the connection will be far more profound, helping to realize the North American Idea. By 2050, the projections suggest that there might be almost twice as many Mexicans in America as the population of Canada.

Each year, about one million people immigrate to the United States, but about 50–60 million people arrive as tourists, and about 60 million Americans tour abroad. What is most interesting about the flow of tourism is the concentration in North America. While the numbers have fluctuated during the past two decades, 50–65 percent of all tourists coming to the United States have been Canadians and Mexicans. At the same time, more than half of all Americans who venture abroad visit our two neighbors. In 2007, 19 million Americans visited Mexico, and 13 million visited Canada. Nearly 18 million Canadians and 14 million Mexicans visited the United States.

➤ The Decline of North America

In the early 1990s, North America emerged as a formidable region that exceeded the European Union in terms of wealth and productivity. The economies and the societies were increasingly connected by businesses, pipelines, tourists, and immigrants, and officials of the three governments at all federal levels were meeting regularly to discuss local, national, and international issues.

In February 2001, the presidents of Mexico and the United States, both of whom had been pro-NAFTA border governors, met in Guanajuato at President Vicente Fox's ranch. They approved a communiqué proposing to consult with their Canadian counterpart to establish a North American economic community. Two months later, they traveled to Quebec City to speak with Canadian Prime Minister Jean Chretien. It seemed like the high point of North American integration, and as it turned out, it was.

The meeting was one of a long series of pleasant, unproductive photo-opportunities by the three leaders. During his administration, President George W. Bush met with the Mexican president eighteen times and the Canadian prime minister twenty-one times, and all three met twelve times. No U.S. president met with his counterparts in Canada and Mexico more and yet accomplished less than George W. Bush. During their many discussions, trade slowed, illegal migration soared, and the income gap widened. Mexico's energy reserves declined, border wait times lengthened, and the cost of shipping goods across the borders rose. Drug-related violence worsened, and favorable opinion among the three publics deteriorated. Tensions were exacerbated by differences on the Iraq war and the response to 9/11, and both Canada and Mexico took offense over the lack of compliance with NAFTA by the United States on two key decisions—trucking as it applied to Mexico and softwood lumber by Canada.

The rise of new problems and the decline of North America were not because of NAFTA but rather because the three governments failed to use it as a platform on which to build a more competitive region and address a new agenda beyond the trade agreement's mandate. By the year 2000, the advantage of NAFTA was spent. If you assess progress by measuring the growth in gross domestic product or trade, the reduction in wait times at the borders, and the public's support for integration, the period since 2001 has been an unmitigated disaster.

As a share of the world product, North America had soared from 30 percent in 1994 to 36 percent in 2001. From there, it declined to 29 percent in 2009. This decline was a reflection of a failed or rather nonexistent North

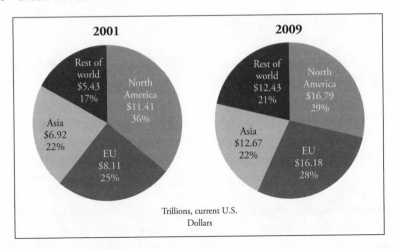

Figure 1.5: Regional Shares of World Product, 2001 and 2009

Sources: UN Stats Division, *National Accounts Estimates of Main Aggregates*; World Bank, *World Databank*; CIA, *World Factbook.* 2001:15.

American policy that also reduced America's ability to address critical economic and security issues at home. In other words, the failure to formulate a North American policy reduced the sovereign capacity of the three countries and the standing of North America in the world.

From 2001 to 2008, the growth rate of U.S. trade with its two neighbors declined from 17.7 percent to 5.9 percent—a reduction by two-thirds. (See Figure 1.6) If one were to incorporate 2009 data when trade plummeted because of the recession, the average annual growth rate in trade for the second period falls to 1.9 percent. The sharp decline in trade since 2001 illustrates the onset of a period of decline for North America.

A similar pattern is evident in foreign investment, which drove the first stage of integration. As Figure 1.7 shows, the average annual growth of foreign investment among the three countries of North America leaped from 7.6 percent before NAFTA to 18 percent in NAFTA's first decade. Then, from 2001–08, the rate fell to 11 percent.

What accounts for the slow-down since 2001? First, the U.S. recession in 2001–02 slowed the economies and trade. Second, the United States introduced security-related restrictions after 9/11 that increased the cost of trade across the border. Trucks were delayed for days; plants were closed. Security inspections transformed the border into giant speed bumps, slowing commerce, and up-ending a corporate strategy of "just-in-time" production that relied on small inventories and rapid shipment of parts across the border. That strategy had given North American firms a comparative advantage. The response

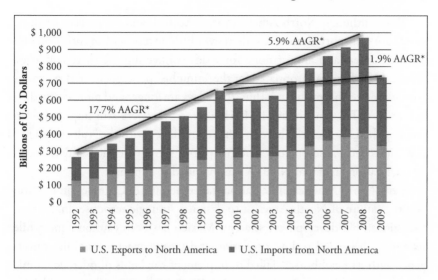

Figure 1.6: U.S. Trade Among the NAFTA Partners, 1993–2009
Note: *AAGR is Annual Average Growth Rate.
Sources: TradeStats Express; U.S. Census Bureau; OECD; World Trade Organization; Industry Canada.

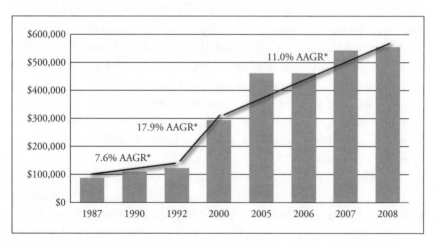

Figure 1.7: North American FDI In North America, 1987–2008
Sources: UNCTAD; Bureau of Economic Analysis; OECD; Statistics Canada.

to the attack on 9/11 also led to a reduction by one-third in the number of people who legally entered the United States, and paradoxically, a rise in the level of illegal migration.[37] (See Figures 5.1 and 5.2) In brief, security was not enhanced, and commerce was harmed.

Third, although North American trade tripled, and 80 percent of those goods are transported on roads, there was little investment in infrastructure on the borders and almost none for roads connecting the three countries. (None of the funds appropriated for the "stimulus" packages in all three countries addressed this problem.) Thus, the delays are longer and more costly than before NAFTA. Fourth, as of March 2011, trucks were still impeded from crossing the U.S.-Mexican border. Fifth, compliance with the "rules of origin" provisions became so onerous that many firms simply use the standard most-favored nation tariff that NAFTA was intended to eliminate.

Sixth, North American integration stalled because of Chinese competition and the failure of North America to design a strategic response. In contrast to China's bold development strategy, Mexico has been cautious, and while its approach has led to lower inflation and greater macroeconomic convergence with its neighbors, it failed to implement the kinds of microeconomic reforms—on energy, education, competition, and taxes—that would have stimulated faster growth.[38]

Finally, North American integration declined because each country decided to widen trade agreements with other countries instead of deepening their partnership. Since signing NAFTA, Mexico negotiated fourteen free-trade agreements, including with Japan and the European Union; Canada negotiated thirteen, including with the EU, and the United States negotiated twelve, mostly with small countries.[39] The motives for pursuing these agreements varied. Mexico and Canada feared dependence on a neighbor that did not take their interests into account and seemed bound to irresponsible economic policies. This caused the countries, in the words of John Manley, a former deputy prime minister of Canada, to "focus more efforts on strategies of market diversification."[40]

The consequence of all of these changes was the decline of intraregional trade as a percentage of North America's trade with the world. This standard indicator of integration looked so promising when it climbed from 36 percent in 1988 to 46 percent of trade in 2001. It then leveled off and declined to 40 percent by 2008. "Even if you are on the right road," Will Rogers once said, "if you sit down, you will be run over." NAFTA sat down, and China ran over it.

In order to capture sufficient support in Congress to approve NAFTA, President Bill Clinton over-promised. He said that NAFTA would reduce illegal migration, but NAFTA was a free trade agreement, not a development strategy. The implicit strategy depended on the magic of the marketplace, but most of the jobs created in Mexico were near the border, and the labor came

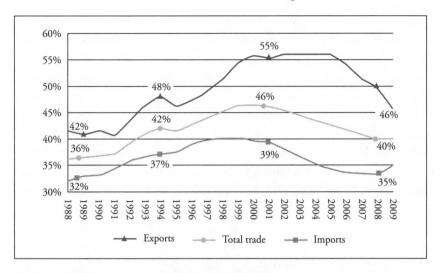

Figure 1.8: Intra-NA Trade as % of Total NA Trade, 1988–2009
Sources: World Trade Organization, *Statistic Database, Selected Regional Trade Agreements.*

from southern Mexico and stayed long enough to learn how to work in a foreign factory and how to cross the border. In other words, the implicit development strategy served as a magnet to encourage undocumented migration to the United States. Illegal migration increased from 3.8 million in 1990 to about 11 million in 2009, with two-thirds of those from Mexico.

On the first day of NAFTA, January 1, 1994, Mexico's great hope of ascending to the first world collided with a small group, who took their inspiration from Emiliano Zapata, a peasant leader of the Mexican revolution. The Zapatista uprising had a theatrical air—a young college professor in Mexico City failed to get tenure, adopted a nom de guerre of "Subcomandante Marcos," and moved in with poverty-stricken Indians in the southern state of Chiapas. After a time, he mobilized them to demand their land and rights by seizing towns and demanding an end to NAFTA. It was a great script, except that it was hard to blame NAFTA because it hadn't started, and Chiapas's problem would not be NAFTA, but its absence. NAFTA would mostly benefit the northern part of the country that was connected to the North American market. Without communications or highways linking it to the north, the poorer southern parts of Mexico had little chance to attract the investment that could help lift the region out of its grinding poverty.

As Governor of Guanajuato, Vicente Fox visited Texas Governor George W. Bush and proposed a number of ideas to promote the development of

Mexico, including a "cohesion fund" to narrow the gap between southern and northern Mexico and between Mexico and the United States.[41] Bush acknowledged he had never heard the word "cohesion" and asked for a definition. Fox told him that it was an English word, and it was the name of a fund that the Europeans used to raise the income of its poorest members. Once Bush heard it was done in Europe and might involve funds, he rejected it, saying the American people would not pay for it. Fox raised the issue again when Bush was in the White House, but the answer was the same. Congress would never approve it. He meant that he wouldn't ask. Fox tried to persuade Canadian Prime Minister Jean Chretien, but ran into a wall there as well.

➤ Recovering the Promise

If NAFTA had created institutions and a new relationship among the three governments, then the day after 9/11, the Mexican president and the Canadian prime minister would have joined President Bush to announce that the attack was against all three countries, and they would respond together. This did not happen, and indeed, 9/11 contributed to an escalation of fears and a downturn in trade and commerce.

The question is whether North America can regain its groove. A first step is for all three leaders to grasp and articulate "the North American Idea"—a spirit of community based on interdependence—to their publics in a manner that will galvanize support for the institutions and policies that will be needed to stimulate the collective economy, address transnational problems effectively, and provide greater security.

All three countries have a special reason why they should assume this new challenge, but they cannot succeed without the help of the others. Mexico's challenge is to find its path to the first world. That is only possible with substantial help from the United States and Canada.

Canada's challenge is to do what it does best—design trilateral institutions that will facilitate decision making in each and all of the countries. The U.S. challenge is to rethink what leadership means in the twenty-first century. In a world of states that are increasingly democratic and accountable to their people, no single nation can rule, and leadership requires adapting to the concerns of other nations. The place to experiment with a new concept of leadership is in one's neighborhood. If the United States can learn to reflect the wider interests of the region not just the narrow interests of a U.S. economic group, then that would mean it is prepared to become a new kind of leader for a new age. We did this after the Second World War. We can do it again.

There will be groups and talk show hosts who will paint our neighbors as untrustworthy or, worse, as threats. And while the three governments are unlikely to adopt this perspective, the strength of the negative argument has inhibited and, at times, even intimidated governments from confronting the real choice, which is between incremental decisions and a bold vision and strategy.

The first option—incremental approaches to the region's problems—has meant that the governments address *one issue, one country at a time* largely in reaction to the crisis of the moment, such as what has happened with the drug-related violence in Mexico. The goal is to seek gradual, minimal progress on a concrete issue. This has been the road taken since 2000. It has accomplished very little, if anything.

The second option—a bold vision of a North American Community and a strategy and institutions to move toward that goal—is the one we should consider. In April 2001, at the Summit of the Americas in Quebec City, Fox proposed that the three leaders designate representatives for a North American Commission to offer proposals on ways to invigorate the region. Bush did not like the idea of multilateral institutions, and "Chretien used up most of the time talking about lumber," recalled Fox. In the absence of new trilateral institutions, the three governments reverted to their traditional dual-bilateral agenda. The problems were rarely solved because they required a leader overruling a strong domestic economic interest in favor of a foreign government. Such cases are rare.

Fox's idea was correct—a vision, institutions, and cooperative policies among the three North American governments were essential to lift the region. But Fox was alone on this agenda. Canada thought it had a "special relationship" with the United States that could only be damaged by cooperating with Mexico. The United States had a full agenda. One out of three is enough to block progress but not enough to move forward. Unlike genuine crises, the problems described above are barely noticeable to the American public—a thicker border, declining competitiveness, and a widening income gap. But their cumulative cost to North America may already outweigh the original benefit of NAFTA.

A fair question is whether a North American Community is feasible. If one asks the politicians in Washington, Ottawa, or Mexico, or the pundits, the answer is resoundingly, "NO!" They will say that there is no way that the U.S. Congress will abandon the Teamsters or approve an investment fund for Mexico. Mexico will never liberalize its energy sector. Canada will not export water or allow the market to price its lumber.

Jacob Viner once wrote that "realism means making the same mistakes as one's grandfather." These answers are similarly "realistic"; they reflect inertia, a lack of imagination, and fear. There is another way. Let us go back in time to the origin of North America. The continent contains within its mountains, rivers, and people a genetic code that may offer some guidance as to where it might go. After we search through its past, let us next turn off the microphones of the blithering pundits and, in the third chapter, listen to the public.

2

The Genetic Code
of North America

Before we ask the question what the people of North America think of their future, it might be useful to explore whether the region has a past. How far back can we locate the North American Idea? To listen to today's critics of North American cooperation, one might think that the United States was endowed by its creator to have borders at the Rio Grande and the 49th parallel, but this not only shrinks our imagination of the future, it warps the past.

A longer view of history is often the best medicine for healing the malady of contemporary preoccupations. To find the cure, it may be useful to locate the genetic code that explains the continent's evolution and predicts its future. So let us begin at the moment of conception—the birth of the continent.

➤ Divine and Planetary Intervention

In the beginning, or rather almost at the beginning, there was an asteroid. About 65 million years ago, a huge rock about six miles in diameter, hurtling through space at a speed of about 60,000 miles per hour since the beginning of time, collided with the earth. The point of impact was the northern tip of Mexico's

Yucatan peninsula, and it hit with the force of a 100-megaton explosion, digging a hole three miles deep and unleashing a fire-storm as hot as one thousand suns. It set all of North America in flames. The age of dinosaurs came to an end in a fiery continental barbecue.[1]

Until that asteroid struck, North America was composed of two long, thin islands separated by a vast sea described as a "bearpaw," because of its shape. The force of the asteroid pushed the sea into the ocean, but then it returned as a tsunami. After the seas calmed, the Rocky Mountains began their slow but inexorable climb out of the earth and into the sky. With each thrust, the Bearpaw Sea emptied a little more and was replaced by a fertile Great Plains that became a land bridge between two grand mountain ranges—the Appalachians and the Rockies—that extend from the northern tip of the continent into the Sierra Madre in Mexico. North America, which became the third largest continent after Eurasia and Africa, was sculpted like a large funnel—6,000 miles at the top and 750 miles at the bottom.

Eight million years later—roughly 57 million years ago—the first of many migrations from Eurasia began—this one by rabbit-sized creatures. A warming trend continued for 14 million years, creating an immense greenhouse for new flora and fauna crossing from Eurasia. Within the borders of North America, wind and water reshaped the landscape. Five million years ago, ferocious pressure from deep inside the earth lifted the Colorado Plateau about a mile high, setting the stage for the spectacular geological carving now known as the Grand Canyon. Beneath and alongside those artistic treasures are natural resources and fertile lands on a scale that people on other continents envy and which has fed and fueled the engines of growth.

The mountains and rivers of North America mostly flow north and south. That north-south axis marks the continent's geography and affects the climate as polar winds from the north confront tropical gales from the south, generating more hurricanes and tornadoes than any other place in the world. Indeed, 90 percent of the world's tornadoes occur in North America.[2]

North America's genetic code was reset by the asteroid. From then on, the continent was programmed to receive and amplify changes coming from elsewhere. If the global climate is warm, North America is warmer. If cold, then North America has even more glaciers. Eighteen thousand years ago, during the most recent Ice Age, North America had 18.5 million square kilometers of glaciers. In comparison, Antarctica today has 12.6 million square kilometers of glaciers. Climate and migration have continually reshaped the continent. "It is as if the continent knows no rest, no equilibrium," Tim Flannery writes in his introduction to the continent's ecology, *The Eternal Frontier*.[3] It is constantly absorbing and adapting to aliens—asteroids, flora, weather, and people.

➤ The Arrival of Humans and the Naming of a Continent

When we think of the human migration to North America, one usually begins with Christopher Columbus's stunning voyage in 1492. The young sailor from Genoa convinced the king and queen of Spain that he could find a short route to the Indies by sailing west. Contemporary myths tell us that the voyage was a historic gamble because people thought the world was flat, but the true story is more revealing.

King Ferdinand and Queen Isabella summoned a group of wise men to evaluate Columbus's proposal. They concluded that the distance to the Indies going west from Spain was much further than Admiral Columbus calculated. They advised against subsidizing the voyage, and the king and queen rejected Columbus's proposal. Of course, the wise men were right. With the boats that he planned to use, Columbus would never have reached India or even China by sailing west. But he was not deterred. He and his brother spent the next eight years seeking a sponsor among the monarchs in Europe. Only after Prince Henry the Navigator of Portugal expressed interest, and the Spanish monarchs had united their country and expelled the Moors and the Jews, did they review their decision and agree to finance him.[4]

Columbus was hardly the first: many adventurers before him reached America. Thousands—maybe tens of thousands—made the trip from Eurasia by traveling East. When Columbus "discovered" the "new" world, he was greeted by the descendants of the earlier migrants. Their numbers had grown exponentially. Some estimate that the two continents of the Americas at the time of Columbus's arrival had a population as large as 100 million people, with about 25 million in the central plateau in Mexico and another 4 million people north of the Rio Grande.[5]

Archaeologists agree that the first immigrants to North America came from Eurasia. The theory—based on geological and anthropological excavations—is that two great glacial sheets in Canada parted at several moments, allowing a comparatively warm, ice-free corridor that allowed migrants to cross a land bridge at the Bering Strait. Once across, they found their way to an area near Edmonton, Canada where they dispersed in many directions. Many scholars now believe there may have been four different migrations, the first as early as 40,000 years ago. There are remains of people in Chile that date to about 20,000 years ago, but the carbon dating is not very precise.[6]

There is more solid evidence of human beings in Australia 50,000 years ago and in Africa before that, so it turns out that the New World is newer, relatively speaking, though it was much older than Columbus. The "Indians" that Columbus observed bore some resemblance to some Asians, but many had prominent noses and narrower faces.

A second migration occurred about 13,200 years ago, and the remains of these people have been found in Clovis, New Mexico. These hardy people were responsible for the first invention in the Americas: the "Clovis Point," a sharp spear that was effective in killing large Mastodons.[7] A third wave—called the Nadene people—arrived some 9,000 years ago, also across the Bering Strait, and a fourth wave of Aleuts and Inuit traversed about 5,000 years ago. Each of these groups and their descendants settled in different areas and adapted differently. In addition to those who crossed the land bridge, there were some who crossed the Pacific by boat.

Anthropologists believe that settled agriculture occurred long after these migrations, and these farmers may have come from a different place than the Clovis or Nadene migrants. A large body of evidence has accumulated that suggests that migration came from Europe 2,500 years before Columbus was born.

Barry Fell, a professor and researcher in Comparative Zoology at Harvard University, studied the Mediterranean Sea Peoples of the Bronze and early Iron Age—about 3,000–4,000 years ago. In the early 1970s, American archaeologists began sending him inscriptions from rocks and pottery, which they found in New England. To his surprise, he recognized the inscriptions as originating in the Mediterranean. He then explored New England and found hundreds of inscriptions and received many more from others.[8] He traced these inscriptions back to Phoenicia, the Celts in Ireland, and Iberia, some as old as 2,500 years. Together, in various Mediterranean languages, they described a very intricate record of voyages to and life in the new world. These inscriptions were on buried temples, tablets, gravestones, and on cliff faces, and were found as far north as Canada, as far south as Georgia, and as far west as the Mississippi. The immigrants left Europe from Spain and Portugal to take advantage of the same trade winds that Columbus rediscovered in the fifteenth century. They built villages, raised Druids' circles, and even used Roman numerals.

Around 1000 A.D., the Vikings began hopping across the northern Atlantic, first from Norway to Iceland, and then Eric the Red went to Greenland. When Bjarni Herjolfsson went searching for Eric the Red, he got lost and kept sailing west until he found a land "level and covered with woods" that was not Greenland. He sailed up and down the coast, and then returned to Greenland where he told Leif Ericsson, son of Eric the Red. Leif was intrigued and sailed west, finding Baffin Island just north of the Hudson Bay, and then Labrador, which they called Woodland, and finally, Vinland. He stayed there for the winter and returned to Greenland the next summer. Others followed in the years ahead, but they fought natives and did not settle.[9]

It was left for Columbus to discover and to make his discoveries known to the wider world, but his voyages were financed because he pledged to the king and queen that his first purpose was to convert the heathens of India. His problem was that he was not sure what he discovered or who the natives were. In a letter dated February 15, 1493, written in the Canary Islands on his way home, Columbus assured King Ferdinand that the people he found in the Indies were "well-formed," but not Negroes. This posed an awkward theological dilemma because the Bible had not accounted for another race. The issue was referred to the pope, who agonized and finally decided they were descendants of sinful Babylonians, most of whom had been killed in the flood. Columbus evidently found the few who escaped the flood, but had been banished to the wilderness.[10] Only after his third voyage in 1498 did Columbus "come to believe that this is a mighty continent which was hitherto unknown."[11]

Of course, the two continents of the Americas were not named after its Genoese discoverer, but after a Florentine, Amerigo Vespucci, who managed the Medici family's financial interests, but became enamored with exploration. On behalf of the king of Portugal, he explored the coast of the southern continent and published several widely read letters in a book *Mundus Novus* in 1502. In it, he described the "Fourth Part of the World"—beyond Europe, Africa, and Asia. His letters and the book were circulated widely and read far more than Columbus's epistle to the king.

A German printer, Martin Waldseemüller (1470–1518), read Vespucci's letters and published a map and a short book of 103 pages in April 1507, called *Cosmographiae Introductio.* In considering a name for the "Fourth Part," Waldseemüller wrote: "Inasmuch as both Europe and Asia received their names from women, I see no reason why anyone should justly object to calling this part Amerige [from Greek 'ge' means 'land of'], i.e. the land of Amerigo, or America." Using modern print, the book sold widely. When Waldseemüller discovered he made a mistake in naming the region "America," it was too late to change the name.[12]

Ralph Waldo Emerson later erupted against the "pickle dealer from Seville . . . who managed in this lying world to supplant Columbus and baptize

Figure 2.1: The 1507 Waldseemüller Map

This was the first map that used the term "America," which can be seen on the lower left panel. Amerigo Vespucci is pictured on the top panel of the third column. North America is distinct—on the top left panel—but it is a poor, scrawny neighbor of South America and especially Africa.

half the earth with his own dishonest name,"[13] but the truth is that Vespucci did not name the continent. A German printer did. And Emerson also got the story wrong: Vespucci was not a pickle dealer, and he wasn't from Seville.

Waldseemüller's map borrows from the available knowledge of the time to show a land mass between Europe and Asia and bearing some resemblance to the two continents of the Americas. That same map was purchased by the Library of Congress in 2003 for $10 million.[14] It is the oldest document that uses the name "America."

North America was first noted on a map published by Gerardus Mercator in 1538—*Americae pars septentrionalis* (North America) and *Americae pars meridionalis* (South America).[15] The continent finally had a name. *Septentrional* is an ancient Latin word that refers to the seven stars of the Big Dipper, which sailors used to find the North Star. Anthony DePalma in his marvelous "biography" of the continent, uses the metaphor of the name to locate the force that binds the continent together. The central idea, in his mind, is "the knowledge that we who live here have inherited the precious chance of starting afresh." This ceaseless journey to start afresh has nonetheless taken many different forms, revealing "different versions of the new world."[16]

In the great American novel, *The Great Gatsby*, Nick Carraway muses about Gatsby's dreams by placing them in the context of the many voyages to this New World: "For a transitory moment, man must have held his breath in the presence of this continent, compelled into an aesthetic contemplation he neither understood nor desired, face to face for the last time in history with something commensurate to his capacity for wonder."

Of course, most Europeans had not bothered to ask the natives what they called the world now known as North America. There were many answers, but the most common was "Turtle Island."[17] A rose by any other name might smell as sweet, but that might not apply to a continent called Turtle Island.

➤ The Great Encounter

After Columbus showed the way, many Europeans followed and named parts of North America after their country of origin. At one time, parts of the continent were known as Spanish America, French America, British America, Russian America (Alaska), and Danish America (Greenland), but three nations— Spain, England, and France—were the principal authors of the third layer of continental definition. The three European powers sliced the continent and injected a different genetic code in each container. The code is defined by the time of discovery, the country responsible, the people they encountered, and the people and nation that they became.

After hearing Columbus's report, the Spanish monarchs sent soldiers to extract gold and dispatched priests to convert pagans. They encountered two grand civilizations—the Incas in the Andes and the Aztecs in Mexico—that were as advanced in many ways as those in Europe. The Pyramid of the Sun in Teotihuacan (just north of the Mexican capital) is the third largest pyramid in the world—200 feet tall and 700 feet on one side. It was built more than one thousand years before Hernán Cortés marched his soldiers into Tenochtitlan in the central valley of Mexico in 1519. Cortés found floating gardens, temples as grand as European cathedrals, and a population larger than that of Paris. In the entire central valley of Mexico, on the eve of the Spanish discovery, the population has been estimated at 25.2 million people, though the estimate is quite rough. In comparison, Spain and Portugal had fewer than 10 million people.[18]

The Aztecs stood on the shoulders of Olmecs, Mayas, and other civilizations that had mastered astronomy and mathematics. The Emperor Moctezuma II had an army of tens of thousands of soldiers, yet Cortés prevailed with 600 men and 16 horses. How that happened has been the subject of many books stretching over 500 years.[19]

Beyond the obvious courage that Cortés and his men demonstrated, scholars credit his success to four factors. Cortés had a technological edge with firearms and horses. The new weapons struck fear in their enemies, leaving some to believe the Spanish had supernatural powers. Secondly, his soldiers were unwitting bearers of the first biological weapons—tiny microbes of diseases—especially smallpox. The natives had no immunity, and tens of millions perished. By 1620, a census located only 730,000 native Mexicans—approximately 3 percent of the population one century before.[20]

Third, the Aztecs had recently come to power by ruthlessly suppressing many other tribes, who were therefore hungry for revenge and eager to help Cortés. And fourth, the Aztecs may have defeated themselves by believing a myth that the god Quetzalcoatl would return to Mexico with a white face and horses. Thus, Moctezuma, the Aztec emperor, welcomed Cortés into the inner sanctum. Cortés reciprocated by murdering Mochtezuma and, by doing so, also decapitated the apex of the Aztec pyramid, replacing it figuratively with the Spanish king, represented by him.

The English who voyaged to Virginia in 1607 and to Massachusetts in 1620 were settlers, not conquerors. Instead of seeking gold and souls, the English immigrants fled religious persecution and sought to build a life on a new land.

Figure 2.2: The 1562 Hieronymus Cock Map

By 1562, the date of this map drawn by Hieronymus Cock, a Dutch cartographer, North America's outlines were much clearer.

They did not want to return to England with new-found wealth; their intention was to stay and build a future in the new world. Instead of facing a proud, hierarchical civilization that they could command only after murdering their leaders, the English faced small tribes of hunters and gatherers.

In North America, above the Rio Grande, scholars have estimated that there may have been as many as 4 million Indians in 3,000 tribes, speaking as many as 2,200 languages. The social organization of these tribes varied widely, from nomadic tribes to settled farmers. Cahokia was a thriving economic center of more than 40,000 people at a point where the Missouri and Illinois Rivers empty into the Mississippi. Close to modern-day St. Louis, Cahokia was the center of a river market that extended from Alberta to New Mexico in the west and to Pennsylvania and the Gulf of Mexico in the east, a trading empire larger than most of Europe. At its height in 1250 A.D., Cahokia had forty-five pyramids, including Monk's Mound, covering sixteen acres, the largest in the world at the time. A temple sat the top of the mound and extended about one hundred feet into the sky. This was the one civilization that the Europeans had not discovered; indeed, only in the 1960s did anthropologists and archaeologists piece together the story, which started in about 600 A.D. with the introduction of new strains of maize and new agricultural techniques, including the hoe.[21]

The French, led by Samuel de Champlain, built their first permanent settlement on the St. Croix River in 1604 and founded Quebec in 1608. More like the Spanish than the English, the French explorers and settlers were sent by the king to establish a province of France to enrich the crown through commerce—primarily hunting and trapping the game that was so abundant in lower Canada. Their numbers remained quite small, and while they ventured wide and, by the early part of the eighteenth century, claimed an area—the Louisiana Territories—that was larger than the English colonies, they did not initially set down roots. Like the Spanish, the French ruled the natives but also used them—in Mexico to mine for silver and in Quebec to trade furs and fish. The northern Indians—particularly the Iroquois, but also the Huron—had developed sophisticated social and political organizations, and they allied with either the French or the English when it served their interests.

The natives—called Indians for centuries, but now called by their tribes or, more broadly, in Canada as "first nations"—left a complex, somewhat paradoxical legacy.[22] In Mexico, the native population was the largest and most stable, and the civilization was most advanced. The Spanish dominated the sixteenth century in the Americas in large part because they were able to build upon the foundation of a great civilization and were able to employ a large workforce. By the time the pilgrims settled in New England, New Spain already had a university in Mexico City that was seventy years old.

Perhaps a better metaphor than the university for the Spanish-Indian encounter can be found under a church on a hill in Cholula near Puebla, southeast of Mexico City. On his march to the Aztec capital, Cortés destroyed villages and temples in his path. The people of Cholula had a magnificent pyramid temple, and they mobilized all the people in the region to cover it with several feet of mud so that when Cortés arrived, he saw only a huge hill. The natives proposed that he build his cathedral on the top of the hill, and that is what the Spanish did. The local people used underground tunnels to burrow into the pyramid. The Spanish thought they were on top of the hill and in full control and that the natives had submitted to their will and that of the Church. The natives viewed the Church as protecting their pyramid and heritage. They kept the secret with a silent chuckle for four centuries. Descendants of the European invaders learned the secret in the early twentieth century.

In the United States and Canada, the British and the French encountered open spaces and a sparse and mobile population. They did not come to plunder, but to settle, grow crops, and raise livestock and their children. In New England, the new settlers farmed with their own hands, not those of slaves, and because many of them came to the new world seeking religious tolerance, they were less intent on converting the heathen. Both settlers and natives were wary of each other, and whether they would share food or attack each other depended on leadership and circumstances. Over time, however, most of the Indians went west for game, and were forced to do so when the settlers took their land.

When the frontier began to close at the turn of the twentieth century, the "first nations" population was estimated by Douglas Ubelaker, an anthropologist, at about 500,000 above the Rio Grande.[23] By this time, most were in reservations. Some had migrated to Canada. As time passed, the newcomers recognized the wrong that they had committed, but even those with the best of intentions failed to find a humane and effective approach. They alternated between helping the indigenous people adjust to the modern world and encouraging them to live apart from it in reservations.[24]

The Spanish who inherited the most wealth and became masters of an empire found themselves weighed down by their treasure. Instead of investing in the land, they extracted its minerals. Instead of learning from the Aztecs and Mayas, the Spanish imposed their religion. Instead of involving the natives in government, they ruled from abroad. Instead of relating to them based on respect, they sought to maintain their racial purity. But over time, many intermarried, and when Mexico achieved independence, the government gave the Indians full rights. By the time of the Mexican revolution in 1910, the country as a whole began to view the native heritage as a source of greater pride than its European heritage. They rebuilt the great monuments and cities of the pre-Colombian era and filled their museums with artifacts. However, race remains a defining characteristic in Mexico. Few pure-blooded Indians are in positions of power, few white Europeans are poor, and an extremely wide gap in wealth and power separates them.

The settlers from England scratched a living from the land while the Spanish used native labor to mine the earth of its wealth. This explains why the region above central Mexico was initially poorer but eventually richer than New Spain. It also explains why the English settlers in the 13 colonies were the first to seek and achieve full independence.

British America was hardly homogenous. Plantation owners in the south did not rely on their own labor; they imported African slaves. This not only compromised the pledge of equality embedded in the new nation, it also made the south more like Spanish America. In the end, slavery divided the country and precipitated a devastating civil war.

The Canadians were faced with a cultural chasm between the British and the French. The French and Indian War, which concluded in 1763, left the British in charge of Canada, but the division between English and French Canada was never truly bridged. That plus the expanding power of the United States left Canadians uncertain as to their identity—a dilemma that continues to this day.

➤ National Codes

Each of the three nations was born of different parents, land, and circumstances. The struggle for independence was long and bloody in the United States and Mexico and only appears inevitable with hindsight. Many Americans who opposed revolution against Great Britain went north to Canada. Canada's own road to independence was peaceful, gradual, and deliberate. "Dominion" status—independent but still tied to England—was achieved in 1867, but Canada waited another century before adopting its own national flag and anthem.

If one conceives of a genetic code as composed of many interwoven threads that evolve over time, the first would be geological. The second was the human migration; the third, the encounter between Europeans and natives, and the fourth was the rise of the nation. Interpreting the national thread is the most daunting, but it offers a key to understanding both the opportunities and the constraints on continental cooperation.

Those who have unscrambled the human genome do not claim to be able to predict human behavior, but scientists can sometimes estimate the probability of having a particular disease. When matched with a particular environment, their estimates improve, but nothing is certain. That is even truer about the national genetic code. Each nation is a complicated organism. In the next section, we shall try to identify the specific threads that have made each nation different as well as those that make them similar because all three often responded to similar global pressures or events.

THE U.S. CODE

The thirteen colonies of British North America marched to independence on two paths—one that was spontaneous, violent, and uncoordinated, and a second that was deliberate, informed, and democratic. The Massachusetts Bay Colony protested British taxation, first by throwing tea into Boston Harbor, and then by fighting British troops on Bunker Hill and on the road to Lexington and Concord in 1775–1776. At the same time, representatives of each of the colonies participated in the Continental Congress. There, they signed the Declaration of Independence that functions as a birth certificate for a nation that views itself as defined more by an idea—freedom—than by geography. "We hold these truths to be self-evident, that all men are created equal, that they are endowed by their Creator with certain unalienable Rights, that among these are Life, Liberty and the pursuit of Happiness." The author, Thomas Jefferson, later wrote that the Declaration "was intended to be an expression of the American mind."[25] It was much more; it became the political creed of the country and also an inspiration for democrats throughout the world. It connects America's sense of itself with its view of the world.

Other threads were woven into the national fabric of the United States. The political framework had many components. The Constitution created a unified state and three independent branches—Congress, the Executive, and the Judiciary—with shared powers so that each would "check and balance" the other. The purpose was *not* to have an efficient government but rather one that would preserve liberty by preventing the concentration of power. The Founding Fathers used the first ten amendments to the Constitution to protect the most essential political rights.

The first president decided to step down after two terms, and this precedent was perhaps as important as any in assuring that democracy would take root. Americans had an inbred antipathy toward concentrated power that permeated public policy for two centuries. When the economic "trusts"—monopolies—grew too powerful at the turn of the twentieth century, Congress passed antitrust laws that divided them and prevented other mergers that could undermine competition. Similarly, Congress or the Supreme Court would restrain the president if he overstepped his bounds.

The social framework was defended by a vigorous civil society that kept the government accountable. Almost all Americans regardless how rich or poor identified themselves as middle-class, and the public school system allowed the poor to be educated and a meritocracy to emerge. Immigration replenished the nation. But the new nation also had a genetic defect: slavery and racism.

The international thread was defined and blessed by two great liquid assets, the Atlantic and the Pacific Oceans, that permitted the new nation to remain aloof from the conflicts of the old world. It meant that the United States could maintain a small standing army. America's view of imperialism was shaped by the Constitution, which granted to Congress the responsibility to set rules for absorbing new territories. Congress then decided that each new territory that entered the union would do so on an equal basis to the other states. In other words, the U.S. government decided that it would have states, not colonies.

The United States, however, was hardly passive or pacifist. It murdered or forced the Indian population to go west. It fought its first war in 1812 to defend the rights of its seamen but also to try to annex Canada. It failed, but the war had a salutary effect of compelling Great Britain to finally recognize in word and deed the independence of the United States, and in 1818, to demilitarize the Great Lakes.

It took more time and another war to define the southern border. In 1819, the United States acquired Florida from Spain. Texas, led by Americans who settled there, rebelled against Mexico and achieved independence in 1836.[26] It asked to be annexed by the United States, but the U.S. government dodged the request in large part because the North and South were at odds about whether new states should prohibit or permit slavery.

In 1844, James K. Polk was elected president and annexed Texas. The Mexican Army crossed the Rio Grande to attack American soldiers and gave Polk the reason to declare war. "Mexico has shed American blood," Polk told Congress, "upon the American soil." Although Mexico initially had more than four times as many soldiers as the U.S. Army (32,000 vs. 7,365), U.S. forces rapidly captured California and Mexico City. The Treaty of Guadalupe Hidalgo was signed on February 2, 1848, and for $15 million, Mexico was compelled to cede to the United States approximately 1.2 million square kilometers that included the future states of California, Colorado, Utah, New Mexico, and Arizona. The main opposition to the treaty in the U.S. Senate came from those who wanted to annex all of Mexico. At about the same time, the U.S. government negotiated with Great Britain the northern boundaries on the east (Maine-New Brunswick) and west coasts (the Oregon Territory). With those treaties, the boundaries of the United States were mostly set. The Russian sale of Alaska in 1867 and the acquisition of Hawaii at the turn of the century added two more territories that in 1959 would become states.

After the Civil War, the United States concentrated on internal development. By 1900, the United States had a population of 75 million people, exceeding Germany's (56 million), and Great Britain's (41 million). It produced twice as much steel as any other nation and as much coal as Great Britain. Its railroads stretched 250,000 miles, and its new entrepreneurs, like Thomas Edison, Henry Ford, and Andrew Carnegie, created entire industries. The U.S. economy was the strongest in the world, but its army was smaller than Romania's.

In the nineteenth century, the U.S. defined itself as a "promised land," a nation that was exceptional and detached from the world's conflicts.[27] In the twentieth century, as it acquired power, it sought to reshape the world to conform to its values and revolutionary vision. With deep roots in the country's unique heritage, an American idea of a new international system crystallized. Its elements were collective security and international organizations; self-determination and the rule of law; and free trade and an end to imperialism. Not every American agreed with this strategy, and as a result, U.S. foreign policy sometimes seemed to swing between unilateral interventions to defend U.S. security and multilateral efforts to secure peace and international norms.[28] In North America, the United States viewed itself as friendly and supportive of its neighbors, though they often saw the United States as arrogant, coercive, or uninterested.

The United States emerged from its civil war with an army so powerful that it could have reshaped the Americas. If the United States had followed the European road of empire, it would probably have begun by subduing and annexing its two neighbors. But it chose instead to heal its divisions and develop itself, allowing Mexico and Canada to do the same. The borders between the three countries stretch over 7,000 miles, but not one fort was built on them, and until the United States became uneasy with undocumented migration in 2007, no troops patrolled them. Indeed, the first border patrol officials were appointed in 1924. The genetic code of the United States is thus a long collective DNA chain. One thread contains a political framework that stresses freedom and resists concentrated power. Another is societal, shaped by immigrants, middle-class values, and a public school system that emphasizes meritocracy. Still another shapes a foreign policy that veers between unilateralism and interventionism on the one side, and international institutions and rules on the other. But the two foreign policy threads joined in their opposition to imperialism and their support for a world of freer trade and self-determination.

THE MEXICAN CODE

Just as the Declaration of Independence, signed by elected representatives, defines the birth of the United States, so too does the "grito" (cry) define Mexico. In 1810, a priest, Father Miguel Hidalgo y Costilla, cried out for the separation of Mexico from Spain. Father Hidalgo was captured and executed, but he was succeeded by another priest. By the time that Mexico achieved independence in 1821, the revolution had turned reactionary, and its first leader, Agustin Iturbide, declared himself emperor. Within two years, however, he was overthrown.

At that time, Mexico and the United States were roughly equal in size (1.7 million square miles) and population (7 million), but Mexico was wealthier because of its gold and silver mines. Between 1821 and 1857, Mexico had 40 changes in the presidency (most by violence), 36 different governments and more than 100 foreign ministers. Instability made Mexico vulnerable to attack by Spain in 1829, France in 1838, and the United States in 1846, with the latter taking the northern third of the country. Ironically, it was the United States after its Civil War that came to the defense of Mexican sovereignty, by sending its troops to the border and persuading the French to depart. Benito Juarez, the first civilian and indigenous leader (Zapotec Indian) to be elected president, introduced liberal reforms.

In 1877, Porfirio Diaz took and kept power for 33 years through many fraudulent elections. Diaz invited foreign investors and modernized the country. He built railroads and developed oil, minerals and a small manufacturing industry. However, inequalities within the country were exacerbated, foreigners dominated the economy, and the lack of free elections evoked increasing resistance.

In 1910, a worldly Francisco Madero led a peaceful rebellion calling for free elections. Diaz abdicated, and Madero won the presidency. Within two years, the authoritarian right, with the complicity of the U.S. Ambassador, assassinated Madero and provoked the first social revolution of the twentieth century. Peasants and workers, led initially by Emiliano Zapata and Pancho Villa, fought the old guard. Nearly 10 percent of Mexico's population died in the revolution that lasted until 1920.

Mexico would be defined by the revolution's struggle against injustice, but also by its pantheon of enemies, which included the Church, the landed aristocracy, foreign investors, and the United States for its interventions in Veracruz to prevent the landing of German arms and in northern Mexico to try to capture Pancho Villa, who had killed Americans. It was also defined by a new constitution approved in 1917 which incorporated the revolution's goals, including national patrimony over its resources, land for the poor, subordination of the Church, strong labor rights, and no reelection for all offices. Assassinations of the revolution's leaders slowed the process by which these principles could be implemented, but over time, a political party, the Institutional Revolutionary Party (PRI), assumed control of the government.[29] President Lázaro Cardenas (1934–40) is one of the most admired of Mexico's presidents for making good on two of the principal promises of the revolution: land reform and the nationalization of the oil industry.

From 1929 until 2000, the leader of the PRI was also the president of the country, and he ruled much as the Aztec emperor and the Spanish viceroy had—with full control. The principle of "no reelection" that was consecrated by the revolution of 1910 was an important political innovation that eliminated *caudilloismo*, or personal dictatorship. Nonetheless, by replacing personal with institutional authoritarianism, the promise of democracy was not fulfilled. Because no official could be reelected, the president had the power, in effect, to appoint the entire government, giving him all of the instruments of patronage that allowed him to dictate government policy.

In foreign relations, the Mexican government followed the *Estrada Doctrine*, which declared that no country has the right to intervene in another country's internal affairs. "Intervention" was defined broadly to mean "influence," and "internal affairs" was also so wide as to cover whatever the PRI wanted to exclude. Mexico would denounce a foreign government, for example, if that government's officials criticized the unfairness of an election. This policy not only aimed to preclude foreigners from influencing Mexico; it also strengthened the PRI's control by making any criticism unpatriotic. The major country to which this policy was directed was the United States. The rationale was articulated by a young intellectual in the 1980s. "In the case of two nations as disparate in size, power, and wealth as Mexico and the United States," wrote Jorge G. Castañeda, "the weight of economic superiority can be crushing and can lead to a permanent loss of significant attributes of sovereignty and cultural identity." Castañeda feared that Mexico could become "less Mexican," and so Washington had to be held at arm's length.[30]

Similarly, Mexico's "import-substitution industrialization" strategy based on high tariffs and restrictions on foreign investment also made it easier to contain foreign influence and create an economic elite tied to the party. The strategy secured substantial growth from 1950 until 1982, and it developed a national market, but at the cost of being uncompetitive internationally and dangerously dependent for its foreign exchange on oil and external debt. When the price of oil plummeted in 1982, Mexico came face-to-face with the limits of its economic and political strategy.

The response to the 1982 debt crisis transformed Mexico's political culture and its economic and international policies so fundamentally that it almost appeared as if a new genetic code had been implanted. Mexico went from a closed economy and an authoritarian political system to one that began to open to the world economy and to free political contests. The changes that began in 1982 reached their culmination with the election of Vicente Fox and the PAN in the year 2000. By that time, Mexico was transformed from a country that kept its neighbors distant to one that offered the boldest ideas for North American cooperation.

THE CANADIAN CODE

Forty-five years passed from the American declaration of independence to Spain's recognition of Mexico's independence in 1821. Another forty-six years would pass until the British Parliament granted Canada substantial autonomy. The three paths could not have been more different. Americans achieved complete independence in five years and established a firm democratic foundation. Mexicans fought twice as long against their colonial masters, and after victory, they replaced a foreign dictatorship with a cruel and unstable national dictatorship.

In Canada, there was no war and no struggle. Its leaders reluctantly met at the request of Great Britain, which realized that it could no longer defend Canada from the strongest army in the world. Canadian leaders respectfully asked the mother country to approve "The British North American Act" to establish a "Confederation of Canada, a Dominion within the British Empire." The British Parliament approved the law in 1867. Canada would *not* be a "fully sovereign state." Foreign and defense policies would still be made in London, and its head of state remained the British Monarch.[31]

"Americans do not know, but Canadians cannot forget," writes Seymour Martin Lipset, "that two nations, not one, came out of the American Revolution." America emerged confident of its revolution and proud of its independence. At the same time, Canada was proud to view itself as "that part of British North America that did not support the [American] Revolution."[32] More than 50,000 American "loyalists" left the United States for Canada before, during, or right after the revolution, and they brought with them a set of values that set them apart, for a time, from those who stayed. Whereas the United States seeks "life, liberty, and the pursuit of happiness," Canadians strive for "peace, order, and good government." Lipset, whose volume traces the differences between the two nations, describes Canada as "more class-aware, elitist, law-abiding, statist and . . . group oriented" than the United States. He posits that English-speaking Canada opposed the liberal, individualistic values of the American Revolution while French-speaking Canada opposed the anticlerical, democratic values of the French Revolution. Both Canadian groups wanted a "conservative, monarchical, and ecclesiastical society in North America"—very different from that of the United States or Mexico.[33]

In seeking to identify the factors that shaped this distinct perspective, Keith Spicer suggests three: climate, geography, and history. To Spicer, the cold, forbidding climate encouraged "caution, conservatism, and an obligatory caring for each other," characteristics that many Canadians admire in themselves. The vast and rich geography offered them a sense of space and opportunity. Finally, in his mind, Canada is shaped by the uneasy relationship between English and French combined with new immigrants from Asia.[34]

The central thread of Canada's genetic code, however, was the combined uncertainty of its identity and its relationship with the United States. Much like Mexico, Canada's relationship alternated between seeking separation and experimenting with economic integration. The first strategy—a "National Policy"—was pursued in 1878 by Sir John A. Macdonald, the first prime minister and a Conservative, to integrate the provinces and build a nation. He raised tariffs and constructed railways and communications across the east-west expanse. But the population was small—only 5.3 million at the turn of the century, as compared to 75 million in the United States.

In the new century, the Liberal Party wanted to reduce tariffs, and so the Wilfred Laurier government negotiated a free-trade agreement with the United States in 1911. The Canadian people, however, were not yet ready to trust the United States, and the Laurier government was defeated before it could implement the agreement. When the Smoot-Hawley Tariff Act passed the U.S. Congress in 1930, raising U.S. tariffs to their highest level in the twentieth century, Great Britain and Canada responded with the Ottawa Agreements, which put a protective shell around the Commonwealth countries.

President Franklin D. Roosevelt reversed course on trade policy and gained congressional approval of the Reciprocal Trade Agreements Act in 1934, which authorized the president to negotiate agreements to reduce tariffs. Canada signed an agreement in 1936, and then in 1948, Liberal Prime Minister William

Lyon McKenzie King negotiated a more extensive free-trade agreement. At the last minute, though, King decided not to sign the agreement, evidently fearing a political result similar to Laurier's. Canada did not, however, opt out of free trade. Instead, it joined the global General Agreements on Tariff and Trade (GATT) in 1948.

After World War II, Canada assembled the accoutrements of an independent nation even while it tried to heal the major division between French Quebec and the other provinces. It acquired its own flag—the Maple Leaf—in 1965 and its own anthem—"O Canada"—to replace "God Save the Queen" two years later. It restricted foreign investment and developed a national energy policy, though the western provinces resisted it.

In 1982, Liberal Prime Minister Pierre Elliot Trudeau "repatriated" the constitution. With that, the British Parliament no longer had the ultimate authority to decide on constitutional changes in Canada. Trudeau then modernized the original British North American Act and added a Charter of Rights and Freedoms to make it the Constitution Act. In consolidating the nation, however, Trudeau also opened some wounds, as Quebec refused to ratify the Constitution unless it was assured a distinct status with French as an official language. After the government negotiated that change in 1987 at Meech Lake, two provinces, Manitoba and Newfoundland, voted against it, believing that Quebec should not have special standing but that the First Nations should. When the Conservative government incorporated those concerns in the Charlottetown Accord, the nation rejected it in a referendum. So the constitutional framework is still not firm.

In part because of internal division and also because of historic caution, Canada moved slowly on to the international stage. It found its place by becoming a world leader in "peacekeeping" and in negotiating treaties on banning landmines and establishing an International Criminal Court. In 1990, Canada joined the Organization of American States and began to play an important role in the Americas, particularly in democracy-building. As a member of NATO and the North American Aerospace Command (NORAD), Canada had long allied with the United States on strategic issues, but—like Mexico—it did not agree with all U.S. policies. Like Mexico, Canada supported the United States during the Cuban Missile Crisis, but it opposed the U.S. embargo against Cuba. Canada sent troops in October 2001 to support the U.S.-led attack on Afghanistan, but it opposed the U.S. invasion of Iraq, much as it had opposed the U.S. war in Vietnam.

On trade issues, Canada, like the United States, preferred its membership in the global trading system (GATT), but it was practical and decided to sign the U.S.-Canadian Automotive Pact in 1965, which dismantled barriers to trade with the United States on autos and auto parts. This facilitated the construction of an integrated auto industry between the two nations.

A review of the history of Canada shows a country that has grown more comfortable in its relationship with the United States, but it remains cautious. Canadians seek opportunities to demonstrate their independence, but they also recognize the advantage of America's market and technology. Over time, there has been a steady trend toward closer economic relationships. Canadian Prime Minister Brian Mulroney's decision in 1985 to explore a free-trade agreement was therefore both a logical extension of this trend and a qualitative shift.

➤ The North American Code

Until the mid-1980s, when both Canada and Mexico decided to open their economies and pursue freer trade with the United States, both countries had devised numerous ways to try to resist the gravitational attraction of the U.S. economy. Actually, the federal governments resisted, but many people, firms, entertainers, athletes, and sub-governments connected across the borders, and the result was an increasing congruence and even synchronization among the societies, economies, and politics.

The three national units are natural points to begin understanding contemporary North America, but if the discussion ends there, one would overlook the many ways our societies have also been sewing a seamless tapestry. Let us therefore review the common themes in the history of the continent, beginning with the natural landscape that was shaped long before surveyors marked the boundaries between the three countries.

All three countries had European-based colonial experiences that were shaped by encounters with indigenous people, who had arrived thousands of years before from Eurasia. Whether the Europeans came from Spain, France, or England, they dominated the local people—first by force, then by encouraging assimilation or insisting on segregation. In the twentieth century, all three countries asserted their pride of this indigenous heritage and permitted autonomy for the tribes.

The movement toward independence took almost a century—from the American revolution of 1776 to Canada's attaining dominion status in 1867. Mexico and the United States struggled through civil war and foreign intervention in the 1860s. In the last thirty years of the nineteenth century, all three countries deployed the new tools of the industrial revolution and turned their energies to creating nations and national economies. In 1862, President Lincoln authorized the construction of an intercontinental railroad, and Canada and Mexico did the same several years later.

At the dawn of the twentieth century, a financial crisis in the United States led to banking failures in the United States and a recession in Mexico, which was so severe that some believe it caused the revolution. That crisis and the concentration of economic power that preceded it catalyzed a progressive movement in the United States, a similar movement in Canada called the Grange, and Madero's "Liberal Plan" in Mexico. The next wave of liberal reforms in all three countries emerged from the Great Depression. The result was the New Deal in the United States, which ushered in Social Security, a jobs program, unemployment compensation, and a similar set of reforms in Canada. In Mexico, Cardenas nationalized the oil industry and redistributed land to the peasants.

By good fortune, in the 1930s, the presidents of Mexico—Lazaro Cardenas—and of the United States—Franklin D. Roosevelt—were progressive leaders, who shared a deep commitment to social justice. When Cardenas nationalized the oil industry, Roosevelt was sympathetic. Had the two leaders not been in synch with each other, the incident would have created a crisis in Mexico and the relationship. All three countries fought in the Second World War, and used the occasion to build the Alaska-Canada and Pan-American highway system that connected the three countries by road. They also worked together to construct the United Nations and other post-war institutions, and all opposed Communism in the Cold War. Again, there were variations in the policies, but in the broadest outline and during pivotal events, e.g., the Cuban Missile Crisis, there was a unity of purpose and direction. The 1960s were a turbulent decade in all three countries—in the United States due to the civil rights movement and the war in Vietnam, in Mexico because of a student rebellion and the "Massacre in Tlatelolco," and in Quebec where the "Quiet Revolution" turned violent.

In 1964, as the United States phased out the *bracero* program for temporary Mexican workers, it collaborated with Mexico to establish the Maquiladora Industrialization Program on the Mexican side of the border. The program allowed U.S. products to enter duty-free into Mexico where they used the cheaper labor to assemble the products for re-export to the United States. Only the "value-added" of the labor was taxed. The program was intended to soak up the labor returning to Mexico from the United States and manufacture more competitively priced products by combining lower-priced Mexican labor with high-priced American know-how.

The next year, the United States and Canada signed an Automotive Pact that allowed further integration of the U.S. and Canadian auto industries. These programs seemed independent of each other and different, but with hindsight, it appears that the countries were responding in similar ways to the need to begin integrating their economies to face more intense global competition.

Still, none of the three governments was ready to formalize a closer relationship or a free-trade agreement. Since the Second World War, the United States led the world in dismantling imperial trading blocs and building and expanding a single world trading system. While it supported European unity for strategic reasons and third world regionalism for development reasons, the United States declined to participate in any regional scheme for fear that could undermine the global trading system. That was the reason that the United States chose a single generalized system of tariff preferences for all developing countries rather than a special one just for Mexico or Latin America.

In the mid-1980s, each country changed its trade policies, and these changes made possible the great leap to a free-trade agreement for North America. First, as oil prices soared, Mexico discovered a vast new oil field in the mid-1970s. President Jose Lopez Portillo had grand designs for using the oil wealth, and he borrowed vast sums of money, believing that the oil in the ground was more valuable than the interest he paid for the capital. He was wrong. When the price of oil fell in the spring of 1982, he was left with a huge debt that Mexico could not pay. The United States and the IMF helped but only after securing agreement from Mexico to open its economy by reducing tariffs, encouraging investment, balancing both the trade and fiscal balance, and privatizing state corporations. Within a few years, Mexico had reduced its tariffs so much that it decided to join GATT. President Ronald Reagan had broached the idea of a North American free-trade agreement in his 1980 campaign for the presidency, but he soon realized that his neighbors were not ready. He did accept a free trade agreement with Israel and a one-way arrangement for the Caribbean and Central America, and these were signals of a new openness to regional agreements.

Canada took the first step. In the 1970s, the Liberal Party had given Canadian nationalism an edge that made many Canadians proud and others very uneasy. Trudeau restricted foreign investment, but when a deep recession struck Canada in 1982, businesses realized that the Canadian market was not large enough to permit them to grow. "They [Canadian businessmen] wanted to become more export-oriented, but were reluctant to make the necessary investment in the face of continued trouble in Canada-U.S. relations."[35]

In 1984, a national election brought the Progressive Conservative Party under Brian Mulroney to power with a large majority. Although his party had opposed free trade with the United States, Mulroney recognized a change in the public mood, and he floated the idea of free trade with President Ronald Reagan, who responded positively. Both governments negotiated and signed a free trade agreement in 1988. In the same year, Mulroney called an election, and with the Liberals opposed to the free trade agreement, a national debate occurred. Mulroney won the election and thus the debate.

The reversal on free trade by Mexico and its president Carlos Salinas was more startling than Mulroney's. Mexico's history of defensive nationalism was always more strident than Canada's. In December 1988, after winning a widely disputed election for president of Mexico, Salinas met with me for a long private discussion. He recognized that Mexico needed substantial foreign investment to move to a first world economy. His first priority was to reduce Mexico's debt, and then he would seek investment from Japan and Europe. He did not oppose investment from the United States, but he thought it would be better if Mexico diversified the sources of its investment.

The Japanese rebuffed his request, fearful that a closer relationship with Mexico could harm its relationship with the United States. In the first months of 1990, he went to Europe and learned that they were preoccupied with the end of the Cold War and incorporating Eastern Europe into a wider system. Several leaders encouraged him to become part of a trading unit with the United States, as that would give Europeans greater confidence to invest in Mexico. Salinas accepted the advice, and in the morning of February 1, 1990, he instructed his Trade Minister Jaime Serra to inform U.S. Special Trade Representative Carla Hills that Mexico wanted to pursue a free-trade agreement.

Hills said that her highest priority was to conclude the Uruguayan Round of world trade negotiations.[36] President George H. W. Bush listened to Hills's argument about giving priority to the Uruguayan Round, and he listened to her Deputy Julius Katz's argument that the United States should maintain its global approach rather than pursue regional trade agreements, but in the end, Bush decided to pursue a new approach for the region. Concerned that Canadian interests could be harmed, Prime Minister Mulroney requested that the negotiations become trilateral. Bush and Salinas agreed. Thus, modern North America was born. The negotiations were so complex that a five-volume text emerged and was signed on December 17, 1992, but each leader signed it in his own capital. It was a potent symbol: they were together, but they were also separate.

The negotiations reached their peak during the presidential campaign of 1992. Many in the Democratic Party, particularly the labor unions, opposed the agreement, and their candidate Bill Clinton found himself on the horn of a dilemma. If he opposed NAFTA, he would be criticized as protectionist, an "un-presidential" appellation, but if he favored the agreement, he could lose the support of unions and others in the party. So he avoided taking a position for as long as possible. Finally, he agreed to speak on the subject at North Carolina State University in Raleigh on October 4, 1992.

I was advising the Clinton campaign at the time and worked with Sandy Berger, his principal advisor on the issue. Some in the campaign wanted Clinton to oppose NAFTA; others insisted that Clinton's support should be made conditional on numerous fundamental changes in the agreement, including inserting enforceable labor and environmental provisions into the agreement. Berger and I proposed that he support NAFTA *and* pledge to ensure that labor and environmental issues would be addressed. In other words, he would not make his support conditional on changes in the agreement, but he would seek to add provisions related to labor and the environment into the agreement. I had spoken to Mexican President Salinas on the issue, and while he said he would prefer not to change the agreement, he would accept these changes.

On the eve of his speech, Clinton phoned former President Jimmy Carter and told him that if NAFTA were passed, American peanut farmers would lose their farms. As I had written an op-ed article for Carter on peanuts and NAFTA, Carter was fully aware of the issue, but he sensed that Clinton was trying to back away, so he made a very strong case for why Clinton needed to endorse NAFTA, and Clinton did.[37]

On taking office in January, Clinton put NAFTA aside while he focused on his priorities. In the summer of 1993, he finally authorized Mickey Kantor, the special trade representative, to conclude the side agreements, which were more symbolic than substantive. Then, he submitted the agreement to Congress and organized a major lobbying effort. Congress approved the new agreement in November 1993.

No single initiative had a more profound effect on North America than NAFTA. Trade and investment sky-rocketed, firms became North American, and immigration increased. A North American market emerged, and the three economies moved closer to each other and became more synchronized.

NAFTA hardly erased the doubts and uncertainties in all three countries about integration, and the Chiapas rebellion raised new ones. More serious was the peso crisis that occurred at the end of the year—a result of too much capital flowing into Mexico at the beginning and then washing out after a year of instability. There were no mechanisms for consulting on a devaluation crisis, and it took three months for the U.S. to help Mexico fashion a response, which amounted to a significant bail-out mostly from the United States. Mexico paid all of the money back before it was due, but many of the hopes that NAFTA had inspired—particularly in Mexico—were punctured by the crisis. Bill Clinton, who had spoken with such pride about the agreement in December 1994 at the Summit of the Americas, hardly mentioned it again after the debt crisis.

The rest of the decade saw quiet but substantial progress toward integration and democratization in Mexico. In 2000, the implausible occurred. The PRI lost a presidential election. Mexico had made a peaceful and gradual journey to democracy, and the electoral process in that year was professional, competent, and fair.

Vicente Fox became the first opposition leader elected president in Mexico in the twentieth century. He knew George W. Bush when they were both governors, and expectations grew after the two of them met at Fox's ranch in Guanajuato in February 2001. There, they promised to establish a "North American economic community." I later asked Fox why Bush agreed. In his view, Bush wanted good relations, but did not have a clue as to what that would entail. He invited Fox to a state visit to Washington in early September, but they made little progress. A few days later, the 9/11 terrorists struck, and this time, it was the United States that built the walls to protect itself.

The North American genetic code is composed of threads that are delicately intertwined—the geological thread, the migrations of flora, fauna, and humans, the collision between a colonial and indigenous heritage, a precarious road to independence, and a continuous struggle to preserve nations while enriching them.

The sum of all those threads is the code, but it cannot predict the future. Indeed, we have seen a history of contradictory behavior. The continent has seen peace and conflict, cooperation and resistance, integration and autarchy, community and nationalism. History is replete with both tendencies, and so the code has its limits. North America is not pursuing a single consistent path. NAFTA lowered barriers among the three countries; 9/11 raised them.

The idea of North America, like the idea of its three member states, was not inherent in the land or handed down by our Creator. It emerged from a complex code. To understand better the future trajectory of North America, we will examine the current views of the people of each country in the next chapter. Those views reflect shared historical themes and also the distinctiveness of each nation. We have enough surveys to test whether the anti-North American pundits are speaking for the people or for themselves.

3

Who Speaks for
North America?

National stereotypes are probably unavoidable. Countries are complex, containing multitudes of contradictions. Stereotypes are useful to help sort through the noise. When Iranian President Mahmoud Ahmadinejad says something nasty about the United States, Americans readily dismiss him as "anti-American" and move on. Although Canadians, Mexicans, and Americans understand each other better, they are hardly immune to using stereotypes to characterize each other. These are the customary ones:

- Canadians and Mexicans view Americans as arrogant, insensitive, or disinterested.
- Americans view Canadians as boring. Some facetiously refer to Canadians as "Americans with national health care and without guns."
- Canadians and Americans view most Mexicans as poor, illegal immigrants with a small minority who are rich and corrupt, and their country as a place that seems chronically under-developed.
- The collective stereotype is that the three countries are so different, so zealous in defending their sovereignty, and so distrustful of each other that any serious effort to collaborate is impractical.

These stereotypes are like negative advertising in a presidential campaign. They are both defensive and insulting at the same time, and they usually work in tainting or taunting their target. They also have a self-fulfilling quality to them. When Americans are accused of being arrogant, they tend to treat their accusers as unworthy, thus confirming their arrogance. When Canadians are called boring, they are likely to fume, privately, thus retaining their invisibility in the United States. And when Americans treat Mexicans with disrespect, Mexicans find ways to express their defiance, allowing Americans to conclude they are not worthy of respect.

The problem with such stereotypes is not that they are completely wrong, but that they are misleading and often produce the opposite of what one wants, making a positive relationship harder to achieve. They also freeze everyone into a single, usually negative frame of an ongoing movie. To move beyond the stereotype, and truly understand each other, one needs to sit through the entire movie and see neighbors doing a lot that is good and some that is not.

In the mid-1980s, I visited senior officials of the Mexican Foreign Ministry. They complained, much as they had done before, that the United States viewed them with disdain and never would accept them as equals. I suggested an experiment. They should undertake a "content analysis" of ten important U.S. newspapers, cataloguing each article on Mexico during the course of a year as "positive," "negative," or "neutral."

In a year, I returned to discuss the results. They were surprised. The analysis demonstrated that the U.S. papers did not have fixed views of Mexico. Quite the contrary, the articles seemed to follow events, policies, or decisions made *in or by* Mexico. If there was violence in Mexico or an anti-American protest, the articles were "negative." When Mexico showed progress on education or cooperation on international issues, the articles were positive. Other times, the reporting was neutral.

"We had always viewed America as dictating to us," said one official, "but these articles suggest that they *react* to us as much, if not more, than they act. What this means is that we can shape the way that the United States looks and behaves toward us." The study, in brief, was liberating. By realizing that U.S. views were not fixed or immutable, and that they responded to events in Mexico or what the Mexican government did, Mexicans felt empowered. They could set the agenda.

Similarly, public opinion in all three countries toward the others is hardly fixed, and opinions are far more sophisticated than the stereotypes. In the days before opinion surveys, governments and intellectuals spoke for the public based on their ideology or the core groups with whom they consulted. But in the absence of surveys, no one really knew what the "public" thought. Today, there is a plethora of public opinion surveys on North America. While it is difficult to interpret some surveys, we have enough data to gain a better understanding of what the public, not just the pundits, think.

➤ Do We Hate Each Other?

Let us be more systematic and begin with mutual perceptions. The conventional wisdom is that Canadians and Mexicans are anti-American, and Americans dislike or have little respect for their neighbors.

When Jorge Castañeda, a scholar and foreign minister under Vicente Fox, and I wrote *Limits to Friendship* in the mid-1980s, Mexican views of the United States were quite negative, partly for historical reasons, but also because of friction due to conflicting policies on Central America and drug trafficking. A poll published in a leading newspaper, *Excelsior*, in August 1986, found that 60 percent of Mexicans viewed the United States as a disagreeable or unpleasant neighbor, and 59 percent considered it an "enemy." Some viewed this poll from the lens of history. Since the U.S.-Mexican war, the United States was regularly viewed as a threat. But opinions in Mexico could have been influenced by a U.S. Senate Foreign Relations Committee hearing that occurred just before the poll. Senator Jesse Helms chaired the hearing and denounced the Mexican government and disparaged the Mexican people.[1]

Fast forward to the year 2000 when surveys found that "favorable" views of the United States by Canadians stood at 76 percent and by Mexicans at 68 percent. Then, in 2005, those favorable views declined by nearly half—to 43 percent in Canada and 36 percent in Mexico.[2]

These snapshots allow us to see more of the movie, and they confirm the point that public opinion in Mexico and Canada toward the United States changes in response to events, and it has changed over time.

A few years after the 1986 poll, Mexican views of the United States began to change, and the North American Free Trade Agreement (NAFTA) played a positive role in the evolution as it signified acceptance by the United States of a genuine partnership with Mexico. Even during the tense years of 2003–2005, Mexicans had a favorable view of the United States by a ratio of 2:1.[3] So did Canadians. Indeed, in the first year of the George W. Bush administration, about two-thirds of Mexicans viewed the United States positively. Opinion began to decline when the United States invaded Iraq and was critical of its neighbors for opposing that decision, and it kept falling because of the poisonous U.S. debate on immigration and the unwillingness by Bush to implement the NAFTA agreement as it related to trucking. Canadian views followed a similar pattern.

Americans had favorable views of Mexico and Canada, but as Mexicans and Canadians soured on the United States, American views of its neighbors also grew unfavorable, though not nearly as much as the neighbors' views of the United States. Even during this period of mutually negative feelings, however, Americans and Mexicans distinguished between people—which all viewed favorably—and governments.[4]

The public has warm feelings toward their neighbors even when they oppose their governments' policies. In 2004, when public opinion in Mexico had turned against President Bush, the Chicago Council on Foreign Relations and two Mexican groups measured "favorability" by asking the public to assign a temperature on a "thermometer scale." The Mexicans reserved their warmest feelings for the United States, and Americans put Mexico third on its scale—behind England and Germany but ahead of Israel.[5] This survey is similar to others undertaken in the last three decades when roughly three-fourths of all Mexicans had a positive view of the United States. About the same percentage of Americans also had a positive view of Mexico.

Beginning in 1974, the Chicago Council on Global Affairs did a major survey of the opinions of Americans toward the world every four years, and more recently, every two years. Americans consistently gave Canada the highest favorability rating of any nation, and Mexico ranked between third and sixth—usually just behind Canada and the United Kingdom and ahead of Israel, Germany, and Japan.[6] Mexico's view of Canada is also very positive, with 91 percent describing Canada as a "partner" or a "friend," and 4 percent as a rival or a threat in a 2006 poll.[7] And Canada's view of Mexico is also quite positive, with 74 percent viewing it favorably, and 13 percent unfavorably.[8]

The public's view of its neighbors is not static. Important events and news reports affect perceptions. Between 2006 and 2010, the rise in U.S. concern about drug violence and illegal migration resulted in an 8 percent increase in the number of Americans who viewed relations with Mexico as "worsening."[9] This is a transitory swing, however. Over a thirty-year span of time, the conclusion that leaps off the pages of these many surveys is that the people in all three nations like each other, though not to the same degree. Asymmetry, which defines the relationship, is visible in the surveys. Americans tend to be more positive, but that may be because they are not paying as much attention. Canadians and Mexicans are far more sensitive to slights or insults by the United States because of its power and their need to defend themselves.

➤ Are Our Values Converging or Diverging?

For a deeper understanding of the relationship, one needs to examine questions of values and trust. Seymour Martin Lipset and Samuel P. Huntington believed that all three countries were built on such different cultural and political foundations that their values would necessarily be quite different.[10] Researchers from the three countries—Miguel Basañez, Neil Nevitte, and Ronald Inglehart—undertook five surveys between 1980 and 2005 to test this proposition of North American divergence. They concluded it was wrong.

Basañez, Nevitte, and Inglehart surveyed people about their views on religion, family, child-rearing, the role of government, the private sector, and different institutions—a total of fifty-four questions about values. They asked, for example, "Should people follow instructions at work? Which qualities would you prefer to foster in children—independence, imagination, or determination? Is God important in your lives?" They found a convergence among the three publics in twenty-five values (46 percent), parallel movement in nine values, and a divergence in only 20 values (37 percent). "Data clearly shows that the value shift on these basic dimensions in the U.S., Canada, and Mexico," the three concluded, "are moving along the same trajectories."[11] They also concluded that this convergence is not due to American predominance. Indeed, the United States also moved in the direction of its neighbors. The convergence was *because all three publics became more alike.*

Alejandro Moreno, a political scientist and pollster in Mexico, tackles the second shibboleth that has been used to make the case for divergence in North America—Mexican distrust toward the United States. Given the history of U.S. interference in Mexico, many scholars have long assumed that Mexican distrust is deep and wide.

The assumption is incorrect. From 1990 to 2005, the proportion of Mexicans who expressed trust in the United States nearly doubled, from 20 to 36 percent. This is low in comparison to Canadians whose trust of Americans increased from 55 to 63 percent during the same period, but it reflects a much higher level of trust by Mexicans for the United States than for any other country, including Canada (trusted by 20 percent of Mexicans) or any in Latin America. Moreover, the doubling in trust toward Americans occurred during the same period that interpersonal trust among Mexicans declined by half, from 33 to 16 percent.[12] In other words, Mexicans trust Americans more than the people of any other country or even themselves. Interestingly, Mexicans trust Mexicans living in the United States more than they trust Mexicans in Mexico or Americans.

"We can safely conclude," Moreno writes, "that Mexicans have had a pre-dominantly favorable opinion about the United States during the last two decades and that anti-American sentiment has been a minority view." He be-lieves that the change is due to NAFTA and growing "social inter-connect-edness." Nearly half of all Mexicans have a close relative living in the United States, and 14 percent receive remittances.[13] The cultural distance that Mexico once felt about the United States has narrowed or disappeared. Mexicans can see their own faces in America.

Because most Canadians speak English and the political culture is similar, they feel a greater need than Mexicans to distinguish themselves from Ameri-cans, but does this mean that they are "anti-American?" No doubt, the national psyche of Canada is fixated on the "elephant"—to use Pierre Trudeau's meta-phor—to its south. There is a minority of Canadians who dislikes anything American and a larger number that can be provoked into such spasms by in-sensitive or unilateral American policies. In the last year of the Bush adminis-tration, Canadian views of U.S. policy were at their most negative, and a survey then suggested that one-third (32 percent) were "consistently against the U.S.," and one-quarter (24 percent) were "consistently pro-U.S." The largest number (44 percent) were ambivalent about their feelings, meaning that it depended on the question and the time.[14] After just six months of Obama's administra-tion, Canadian views of the United States had become much more favorable, by 13 percent (from 55 to 68 percent), and Mexican views had improved by 22 percent (from 47 to 69 percent).[15]

Canadians and Mexicans distinguish between U.S. policy and the U.S. as a country, and they tend to be more positive about the latter. Both Canada and Mexico have had serious differences with the United States, but when asked whether those differences are a result of different values or policies, 57 percent of Canadians and an equal percentage of Mexicans said it was because of dif-ferences in policy, while only one-third of Mexicans and Canadians said it was due to different values.[16] In fact, American views of President Bush's policies by the end of his administration were as negative as Canadian and Mexican views. In brief, the public in all three countries share values and sometimes share views on policies.

Karl Deutsch, one of the great political scientists of the twentieth century and a refugee of Europe's wars, focused his research on trying to understand how states could collaborate. His theory was that as states develop closer rela-tions and communications, they begin to develop a sense of *community*, which he defined as an assurance "that they will settle their differences short of war."[17] The key factors in shaping those expectations are trust and a convergence of values. The surveys that we have examined suggest that the three countries of North America have quietly crossed a threshold where they have come to trust each other and share values. The next step toward a community is not as far as some would think.

➤ How Do We View NAFTA and Free Trade?

Although opponents of the U.S.-Canadian Free Trade Agreement and NAFTA have been fixed in their opposition, overall public opinion in the three countries has experienced wide fluctuations in the past fifteen years. In Mexico, almost 80 percent supported NAFTA when it was first proposed in 1990, but support plummeted to about 25 percent in 1995 after the full effects of the peso crisis were felt. From there, support steadily climbed to above 60 percent. Canada also experienced a wild swing, with support for the U.S.-Canadian Free Trade Agreement at nearly 80 percent when it was first announced in 1988, followed by a recession-driven decline until 1992. Since then, Canada's economy has done well, and support for NAFTA rose above 60 percent. (See Figure 3.1)

U.S. public opinion has followed a similar, although slightly more volatile pattern. A plurality between 1991 and 1996 supported NAFTA although the

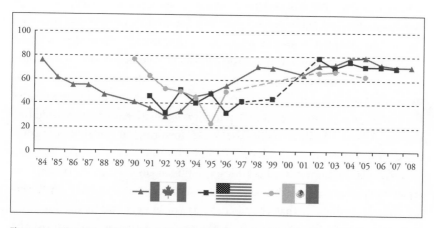

Figure 3.1: Support for Trilateral Free Trade Agreements, 1984–2008

Percent In Favor of Free Trade between Canada, the U.S., and Mexico.

Base: Most recent data points: Americans, Sept. 2007; Canadians, July 2008; Mexicans, June 2005

Source: Frank Graves, "Public Perspectives: Emerging Opportunities for Canada-U.S. Cooperation." Presentation for the Canada-U.S. Project, Government Conference Centre (Ottawa), Dec. 8, 2008, p.5.

margin was sometimes extremely narrow, and the supporters only approached a majority once. From 1996, however, support for NAFTA climbed from 35 percent to nearly 80 percent in September 2002 and 70 percent in March 2007. After that, U.S. support for free trade declined as the economy sank. By the time of the March 2008 presidential primary in Ohio, public opinion had turned staunchly against it, and the two Democratic presidential candidates reflected those views in their critical statements of NAFTA.

Based on slightly different questions, other surveys on American views of trade policy vary in the amount of support or opposition, but the overall trends are similar to the ones above. For example, in fourteen separate surveys from September 1997 to November 2010, the Pew Research Center asked: **"In general, do you think that free trade agreements like NAFTA, and the policies of the World Trade Organization, have been a good thing or a bad thing for the United States?"** A plurality answered "yes" from 1997 until November 2007 when the public divided 40-40. Then as the economy slipped into recession, views turned negative. In April 2008, only 35 percent said free trade was "good" and 48 percent described it as "a bad thing." One year later, however, in April 2009, 44 percent answered "yes," and 35 percent answered "no," and a similarly positive view was reported in November 2009. However, the economy did not recover as quickly as many had hoped, and by November 2010, the positive views about NAFTA and free trade had turned negative again.[18]

A more nuanced set of questions on trade was asked in June 2010 by the Chicago Council on World Affairs. At that time, a plurality (43 percent) of Americans favored trade agreements that lowered trade barriers, provided that the government would help workers if they lost their jobs due to trade. Another 14 percent favored free trade without assistance to workers, and only 36 percent opposed such agreements.[19] In brief, with the exception of relatively short periods during the recession (2007–2009) and in the period after the 2010 Congressional elections, a plurality of Americans has supported free trade and NAFTA. Regrettably, the worst downturn in the economy coincided with the presidential debates of 2008.

In the 2004 survey by the Chicago Council on Foreign Relations, the American public was asked to assess the costs and benefits of NAFTA. Overall, Americans believe that they benefit as consumers and as producers of exports, and these benefits outweigh the costs in terms of lost jobs. At the same time, Americans believe that trade with Mexico and Canada (NAFTA) has benefited the United States less than trade with the rest of the world, and that may partly explain why NAFTA became a piñata for a wide range of problems.[20] The 2010 Chicago Council on World Affairs survey asked a similar set of questions about whether globalization was good or bad for different reasons. Americans said globalization was good for "consumers like you" (59 percent good, 37 percent bad) and for American companies (51 percent and 44 percent), but bad for the U.S. economy (50 percent bad, 46 percent good) and for creating jobs in the United States (68 percent bad, and 36 percent good).[21]

How are we to explain the changes in public opinion over time? First, the views of NAFTA and free trade agreements have less to do with NAFTA or trade than with the performance of the economy and expectations about the future. If the economy performs poorly, people look to apportion blame, and trade is a usual suspect.

Secondly, leadership matters. After President Herbert Hoover signed the disastrous Smoot-Hawley Tariff of 1930 raising tariffs to their highest level in the twentieth century and exacerbating the Great Depression, presidents have tended to support freer trade policies. Congress generally seeks to protect uncompetitive industries, but defers to the president on trade policy, provided he makes the case and uses his political capital well. In the case of NAFTA, if Vice President Al Gore had failed to defend it against Ross Perot, opposition might very well have blocked the agreement.

In almost every year prior to the 2007–09 downturn, there has been a consensus that free trade benefits all three countries, but that the other two countries benefited more. In a 2004 survey, a plurality of Mexicans (44 percent) believed NAFTA was good for Mexico, but 78 percent believed it was better for the U.S. economy. Similarly, Americans were divided on whether NAFTA benefited the U.S. (43 percent), but 69 percent believed that Mexico benefited more. (See Figure 3.2)

In addition, all three peoples believe that their country has complied more with NAFTA than the others. This point, plus the fact that firms attribute their failure but not their success to trade, explains the logic that makes it politically difficult to reach trade agreements. However, strong presidents, who used their political capital well, have been able to persuade Congress and the public to support freer trade.[22]

➤ Is There A North American Identity?

How many North Americans can we find? There are many reasons why one would expect the answer to be "none" or "few." First, most leaders have tended to stress the differences separating the three countries, not the shared values. Second, drug trafficking, terrorism, illegal migration, trade disputes—all these

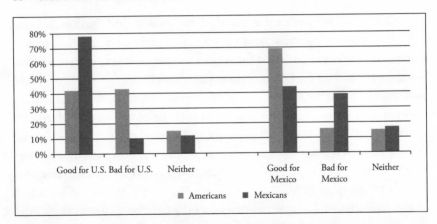

Figure 3.2: Percentage of Mexicans and Americans Who Think NAFTA is Good for Each, 2004
Source: Chicago Council on Foreign Relations, CIDE, and COMEXEI, *Global Views, 2004: Comparing Mexican and American Public Opinion and Foreign Policy* (Chicago: Council on Foreign Relations), p. 25.

issues underscore the problems separating us, and these are amplified by a critical media. Third, no leader in any of the three countries has articulated a vision of North America that would encourage people to view themselves with a wider identity. Fourth, there are no credible or effective trilateral institutions and no North American symbols that would encourage a sense of a regional community. And fifth, nations remain the most important political unit, and most people identify with their nations.

Even with a thousand-year history and a declared goal of unification, Europeans have not adopted a European identity. Surveys repeatedly ask individuals if they view themselves as citizens of a country *or* European, and they select their country. Only 4 percent of the people in fifteen European nations identified themselves as "European Only." In a comparison of two sets of Eurobarometer surveys in 1999 and 2007, one can see a slight but growing plurality choosing "Nation and Then Europe" as an identity (up from 42 percent to 45 percent), and a comparable decline for "Nation Only" (from 49 percent in 1999 to 43 percent).[23] In brief, there has been a gradual emergence of a supplementary identity in Europe that sits alongside national identities. And as Citrin and Wright have shown, identity influences policy, particularly on immigration and the degree to which nations seek to collaborate with each other.[24]

Beyond the impediments mentioned above to framing a North American identity, the three countries have an additional set of problems that stem from the struggle that each had in defining a national identity. After suppressing the indigenous people for centuries, all three countries have explored ways to incorporate them into a national identity. Because it encountered the most advanced civilization, Mexicans have been more credible in taking pride in their indigenous heritage, but in the face of numerous interventions and defeats, Mexico had to wait till the twentieth century to construct a national identity. The United States needed to fight a civil war before it could heal its social and geographical division and nurture a national identity. Canada's journey has been the most difficult—in defining an identity separate from that of the United States, inclusive of a special role for Quebec, and expansive enough to include the new Asian immigrants.

Given the multidimensional identity challenge faced by each of the three North American countries, and given the lack of attachment to the North American idea by its leaders, one would expect that no one would call themselves North American, but a few do: in the United States (5 percent), Canada (4 percent), and Mexico (1 percent). Those numbers correspond to the number of Europeans who see themselves "solely as Europeans." When the choice is between "nation" and "continent and nation," then the answers suggest there is an attachment to North America that is less than Europe's but more than one would expect. Twenty-seven percent of Mexicans, 41 percent of Americans, and 31 percent of Canadians identified with *both* nation and North America.[25] (See Figure 3.3) Some might interpret this data to conclude that a majority is nationalistic, and they would be right, but that is not the surprising news. The bigger story in this table is the opposite of what we expected: there is an attachment to North America—over 25 percent in all three countries and, most surprisingly, 41 percent of Americans. Given the lack of leadership in North America, and the differences, how are we to explain this? It seems unlikely that this is a deep attachment, but perhaps, the idea of North America is not as foreign or frightening to the people of the three countries as some pundits would want us to believe.

Even before NAFTA was negotiated, John Wirth and Robert Earle assembled a group of intellectuals from the three countries to consider the prospects for a North American identity. They viewed the "transborder areas" as "the testing grounds of socio-economic integration in North America."[26] They were prescient. NAFTA speeded up both economic and social integration among all three countries, and the people on the borders felt the transformation most acutely.

Robert Adrian Fiero Bartlett, a young, ambitious congressional aide, helped organize the Congressional Hispanic Institute in Washington, D.C. in the spring of 2009. He recruited a Hispanic congressman and several Washington experts, including me, to discuss ways to promote the development

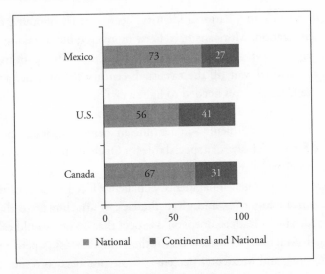

Figure 3.3: Identity: National and/or North American?

Q: Would you say you see yourself as a "national" or "continental and national"?

Source: Frank Graves, "North America: Mosaic, Community, or Fortress?" *Norteamerica*, Vol. 2, No. 2 (July–December 2007), p.108. "Continental and national" actually combine three categories: "national and continental," "continental and national," and "continental."

of Mexico within a more integrated North America. Before introducing the panel, Fiero introduced himself:

When someone asks me where I'm from, I'm always hesitant to give a response because I know that my response will be heavily influenced by my perception of the person asking me. For instance, if I believe the person is Hispanic, then I'll say I'm from Mexico, de la ciudad de Tijuana. If, however, I think that person's primary language is English, then I'm from San Diego, California. Now if the person is familiar with California's borderlands, I can then say that I'm from what my friends and I refer to as Santi Diegojuana. You see because for us, the San Diego/Tijuana border region was never about two cities in two different countries, but instead an interconnected area with diverse cultures. We learned at an early age to interchange and mix our cultures, our languages, and even our nationalities. It makes sense, then, that we considered the border nothing more than an imaginary line. Unfortunately, the U.S.-Mexico border is anything but imaginary; and millions of people who have not been as fortunate as I embark on the perilous and sometimes fatal journey across the border in search of greater opportunities to secure a better quality of life.[27]

Fiero is comfortable in his bi-nationality as are many people on the borders, but when the speed bumps make the journey costly and difficult, these affect the whole region. What is interesting about this perspective is that it is not unique to the U.S.-Mexican border. Sarah Hubbard of the Detroit Regional Chamber of Commerce feels much the same way. "We treat Canada like going to Ohio or to Chicago for the weekend. We have families living on both sides of the border," she said. "We have business partnerships on both sides of the border. We believe our community is unique because it is bi-national. It's seamless in many ways."[28]

The closer you live to the borders, the more you see them connecting the people on both sides. The further you live from the borders, the more you see them as separating the countries. The tension between these two perspectives and identities defines the ambivalence and the contradictory policies of the countries.

While the question about a North American identity refers to the continent, the term North American has a distinct connotation in each of the three countries that may explain how the publics could respond differently to questions. Canada has the most familiarity and comfort with the term "North American" because it has long used the term to apply just to its relationship with the United States. In a lecture at Vanderbilt University in 1917, James A. MacDonald, editor of the *Toronto Globe*, Canada's leading newspaper at the time, spoke of the North American idea as one based on "the right of a free people to govern themselves." He viewed the idea as central to the future relationship with the United States and to global leadership by both. He acknowledged that Mexico "shares in the geography of North America, but not in its idea . . . Mexico does not cherish the American standards of freedom . . ."[29] To this day, Canada remains uncomfortable with the idea of Mexico as a part of North America, and that has led to tensions with Mexico.

For Mexicans, the word *Norteaméricano* has always referred to U.S. citizens, but after NAFTA, most Mexicans adapted. Instead of viewing themselves as *Norteaméricanos*, which is a bridge too far given the history, one survey found that 43 percent of Mexicans view themselves as North Americans—a part of *América del Norte*—as compared to 41 percent who view themselves as "Latin Americans."[30]

Finally, having appropriated the term America at its birth, most Americans don't feel they need to include the word North to apply to themselves, but there also does not appear to be any objection to the use of the term, except among the anti-North American Union crowd.

The point is that all three publics approach the term North American from different directions, but few object to having it applied to them. Nor is there much of a sense as to what the identity means because only a few intellectuals have tried to find the connecting thread, and no political leader—except Vicente Fox of Mexico—articulated it beyond the general rhetoric of good neighborly relations. Identity, however, does influence public policy. We have seen that in Europe, and there are comparable signs in North America that those who are more nationalistic in each country are the most opposed to immigration and collaboration.

➤ Should the Three Countries Deepen Their Relationship?

The real test of the future of North America is whether the three countries want to collaborate in new and different ways in order to promote shared interests. Here again, the conventional wisdom is that Mexicans, Canadians, and Americans do not want a customs union, a security perimeter, or any proposal that could reduce the border as a barrier or lead to a European-style union.

Frank Graves, president of Ekos, a leading Canadian polling firm, has conducted surveys over a period of time in all three countries in North America, and his conclusions collide with conventional wisdom. A survey in the summer of 2005 found strong majority support in Canada (57 percent) and Mexico (59 percent) and a plurality in the United States (45 percent) for forming a common market or economic union like Europe. In the case of the United States, the same question asked three years before yielded 58 percent support.[31] (See Figure 3.4)

Not only do people say they want an economic union, 61 percent of Mexicans, 58 percent of Canadians, and 51 percent of Americans believe that it is very or somewhat likely that a North American economic union will arrive by 2015.

These are startling numbers. We have seen that a plurality of Americans viewed free trade agreements as positive except between November 2007 and April 2009, and in November 2010, but it is surprising that so many seem open to a customs union. Technically, the move from a free trade area to a customs union is not a great leap. All three countries would agree to a common external tariff. A customs union would yield substantial benefits for the three economies, but politically, it would not be easy. Of course, the question was not precise, and it is not clear that the public was informed as to the distinctions between a free trade area, a customs union (free trade + common external tariff), a common market (customs union + free movement of labor), and an economic union (common market + a common currency). Each of those options involves

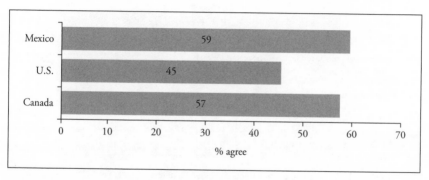

Figure 3.4: Interest in Forming a Common Market Like in Europe

Q: . . . should have an economic union like the European Union

Mexican data based on a 7-point scale whereas other data points represent a 4-point agree/disagree with no neutral category. Canada n=1002; U.S. n=752; Mexico n=1510.

Source: Ekos, *"Wave 1—General Public Survey: Canada, the U.S. and Mexico"*, June 2005, p. 49.

a depth of commitment that goes significantly beyond the status quo, and each step has been exceedingly difficult and time-consuming in Europe. Whether or not the public is ready for proposals along these lines, perhaps the most important conclusion to derive from these survey answers is that a substantial number of people are not frightened by the association with Europe.

The public in all three countries have been asked if they would consider forming a single North American country "if it meant that you would enjoy a higher standard of living," "a higher quality of life," or an improved environment. Pollsters sometimes refer to these types of questions as "push" questions in that they encourage the public to respond positively, and indeed, the responses to these questions by Americans, Mexicans, and Canadians were, on the whole, very positive. (See Figure 3.5) But a closer look at the results indicates the limitations of the "push" critique. One can see variation among the three countries, suggesting that national perspectives are different, and change over time. Events alter opinions. Since the onset of NAFTA, expectations of the benefits of integration may have declined as relations experienced setbacks.

Whether or not one takes the answers at face value, it would appear indisputable that the public in each of the three countries is more pragmatic than ideological and more interested in improving their lives than in defending specific forms of government. In that sense, the public differs from their governments and the elite, who seem more intent on defending their governments than in proposing new initiatives.

	U.S. with Canada		Canada with U.S.		Mexico with U.S.	
Survey Year	1990	2000	1990	2005	1990	2005
Better quality of Life	81	77	50	41	64	53
Environmental issues	79	66	56	41	53	NA
Higher standard of living	72	59	38	27	61	49

Figure 3.5: Forming One Country Under Specified Conditions (Percent in Favor)

Source: Basáñez, Inglehart & Nevitte, "North American Convergence, Revisited," *Norteamerica*, Vol. 2, No. 2, (July–December 2007), p. 35.

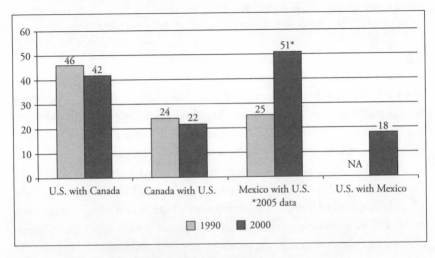

Figure 3.6: Abolishing North American Borders: Percent in Favor

Source: Basáñez, Inglehart & Nevitte, "North American Convergence, Revisited," p. 34.

The public's view of the border is also more flexible than those of their governments. In surveys in 2000 and 2005, 42 percent of Americans and 51 percent of Mexicans favor abolishing the border with their northern neighbors, but only 22 percent of Canadians and 18 percent of Americans favor abolishing it with their southern neighbors. (See Figure 3.6) These surveys suggest that both Mexico and the United States are comfortable with allowing freer movement of their labor going north, but only about one-fifth of Canadians and Americans are prepared to open their southern borders. Again, the fact that 20 percent of Americans and Canadians are ready to open the more problematic borders might be as telling as the larger numbers wanting to open the northern borders because the 20 percent may favor a North American Union, and this group may be larger than the anti-NAU group.

The public is clear in their preference for North American approaches to a wide group of issues. In an explicit question as to whether people in each of the three countries would prefer independent, national policies or integrated, North American approaches in eleven separate issue-areas, a majority of the citizens of all three countries preferred more integrated and cooperative policies on the environment, transportation, defense (security perimeter), energy, and the economy. (See Figure 3.7) This is very significant, in part, because the three governments have shown very little interest in pursuing any of these areas. There are more divided views within and among the three countries on the issues of immigration, currency, foreign policy, banking, and culture.

The surveys suggest that Mexicans are the most committed to the North American Idea. Indeed, in all eleven areas, a majority of Mexicans favor collaboration. A majority in the United States favor collaboration in nine issues and a plurality favor cooperation on a tenth, banking. Canada is clearly the reluctant suitor on North America. A majority favor trilateral cooperation in six areas. Canadians are closely divided on immigration and foreign policy, and are opposed to an integrated approach in cultural policies, banking, and currency. Of more concern, the Canadian government is less interested in North American cooperation than its public.[32]

The public is aware that their leaders have adopted a gradual, quiet, and incremental approach to North America, but 56 percent of Americans and 61 percent of Canadians would prefer a bolder approach. (See Figure 3.8)

➤ A Cooperative Public and Timid Leaders: Explaining the Puzzle

So where is the opposition to North American integration that Lou Dobbs and his anti-North American Union comrades insist is the majority view? By significant numbers, in numerous surveys, the public seems supportive of much deeper collaboration. On the other hand, the leaders are not listening or leading. They have pursued no grand ideas, and their few ad hoc initiatives have been pursued half-heartedly and unsuccessfully. What explains the puzzle of a supportive public and an inhibited leadership?

The explanation of the puzzle might lie in answers to questions that were not asked about the intensity of one's views. Though the numbers of the

Figure 3.7: Desirability of Integrated Policies, June 2005

Q: In the future, would you like to see the countries develop policies in a more independent fashion or develop integrated North American policies for each of the following areas?

Source: Ekos, "Wave 1—General Public Survey: Canada, the U.S. and Mexico", June 2005.

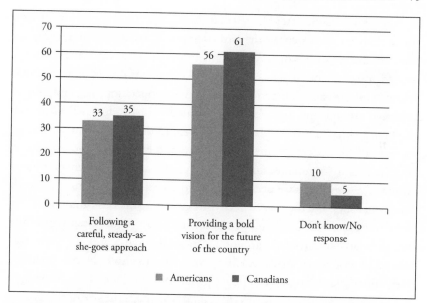

Figure 3.8: Should Leaders Go Slow or Be Bold?

Q: Which way would you prefer the United States/Canadian federal government to operate?
Source: Ekos. Survey of Americans: U.S. Wave of the Security Monitor 2006–7, July 2007.

opponents of integration may be small—perhaps equivalent to the advocates of a North American Union—their intensity and activity might be sufficient to stop initiatives, and conversely, though the numbers favoring a cooperative approach might be high, they might be relaxed about the subject. They might be prepared to state their views for a public opinion survey, but they are unlikely to write a letter to a congressman or participate in a demonstration. In a democratic political system, particularly one with an independent congress such as in the United States, a few interest groups with very intense followings are capable of skewing the debate by pre-empting initiatives and steering policy.

The surveys that are available for assessing public opinion on North America suggest four distinct perspectives, and while it is hard to identify precisely the percentage of the public which each group represents, nonetheless, estimates are possible.

Sovereignty Zealots are those who will defend national sovereignty and oppose continental cooperation strenuously. In the United States, this group follows the line of Dobbs, Buchanan, Corsi, and Ron Paul, and it found its voice in 2005 after the announcement of the Security and Prosperity Partnership by concocting a conspiracy theory that the George W. Bush administration was secretly trying to deprive the United States of sovereignty and merge the three countries into a North American Union. The idea was not just false, it was preposterous, but it served to animate a segment of the population that feared Mexican migration and any continental cooperation. The groups who coalesced around this approach are associated with Lyndon LaRouche, the cult figure who swung from Marxism to fascism, and was sent to prison during the Reagan administration for tax violations and mail fraud; the John Birch Society, an anti-Communist and anti-U.N. group; and Phyllis Schlafly's Eagle Forum. These groups have been the most vocal, active and intense on North American issues, and they were effective in inhibiting the Bush administration and deterring the Obama administration from any grand initiatives. While the most fervent anti-NAU groups are in the United States, there are also nationalist groups in Canada and Mexico opposed to greater North American integration. The question is how many people inhabit this compartment.

In considering survey answers that could help judge the size of this group, one might start by identifying those with a strongly negative view of their neighbors. In a 2009 survey, 26 percent of Canadians had a negative image of the United States, viewing its greed, arrogance, and aggression as the cause of the region's problems. The same percentage of Mexicans—26 percent—resented the U.S.[33] With regard to American views of Mexico, polls by Gallup in 2001, 2003, and 2004, indicated that 20–27 percent of Americans had a "mostly" or "very unfavorable" view of Mexico, and in a 2005 Pew survey, 9 percent of Americans had an unfavorable view of Canada.[34] To get a better estimate of the size of the "zealots" within this group, Zogby's survey in March 2006 asked both Americans and Mexicans "how you believe the U.S. sees Mexico?" Only 6 percent of Americans viewed Mexico as a threat, but 18 percent of Mexicans thought that the United States viewed it as a threat.[35] Based on this data, we estimate that about 15 percent of Americans and 25 percent of Mexicans and Canadians might compose this group.

North American Unionists are at the other end of the policy spectrum. They want a merger of some kind among the three countries and want to abolish the borders with both countries. In one survey, 59 percent of Mexicans, 57 percent of Canadians, and 45 percent of Americans said they wanted a union like Europe's. These numbers seem high and while they may reflect an interest in collaboration, one doubts that a North American Union is as much in demand.

Another pertinent question is whether people want to abolish borders. (See Figure 3.6) The answer was that 22 percent of Canadians were in favor of abolishing their border with the United States, and 18 percent of Americans were prepared to abolish it with Mexico, while 42 percent of Americans wanted to abolish it with Canada. Of Mexicans, 57 percent think they "should have the right to enter the U.S. without U.S. permission." That does not mean that the Mexicans want to establish a Union, but it suggests that Mexicans do not identify the border with sovereignty. Let us estimate that roughly 20 percent of each of the three nations fall in this category.

Nationals and North Americans want to deepen cooperation among the three governments. The surveys suggest that 42 percent of Americans, 32 percent of Canadians, and 27 percent of Mexicans view themselves both national and continental. The fact that such a high percentage of people in all three countries have a supplementary identity does not necessarily translate into specific policies. There is likely to be considerable overlap between this group and "North American Unionists" and "pragmatists."

Pragmatists decide whether they support the status quo or new initiatives based on the logic of the argument, the state of the economy, and trust in leadership. The pragmatists are the "great deciders." When they swing from the status quo to favor integration, they can often win the debate. They tend to respond to events rather than ideology and focus on the central question: Will the proposal improve our standard of living and the environment? This group represents close to 50 percent of the three publics as reflected in the three graphs on cooperation on eleven issues. (See Figure 3.7)

Of course, the numbers do not add up, or rather they add up too much. That is partly because there is considerable overlap among the last three groups. Moreover, the size of each group fluctuates with events and leadership. When leaders fail to make the case for North America, when the economy declines or fears of terrorism and massive waves of undocumented immigrants increase, and when events occur that reinforce the U.S. stereotype of Mexico as violent or corrupt and Canada as unhelpful or "anti-American," the number of "sovereignty zealots" is likely to increase. On the other hand, the data is clear on one point. The vast majority of the people in all three countries are in favor—to different degrees—of more cooperation and collaboration, including perhaps a customs union and other significant initiatives.

How do these four groups interact to make or pre-empt policy? Essentially, the sovereignty-zealots, though a small minority in all three countries, but particularly in the United States, are so intense and active that the status quo has become the default option. The three leaders have chosen not to contest this group, which has been able to steer the debate away from the critical issues, and the group has been assisted by a steady stream of negative stories about Mexico and passivity by Canada. The capability of a single-interest or a single-minded group to stop the process is substantial in most democracies; in the United States with its strong federal system and its campaign finance system, such groups often can stalemate the system. Neither the Clinton, Bush, nor Obama administrations has been willing to override this group or sail around it. The supporters of integration have also been silent.

In the case of North America, it appears that the U.S. presidents have paid more attention to the 20 percent who are zealots than to the overwhelming majority looking for leadership to move the agenda forward. And while one-quarter of both Canadians and Mexicans may be reluctant to embrace the United States, three-quarters are also looking for more serious initiatives to cooperate. The problem, in brief, is that the three governments have paid too much attention to the strident voices and too little attention to the broader North American public.

Although the European model is quite different from North America's, Europe's path toward integration contains lessons that could be of great value in North America. Europe's journey was not straightforward and never easy. Indeed, it seemed on the verge of a breakdown each time that it stretched to fulfill the promise of a union. But somehow, each time, the Europeans stopped bickering and approved the big initiative—whether Cohesion Funds, a European Court, the single market, the Euro, or a restructuring of supranational institutions and power under a new constitution.

Even with these initiatives, however, the European Union is not really a union. A union is a unified national state, and the EU has twenty-seven sovereign states. The clearest confirmation of that fact is that only 1 percent of Europe's GDP is collected as taxes by the EU whereas approximately 40 percent is collected by states. So Europe's vision was larger than its policies, but that vision permitted the region to move forward together and further than any contemporary compact among states.

While the principal aim of European integration has been to develop a unified framework that would ensure peace, the three governments of North America had no such ambition. Lacking such a goal, North America has slipped backward, hurting the economies, undermining initiatives aimed at increasing integration, and jeopardizing the region's security. To move forward, North America needs a bigger idea, and it needs leaders to advance the agenda. The good news is that most of the people of North America are ready to be led. The North American Idea exists, and in this chapter, we have allowed the people of North America to speak.

Here is a summary of what they have said: We—Mexicans, Canadians, and Americans—are alike in values and aspirations. We believe in democracy, free speech, press and association, tolerate other religions and beliefs, accept a limited role for the government, and agree on the utility of the market. Although we may disagree on certain policies, we like, respect, and trust one other. We view NAFTA positively, though less so when our economies are doing poorly, and we all agree that the other countries have benefited more than us. A growing minority of us think of ourselves as both nationals and North Americans, and if the surveys are correct, would like to have a North American Economic Union, though admittedly, the definition of a union remains unclear. Moreover, we think it will happen in a decade. We want our governments to work together across the full spectrum of issues and be bolder in their efforts to strengthen cooperation.

North Americans have already traveled a considerable distance in establishing a formidable region and in combining their views and aspirations. In the next two chapters, we shall see the promise of North American integration and evaluate the pitfalls.

Part II: Trespassing

Nothing else in the world . . . not all the armies . . .
are so powerful as an idea whose time has come.
    —Victor Hugo

4

Transcending the Borders

I n a small town called Postville in the northeastern corner of Iowa, on May 13, 2008, federal authorities swooped in with helicopters in a coordinated assault on a Kosher meat-processing plant. It was the largest raid against a single plant in the country's history. The Immigration and Customs Enforcement (ICE) officials arrested 389 illegal migrants, mostly from Mexico.[1] The incident was so surreal that few people realized it turned upside down a pitcher of conventional wisdom. Think about it:

- What is a Kosher meat-processing plant doing in Iowa?
- Ross Perot had warned us that American companies would move jobs and factories to Mexico, and yet this factory moved from Brooklyn to Iowa to employ Mexicans. Huh?
- How did Mexicans find out about these jobs in Postville, Iowa and relocate there, while unemployed Americans in Des Moines or Chicago did not know about the jobs or did not apply for them?
- And helicopters? Didn't the "Minutemen," that group of vigilantes "protecting" our borders, warn us that blue-helmeted UN soldiers would be coming by helicopters to rob us of our sovereignty? If so, why were the Minutemen cheering when it happened in Postville?

The reason for the helicopter-led raid was that President George W. Bush had to prove to his own Republican party that he would enforce immigration laws after failing to do so for seven years.[2] He also wanted to fulfill his promise to Mexican President Vicente Fox in February 2001 to enact a comprehensive immigration plan. Never mind that Bush waited until the end of his term before giving it the old college try. Despite his efforts, he failed to persuade Republicans or pass an immigration bill. Instead, he signed a new law to build a 670-mile wall across the border. Why did he reverse course?

Bush's immigration plan provoked a furious reaction from conservative Republicans, who accused the president of promoting "amnesty" for people who violated U.S. immigration laws. To regain his political footing, the president dispatched the Department of Homeland Security to secure the border. But when did the Mexican border move to Iowa?

It used to be that the borders defined the relationships among the three North American countries and that sovereignty could be defended at the border. The borders are still important, but people, ideas, culture, the Internet, and cell phones are transcending the border—going around, over, and under the border. Or simply ignoring it.

The BlackBerry cell phone, designed and manufactured by a company called Research in Motion in Waterloo, Ontario, and Cirque du Soleil, the Montreal-based futuristic circus, are just two examples of how imagination can leap the borders. Televisa and Univision are two others that bring Mexican programs to the United States and American soap operas to Mexicans.

Mexicans, Canadians, and Americans have spilled over the borders and into the heartland, the crevices, and far-reaching corners of all three countries. Forty years ago, in the poor southern state of Michoacan, many of the Indian villagers could hardly speak Spanish, and a trip to Mexico City would have been out of reach for all but a few. Today, entire villages from that state have moved—not just to Mexico City, but to Los Angeles and North Carolina, and some villagers can be found as far afield as Calgary, Alberta. Forty years ago, few Americans would cross their borders to purchase medicines. Today, buses of elderly people from Minnesota and California go to Canada and Mexico not only to buy less expensive generic medicines but also to seek medical treatment. Today, Georgia and North Dakota have large Mexican populations; Canadian entrepreneurs seek their future in Los Angeles and New York; and Virginians retire in Baja.

A vast change in the life of all three countries has occurred. Two decades ago, when I taught in Mexico City, the first McDonald's restaurant opened in the southern part of the city. The reaction came in two waves. For the first two months, lines circled the building, and Mexican families waited hours to get Big Macs. Middle-class Mexicans could not get enough of the burgers, even though the price was equivalent to the finest food at some of the city's best restaurants. The embrace of American fast food was more than Mexico's nationalistic intellectuals, political party dinosaurs, and labor leaders could stand. Late one night, a few radical labor organizers broke some windows and shut down the Golden Arches. Today, the Golden Arches can be seen all over Mexico, and they are hardly alone. Wal-Mex, Wal-Mart's Mexico branch, has 1,400 stores and is the largest employer in Mexico. Starbucks is as ubiquitous in Mexico as Taco Bell is in the United States and Canada.

Canada and Mexico have been coping with the dominance of the United States for two centuries; what is new is that the United States is now feeling the influence of its two neighbors. The Canadian presence is widespread but less visible. Leaving aside Jim Carrey, most Canadians are modest and polite, and most Americans cannot recognize them or their accent. And those Americans who live in Canada do so because they prefer the lower-key ambience. So there is less awareness within both countries of the others' presence.

That does not apply to poor Mexicans slicing Kosher salami in Iowa. The United States is absorbing Mexico in many different ways—from the bilingual messages at city hall, to the daily interaction with workers who cut lawns, to the fajitas at the local restaurant. Mexicans are working in the most exclusive New York law firms, and sixteen Mexicans were in the World Trade Center when it was attacked.

In this chapter, we shall tell the story of the spread and deepening of North America. This is about a continental market that is being constructed, but that market is not just a place where goods are bought and sold, it is also about entrepreneurs and entertainers in all three countries creating new products and shows together. It is about three societies that have been unleashed to interact in new ways, and it is about each country redefining itself to incorporate the best of the others. No single example was more profound than Mexico's journey to democracy since NAFTA. To transform its election administration from the most fraud-prone to one of the most professional and honest in the world, Mexico borrowed from Elections Canada and purchased advanced technology from IBM. That is the new model, but it coexists with an older one.

North America is at the midpoint between an old border mentality and a new kind of continental market. The three governments can hardly conceive of a continental labor market, but it is taking shape in front of their eyes. Like any new phenomenon in the midst of a prolonged spasm of creation, this new North American market is filled with imperfections and contradictions.

It contains a legal market, but also illegal and "informal" markets. The actors shaping the markets are small and multinational companies and drug traffickers that employ more workers than most of the legitimate firms. Rooted in each nation, the television and film industries seek to entertain all three, and, in doing so, they are developing a common language of laughter and drama.

This chapter is about these new markets that are taking shape while the three governments try to extinguish the fires sparked by the creative processes and the new tensions that they emit. We shall start with people. Their movements were not contemplated by NAFTA, but they are transforming North America. We will then discuss the emerging agricultural market and the role of business as an agent of integration. Finally, we will examine the impact of the illegal transnational market of drug trafficking.

➤ Old Borders and New Faces

In the beginning, there were just rivers and deserts in the south, and the Great Lakes and wide, open ranges in the north. By 1850, after annexing Texas and the southwest, and negotiating its northern border, the United States and its neighbors largely forgot about the borders. People crossed them freely. The father of future Mexican President Vicente Fox galloped down from Cincinnati to Guanajuato to make a new life for himself, and many more Mexicans rode or simply walked north. Canadians moved south for the weather or when wages were much better, and Americans moved north when they were displeased with their government or wanted a change.

The United States almost always encouraged immigration, but that did not mean that Americans were hospitable to all of the new immigrants. In the nineteenth century, the United States excluded Chinese and Japanese, and it always sent home those with physical or mental problems, but it did not set any quantitative limits on the flow of immigrants until the 1920s. The debate that led to the passage of two immigration laws was precipitated by the largest flow of immigrants in one period in the nation's history. From 1890 to 1910, more than 25 million new immigrants arrived in the United States. At the time, this was more people than the combined population of Canada and Mexico. The new immigration laws established the Border Patrol with 450 inspectors on horseback. The Patrol was instructed to permit Mexicans to enter the United States, but to prevent entry by undocumented workers from Europe.

During the Second World War, as its men went into the armed forces, and its women replaced them in the workforce, the United States needed more workers. Washington signed a "Bracero Agreement" with Mexico in 1942 that permitted Mexicans to work on contract with U.S. farms and some firms, but they needed to return to Mexico at the end of their contract. Although the program was supposed to end when soldiers returned home, American businesses and farms had come to value the hardworking Mexicans, and the program was renewed. Nearly five million Mexicans participated in the program until 1964 when U.S. labor unions and Mexican-American citizens, feeling at a competitive disadvantage with the cheaper labor, persuaded the U.S. government to terminate the agreement.[3]

To absorb workers returning to Mexico, the United States and Mexico established a *maquiladora* program that allowed companies on the Mexican side of the border to assemble manufacturing products with parts coming duty-free from the United States. The assembly plants stimulated industrial development in the border area, but they did not reduce migration to the United States. In fact, some believe that they planted the seeds for a much larger migration in the future.

The 1965 Immigration Act was the turning point in modern U.S. immigration policy; it unlocked the ethnic-based restrictions of the laws of the 1920s and permitted 20,000 immigrants from every nation. This changed fundamentally the composition of immigration. Between 1900 and 1975, 85 percent of all immigrants came from Europe. Since 1975, 89 percent of all immigrants have come from Asia and Latin America, with the highest proportion coming from Mexico—nearly one-third of all immigrants. That is because family reunification provisions in the 1965 law permitted Mexicans to greatly exceed the annual quotas. In 1970, Mexico had the fourth largest foreign-born population in the United States—behind Italy, Germany, and Canada. Within a decade, Mexico leaped to first, and soon the United States had five times more Mexicans than from any other country.

The Spanish had encouraged immigration to Mexico, but by the seventeenth century, just as the English began to move to the New World, Spaniards lost interest. During Mexico's war for independence, the Spanish viceroy offered huge tracts of land to lure new immigrants, but the people who responded were mostly from the United States. They settled in Texas and soon out-numbered the Mexicans. When the Mexican government tried to reassert its control, they rebelled. Throughout the rest of the nineteenth century, few immigrants came to Mexico, and by 1910, only 116,000 foreigners resided in Mexico.[4]

During the last three decades, Mexico began receiving large numbers of Central American refugees largely because of the wars in the 1980s. Many were simply trying to transit through Mexico to the United States, but some stayed. In 1989, the government deported 110,000 people in order to try to discourage further migration. Nearly one million Americans also moved to Mexico, representing the largest numbers of Americans in any country outside the United States. Most of these were retirees, but some younger professionals also moved there.[5]

Canada made a great effort to recruit immigrants, but initially only from Western Europe, and so by 1901, 88 percent of the population still claimed to have French or British origins.[6] Like the United States, Canada and Mexico discriminated against the Chinese and Japanese. Only in 1976 did Canada enact a new Immigration Act that was quite similar to the U.S. law of 1965 and allowed a dramatic increase in immigrants from the third world. However, while U.S. laws gave priority to family reunification, Canada's criteria for admission emphasized skills and education.[7] In recent years, immigration has had a huge effect in Canada where 18.4 percent of the population is now foreign-born (as compared to 12.4 percent in the United States). The largest proportion of immigrants is from Asia. Five percent are from the United States, and 1 percent are from Mexico, although that number is growing.[8] In 2006, Spanish became the third most spoken language in Canada—behind English and French.[9] Immigration has defined Canada and the United States, and since the 1970s, emigration has defined Mexico.

The growth in the Mexican population in the United States has been rapid and recent. The number of Mexicans living in the United States barely increased from 641,000 in 1930 to 760,000 in 1970, but from then till the present, the Mexican-born population increased thirteen-fold. (See Figure 4.1) Mexicans now account for about 31 percent of all immigrants, more than five times the next largest group. And Mexicans in the United States—including those born in the United States of Mexican parents—represent an increasingly important share of the Mexican people, from 1.5 percent in 1970 to 11 percent in 2009. In other words, today, one out of every ten Mexicans lives in the United States.

In the past twenty years, a new generation of Mexican immigrants leapfrogged over those living on both sides of the border and have moved to the interior of the United States. In 1990, 750,000 Mexicans lived in Los Angeles, and 58 percent of all Mexican immigrants living in the United States resided in California. By 2006, though the Mexican population in Los Angeles more than doubled, the number of Mexicans living in California declined to only 28 percent of all those in the United States. They spread to virtually every county in the country. Since 2000, the Hispanic population grew in 3,000 of

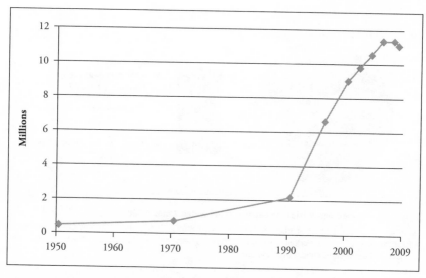

Figure 4.1: Mexican Immigration to the U.S., Legal and Illegal, 1950–2009

Sources: Decennial censuses through 2000 (Campbell and Lennon 1999), Urban Institute and Pew Hispanic Center tabulations of March CPS for 1995–2004; Rakesh Kochhar, "Survey of Mexican Migrants: The Economic Transition to America," Pew Hispanic Center, December 6, 2005; Jeffrey Passel and D'Vera Cohn, "U.S. Unauthorized Immigration Flows are Down Sharply Since Mid-Decade," Pew Hispanic Center, September 1, 2010).

the nation's 3,141 counties, and the highest growth rates were in states in which the Mexican or Hispanic population had been negligible, e.g., Georgia (60 percent), North Carolina (57.9 percent), and Iowa (50 percent).[10]

According to U.S. Census projections, the U.S. population is projected to grow from 310 million in 2010 to 350 million in 2025; Canada, from 34 to 38 million, and Mexico, from 113 to 130 million. Immigration will account for two-thirds of population growth in the United States, and 70–90 percent in Canada.[11]

The Pew Center estimated there were about 30.7 million Mexicans—representing two-thirds of 46.8 million Hispanics—in the United States in 2008. Of these, 19.4 million were born in the United States of Mexican parents, and 11.4 million were born in Mexico. Of the Mexican-born, about 5.1 million are legal residents or naturalized citizens, and 6.3 million are undocumented.[12] (See Figure 4.2)

First generation immigrants are the bridge that connects and changes both host and home countries. While trying to adapt to their new country, the new immigrants also help the relatives that remain behind. As the number of Mexican immigrants in the United States increased, and their wages improved, the

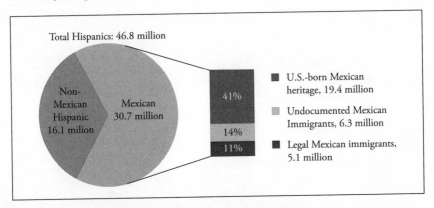

Figure 4.2: Hispanic and Mexican Population in the United States, 2008

Sources: "Statistical Portrait of Hispanics in the United States, 2008," Pew Hispanic Center; Jeffrey S. Passel and D'Vera Cohn; "A Portrait of Unauthorized Immigrants in the United States," Pew Hispanic Center. Available at http://pewhispanic.org/topics/?TopicID=1.

amount of wealth transferred to the poorest villages in Mexico quintupled—from about $5 billion in 2000 to nearly $25 billion in 2007.[13] This amount exceeded revenues Mexico received from tourism and the export of oil. The immigrants also transmitted the shock of the U.S. recession by reducing remittances to about $21 billion in 2009.

Mexican President Vicente Fox tried to multiply the effect of these remittances by offering three pesos in a matching grant for the local communities for every one peso invested by immigrants in the towns. The idea, unfortunately, did not achieve its promise because it was based on a flawed premise that remittances were a form of investment. In fact, remittances should be viewed as transnational welfare payments for dependent families. The workers who move to the United States leave behind an extended family with limited, if any, ability to earn income, and a community denuded of young workers. The remittances are therefore used for food, housing, and essentials. There is little, if any, remaining for investments.

The dramatic surge in undocumented Mexican migration to the United States in the past two decades created an unusual transnational labor market. The flow of migrants has been largely unregulated and constitutes a kind of transnational informal sector in the United States. The funds sent to Mexico are of such a scale as to affect the nation's exchange rate, but Mexico loses the human energy of its immigrants. The lesson is ironic. The country—like the United States—that receives immigrants grows faster than the one sending them. The receiving communities have a future, and the sending towns have a past.

The public in the three countries has contrasting views about immigration and the integrated labor market, but they also share some opinions. President Bush's proposal for immigration reform generated a heated and often poisonous national debate from 2005 through the presidential election in 2008 in the United States. Surveys suggested that American concern was focused on illegal, not legal migration. A survey in September 2008 showed that 43 percent of Americans were "worried about illegal immigration," but only 3 percent were worried about legal immigration.[14] Two years earlier when the debate was much more intense, 60 percent said that illegal migration was a serious problem. Only 4 percent said they were worried about legal migration.[15]

When asked in March 2006 whether Mexican workers benefit the United States, 68 percent of Americans said "yes," and only 27 percent disagreed. Mexicans shared those views, only more so, with 80 percent agreeing that they benefit the United States and only 16 percent disagreeing. On whether the United States should build a wall to keep out illegal migrants, 69 percent of Americans, and 90 percent of Mexicans said "no." Only 28 percent of Americans and 7 percent of Mexicans said "yes."[16] But these surveys do not reflect the intensity of the opposition to illegal migration nor the emotional effect that angry comments have on all Mexican immigrants. The most strident critics of illegal migration tend to describe them as criminals or welfare cheats. They rarely recognize those who work hard and pay taxes.

Antonio Garza, the U.S. ambassador to Mexico during the George W. Bush administration, is tall, light-skinned, and very much a Texas Republican. An old friend of Bush's, he had been attorney general of Texas. During a week in which the congressional debate on immigration heated up, he saw a Mexican-American journalist, whom he had known for years. The journalist's politics were far to the left of Garza's, but Garza didn't mind speaking with people who did not necessarily agree with him. Commenting on a congressman's verbal attack on Mexican immigrants, Garza said: "Sometimes, I feel as if they are talking about me!"

This was a very unusual feeling for Garza, who had risen quickly and to the very top of America, but it was no surprise to the journalist: "Bro," he said, "I've been telling you that for years. You're not one of them, and they don't like you, me, or anyone from Mexico." Garza, of course, did not accept that, but in recounting the story, he also acknowledged that the debate left him uneasy, as if America might never really accept Mexico or the Mexicans within.

American views of migration have fluctuated with the economy and the perception of threat. Canada's views have been more stable and positive. In an Ekos survey in the fall of 2006, 57 percent of Canadians said that immigration had a positive effect on their nation.[17] Unlike the United States, Canada does not have a problem with illegal migration. Canada employs Mexicans as temporary agricultural workers in the summer, but few remain beyond the expiration of their contract. It might be that Canada's winter is a more effective deterrent than the U.S. Department of Homeland Security.

The Mexican views of immigration have probably undergone the most dramatic transformation over the past thirty years. Mexico had long mocked the people who migrated north. Octavio Paz, the Nobel Prize-winning author, wrote that migrants lost their culture and represented the "worst of both worlds."[18] *Pocho* or "overripe" is a derogatory slur used by Mexicans to describe those who went to the United States and came to prefer hamburgers to tamales, and English instead of Spanish.[19]

But this changed. The surge in migration in the 1970s and 1980s coincided with a post-civil rights revolution in America that celebrated ethnic diversity and offered preferential treatment in admissions to universities. Bilingualism was introduced on the ballot and spread to labels on consumer goods and street signs. Hispanic groups like La Raza and LULAC (League of United Latin American Citizens) organized the community into a formidable political force.

At the same time, Mexico was rethinking itself because of NAFTA and the movement toward democracy. Salinas, with a Ph.D. from Harvard, reached out to Mexican-American leaders for help in persuading the U.S. Congress to pass NAFTA. His successor, Ernesto Zedillo, with a Ph.D. from Yale, spoke to the annual convention of La Raza in 1997 in English, and "proudly affirmed that the Mexican nation extends beyond the territory enclosed by its borders." Mexico then changed its constitution to permit its immigrants to the United States to retain Mexican citizenship. President Vicente Fox established a cabinet-level Office for Mexicans Abroad and appointed Juan Hernandez, a Mexican American, as director.[20]

Old stereotypes were evaporating. Joe Contreras, a self-described *pocho* from Los Angeles, wrote a wonderfully picaresque voyage of discovery of his Mexican roots. By the time he was posted as bureau chief in Mexico for *Newsweek*, he was ready to relate to his mother country as he had studied it— nationalistic, authoritarian, anti-American. Of course, he found a different Mexico, one that was post-nationalistic, chaotically democratic, and very positive about the United States. He acknowledged his surprise and accepted the curious juxtaposition of the twin journeys, passing each other from opposite directions. A young Mexican-American enamored with his parents' country and its nationalistic past, Contreras returns to a Mexico that had left its past behind and was searching for a better life in a North American future.[21]

To serve the widening Mexican community in the United States, the Ministry of Foreign Affairs expanded its consulates to 50 cities in the United States during the past decade. Each one helped their community get a *matricula consular*, a photo identification card that could help Mexicans get drivers' licenses or open checking accounts.

A Mexican professor visited governors throughout the south, urging them to recognize the ID card. Alabama Governor Don Siegelman was so impressed by the presentation that he immediately agreed, and as she left his office, he said: "Please remind your people to vote for me on election day." A little startled, she turned and said: "But most of the people are not here legally." The governor winked and whispered: "That's O.K." His aide later called to retrieve the remark.[22]

With roughly half of all Mexicans having a close relative living in the United States, it is easier to understand why many are beginning to feel North American. In a survey in 2003 asking whether they would immigrate to the United States if they could, 81.4 percent of Mexico answered affirmatively.[23]

Some Mexicans have come to believe they have a right to be in the United States. Several undocumented workers asked her to fix their papers. When she told them that was illegal and improper, and she would not do it, they protested. In the course of my research on migration from the Caribbean in the mid-1980s, I encountered a similar reaction. Caribbean people took for granted their "right" to migrate to the United States. Mexicans now have similar views.

Canadians also feel a sense of entitlement. They remain distressed that the United States decided to require passports to enter the United States. When Christopher Sands, an astute analyst of bilateral relations, spoke to a group in Waterloo, Canada, he defended the U.S. passport requirement. An aging Canadian protested, saying the requirement "made a lot of Canadians feel like you think we're second class citizens."[24]

Canadians have always immigrated to the United States, but the magnitude of the Mexican migration raises the question as to what motivates them. Many Americans think they are looking for jobs, but the Pew Center interviewed thousands of Mexicans, who were applying for an ID (*matricula*), and found that 95 percent had jobs when they left Mexico.[25] The migrants view the United States as an extended labor market where they can earn six to ten times as much as in Mexico with better prospects for advancement. They have a family network that facilitates their transition, and until the recession of 2008, they had little difficulty securing work. Most undocumented Mexican immigrants are relatively poor and uneducated, but the motive that brings them to the United States is not all that different than the one that brings Canadians to the United States and Americans to both countries—i.e., they seek ways to improve their lives.

Despite the fear of some Americans that the Mexicans will not assimilate, Mexicans adapt, intermarry, and learn English faster than other ethnic groups. By the second generation, most immigrants are improving their job status, paying taxes, and speaking English.[26] At the same time, and like every previous immigrant wave, the Mexicans are changing America, and that is occurring rapidly.

As long as the income gap is as wide as it is—whether it is between Mexico and the United States or between Mexico and Central America—immigration restrictions are still needed.

A free market in labor is conceivable, though politically difficult, between Canada and the United States, but it is not in the interests of either Mexico or the United States. The Alducin 2003 survey noted above suggested that as many as 81.4 percent of Mexicans—or about 85 million people—would immigrate north if they could. Even if one-third acted on that wish, it would mean severe dislocations in both sending and receiving countries. Nonetheless, the logic of an integrated North American market means that people will continue to seek the highest wages within or beyond their borders. Mexican legal migration will continue at a high level until the development gap between Mexico and the United States begins to close.

Whether the U.S. Congress passes a bill that would prevent illegal migration remains questionable. That would require effective enforcement in the workplace, but the only way to do that would be if all Americans had to present a biometric national identification card. Groups on both ends of the political spectrum oppose such a card, and the growing power of Hispanic advocacy groups would prevent any restrictions that could have a discriminatory effect. Over time, Americans will accept the Mexicans in their midst because, like other ethnic groups, they will be Americans. Actually North Americans.

➤ North American Food

When Americans think of a Mexican farmer, the image that comes to mind is of a poor *campesino*, a rugged peasant, who struggles to grow corn on a small patch of infertile land. There are still Mexican campesinos that fit this image, but they are fewer and fewer each year. Mexico's rural population has declined from 26 percent to 15 percent between 1980 and 2005, and their contribution to Mexico's gross domestic product is small, only about 4 percent.[27] The movement of people from subsistence agriculture to small towns and larger cities reflects a long-standing global trend. It is worth recalling that fewer than 2 percent of Canadians and Americans still farm.

On January 1, 2009, fifteen years after NAFTA came into effect, the last tariffs were phased out. These tariffs were on agricultural products—corn, beans, sugar, powdered milk—and they had gradually descended from a high of 200 percent in 1993. Mexico's small farmers—particularly in corn—were fearful of unfair competition by United States subsidized farmers, but during the transition, from 1990 to 2004, Mexico's corn production increased by nearly 50 percent, from about 14 million to about 22 million tons.[28]

During the same period, each country found its comparative advantage. From 1990 to 2009, United States and Mexican agricultural trade more than tripled from $3.6 billion to $12.1 billion, with a slight surplus for most of that time in favor of the United States. Mexico specialized in exporting fruits and vegetables to the United States. The major U.S. exports to Mexico were grains and animal products. Corn represented only about 11 percent of U.S. agricultural exports during most of the period.[29]

To locate the new image of Mexican farmers, one needs to look in the northern, more productive part of the country, and there one finds Ms. Alicia Bon Martin, the CEO of a successful vegetable farm in Sonora, and a former chairwoman of the Fresh Produce Association of the Americas. Sonora borders Arizona and together with neighboring states in Mexico produce about half of all the vegetables Americans consume each year, allowing Americans to eat fresh vegetables year around. Martin is confident, bilingual and dual national. Her family lives and has been educated on both sides of the border. Since NAFTA, her farm has roughly doubled in size and has prospered.[30] She is not alone, and as the northern farmers prosper, more of them are dual-nationals, living, working, and connecting both sides of the border.

NAFTA has had a schizophrenic effect on Mexico, and that is seen most clearly in agriculture where the north hitched a ride on the most modern agricultural market, and the south remained unconnected, subsistence-based, and backward. The decline of the south is due to a long-term trend and to the absence of effective government support for small farmers. The northern part of Mexico has taken full advantage of NAFTA and has introduced more balance to what had been a chronic national deficit in agricultural trade.

Jeffrey Jones, a rancher from Chihuahua, was elected to the Senate of Mexico, and after a term, served as an undersecretary of agriculture in Mexico

City. Jones' family had come from the United States and helped shape the economy of northern Mexico. Jones is candid about Mexico's problems and intent on trying to solve them. He moves easily between both cultures and also between the worlds of business and public policy.

While descendants of Americans, like Jones, Martin, and Fox, can be found in the northern part of Mexico, most of the people on both sides of the U.S.-Mexican border were born in Mexico or descended from Mexicans. They feel far more distant from their own capitals than they do from their friends and relatives across the border.

The future of North America will be shaped by people traversing the border but also by the crops. The history of trade in avocados may illuminate both past problems and future opportunities. The fruit's name comes from the word *ahuacatl* from the indigenous Nahuatl language. It means testicle for its shape and supposedly stimulant qualities. It is native to Mexico, but seeds were exported to California in the early part of the twentieth century to a farmer who experimented genetically to find the strongest variety. Rudolph Hass, a postman, purchased some of the seeds and subsequently patented it as the Hass avocado in 1935. This variety became the most popular in California and Mexico, but California producers lobbied the U.S. Department of Agriculture (USDA) to prevent avocado imports from Mexico. They claimed the fruit had diseases.

The Mexicans tried to overturn the ban during the NAFTA negotiations, but the United States resisted until 1997 when it allowed exports to several northeastern states. Only when Mexico began to restrict U.S. corn exports did the U.S. Department of Agriculture accept a long-standing invitation to send disease experts to Mexico. They found no problems and cleared exports to the United States.

California producers, seeing the handwriting on the wall, sent their own marketing experts to Michoacan, the center of avocado production in Mexico, to set up packing operations and negotiate contracts with the native producers to market their product in the United States. When the United States market opened, the exports of Mexican avocados to the United States ascended from $34.5 million in 1995 to $407.6 million in 2005, and it so enlarged the market in the United States that California producers also expanded production and profits significantly. Today, avocado production represents 62 percent of agricultural production in Michoacan, generating 47,000 direct and 70,000 seasonal jobs, and 197,000 indirect but permanent jobs, and Mexico is the largest producer, consumer, and exporter of avocados in the world.[31]

The conventional wisdom was that trade in avocados would hurt American farmers and help Mexicans, but when the market opened, both profited.

The case also confirmed that the United States used phytosanitary measures to protect U.S. farmers not American consumers, contrary to the provisions of NAFTA. Finally, it showed that if U.S. businesses moved from a sovereignty-based, defensive posture to one that was more entrepreneurial and based on partnership with Mexico, all sides could benefit.

➤ North America's Business

Businesses—multinational corporations (MNCs), banks, and small and medium-sized firms—have been the main agents for economic integration. Over 18,000 U.S. companies have operations in Mexico. Most of these are connected to their home firm in the United States, and many have subsidiaries in Canada.[32] From the eve of the U.S.-Canadian Free Trade Agreement in 1988, all three countries have witnessed an explosion of foreign direct investment—both inward and outward. (See Figure 4.3)

From 1987–2008, U.S. foreign direct investment in Canada increased almost four times, from $59.1 billion to $227.3 billion; and in Mexico, nearly twenty times, from $5.4 billion $95.6 billion. Canadian investment increased at a faster rate to both destinations—nine times from $24.7 billion to $221.9 billion in the United States, and twenty-three times from $190 million to $4.3 billion in Mexico. Finally, Mexico increased its outward foreign direct investment by the fastest rate, albeit from the lowest level, in the United States by over forty times from $180 million to $8 billion, and over 20 times from $11 million to $253 million in Canada.[33] The ascent was triggered by NAFTA, and while many analysts predicted that U.S. investment would drive North American integration, the great surprise was that Canada and Mexico became important sources of investments—not just destinations.

Canada and Mexico wanted more investment from the United States but not so much that they would lose control of their economies. Their fears proved unfounded. U.S. investment increased sharply in both countries, but investments from the rest of the world increased even more; the U.S. share of total foreign investment in Canada declined from 73 percent in 1987 to 55 percent in 2008, and in Mexico from 40 percent to 32 percent. (See Figure 4.4)

Canadian and Mexican investment also increased in the United States in areas like telecommunications, cement, and mining, but there were also new forms of investment by individuals. Canadians, for example, became the No. 1 foreign buyers of homes in the United States, accounting for 23.6 percent of

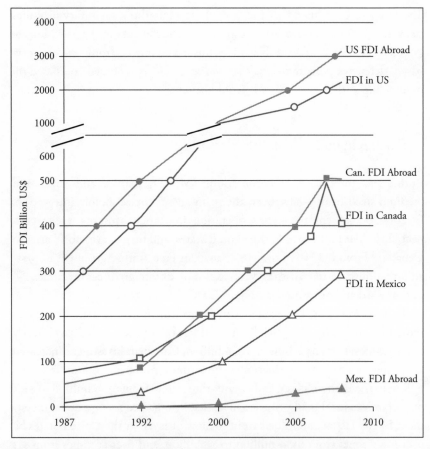

Figure 4.3: North American Foreign Direct Investment: Inward and Outward, 1987–2005
Source: Appendix, Table 12.

all purchases, twice as much as the next country, and Mexicans were the third largest buyer.[34]

The growth of foreign investment among the three countries of North America was, of course, part of a worldwide phenomenon, but what appeared to be globalization was actually regionalization, and North America was the strongest region. Pankaj Ghemawat, a professor at the Harvard Business School, is critical of the idea of a "borderless world." Instead of the "flat earth" that Thomas Friedman chronicles, Ghemawat sees mountains and deep valleys—restrictions and impediments—that impede globalization and encourage investments in near regions.[35]

Alan Rugman and Chang H. Oh agree that the concept of globalization masks a trend that is actually regional. They examined the geographical sales

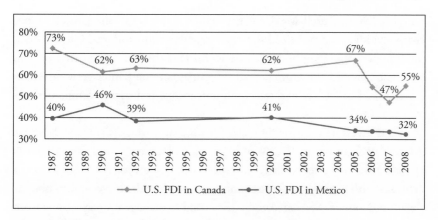

Figure 4.4: U.S. FDI as % of Total FDI in Mexico and Canada, 1987–2008
Source: Appendix, Table 12.

of 348 of the 500 largest multinational corporations (MNCs) in the world. Here is what they found:

- 154 firms are North American with 75 percent of their sales in North America and only 15.6 percent in Europe and 7.5 percent in Asia;
- 127 firms are European with 64 percent of their sales in Europe; and
- 67 firms are Asia-Pacific with 76 percent of their sales in their region.

The "world's largest firms," they conclude, "are regional, not global. . . . They both produce and sell on a home region basis."[36] Of course, many of these regional firms have a global reach, but when their total sales are considered, they are firmly rooted in a region, and the one with the largest market and the most MNCs is North America. Mexico and Canada have an increasing number of those MNCs.

CEMEX, a Mexican cement company, based in Monterrey, controlled about two-thirds of the Mexican market in 1989, when it decided to invest abroad. Part of the reason was that the U.S. International Trade Commission, reacting to pressure from uncompetitive U.S. firms, imposed a 58 percent countervailing duty on Mexican exports of cement. CEMEX responded by buying a large cement company in Texas and used that as a base to expand across the United States. Then, it went global, operating cement plants in fifteen countries and exporting cement to sixty countries. It quintupled sales to $5 billion, and by 2000, it was the world's third largest cement company.[37]

CEMEX reassured Mexicans they could compete in the United States. Grupo Modelo did not need the encouragement. It produced Corona beer, the fourth best-selling brand in the world and the No. 1 imported beer in both Canada and the United States.[38] Canadian companies grew fastest in North America with banks, telecommunications, and energy companies taking the lead.

It was investment by medium-sized firms that distinguished post-NAFTA investment from before. Jeld-Wen began manufacturing windows and doors in Klamath Falls, Oregon in 1960 with fifteen employees, and it grew to 150 divisions with more than 20,000 employees worldwide. In 1996, they bought a plant in Nogales, Mexico. At first, they tried to manage it by telephone from their headquarters, but that did not work so they asked Tony Vartola if he would relocate from Oregon, and he agreed. He moved his family to Rio Rico, Arizona just across the border from Nogales, and each day, he commuted to work at the plant.[39] Instead of losing workers, the plant in Nogales saved and expanded the labor force in Oregon, and the company expanded throughout North America and beyond. It supplies windows and doors for Wal-Mart and Home Depot.

Needless to say, there are thousands of examples of firms from each of the three countries of North America that have decided to expand by building or purchasing plants in the other countries. Some fail, and some succeed. All begin by visualizing the business equivalent of the North American Idea, a continental supply and marketing chain.

Some firms are very creative. Many Texans who lack health insurance go to Mexico and pay half the cost of going to a doctor in their state. To cater to middle-class Mexicans and a growing number of Americans, U.S. health care firms are building hospitals across the border.[40] This is the way integration is supposed to work. Entrepreneurs develop markets, and if consumers respond, they succeed. Governance, however, can facilitate or limit expansion. To grow, these hospitals need for the United States and Mexican governments to certify the quality of care, ensure adequate standards, and permit American retirees to use Medicare at these hospitals. Thus far, the governments have not pursued this issue.

As the economic bonds connecting the three countries have grown tighter, the very nature of trade has changed. Initially, each country exported products to each other. The United States exported airplanes; Canada sold lumber; Mexico sent vegetables and welcomed Canadian tourists to the Mayan ruins in the Yucatan. As trade barriers declined, U.S. auto companies began purchasing parts in Mexico and Canada. Soon, autos were assembled in each of the countries using parts from the others. Today, there are no American, Canadian, or Mexican cars; they are virtually all North American.

Martinrea International, a Canadian-based automotive supplier, employs more than 5,000 workers at thirty-two divisions in all three North American countries. The rear suspension assembly, which fits into a Chevy Equinox, is composed of parts that come from thirteen separate companies in the United States and Canada. Other parts come from Mexico.[41] (See Figure 4.5) In 2008, 25 percent of the average car produced by the three major U.S. auto companies was composed of international parts. Of that, Mexico supplied 30 percent and Canada 20 percent. Mexico overtook Canada in 2003 to become the leading international supplier of new car parts, and Canada and Mexico remain the top markets for U.S. car exports and, with Japan, the main source of U.S. car imports.[42]

Seventy percent of Canada's trade with the United States is intra-industry while close to 40 percent is within the same company.[43] To take advantage of NAFTA and reduce the costs of inventory and logistics, firms shifted to "just-in-time" production. When they need a part or a car, the computer would notify their partner across the border, and it would arrive that day or the next. The auto and auto parts industry remained the standard and, indeed, amounted to nearly 40 percent of the trade among the three countries, but other industries are replicating the model. In the new North America, businesses sell products across borders, but more often, they make products and do things together.

The degree of interdependence of the three countries is not understood very well by the three governments. During the deep recession of 2007–2009, the U.S. Congress grafted "buy American" provisions on the recovery package though it was contrary to the terms of NAFTA. After hearing concerns from Canada and Mexico, President Obama pledged U.S. procurement decisions would not violate its international obligations. The challenge was to make sure that subnational governments—states and communities—would not violate these agreements. American companies soon complained that their subsidiaries in Canada and Mexico were denied the chance to bid on contracts. The U.S. Chamber of Commerce therefore found itself in the awkward position of complaining to Congress that the "buy American provisions" were harming their ability to compete in the U.S. market.[44] In the end, the cross-investments compelled all levels of government in the United States and Canada to negotiate a fairer, more open procurement policy. The challenge is for the three governments to anticipate and plan such agreements, not just react after they have made a mistake.

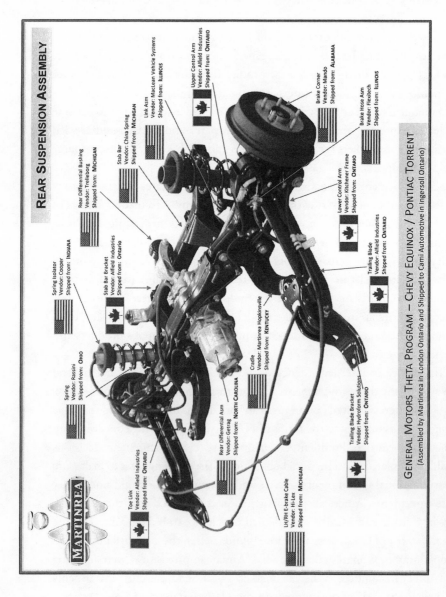

REAR SUSPENSION ASSEMBLY

Spring Isolator
Vendor: Cooper
Shipped from: **INDIANA**

Rear Differential Bushing
Vendor: Trelleborg
Shipped from: **MICHIGAN**

Stab Bar
Vendor: China Spring
Shipped from: **MICHIGAN**

Link Asm
Vendor: MacLean Vehicle Systems
Shipped from: **ILLINOIS**

Upper Control Arm
Vendor: Allfield Industries
Shipped from: **ONTARIO**

Stab Bar Bracket
Vendor: Allfield Industries
Shipped from: **Ontario**

Brake Corner
Vendor: Mando
Shipped from: **ALABAMA**

Lower Control Arm
Vendor: Kitchener Frame
Shipped from: **ONTARIO**

Brake Hose Asm
Vendor: Flexitech
Shipped from: **ILLINOIS**

Spring
Vendor: Rassini
Shipped from: **OHIO**

Trailing Blade
Vendor: Allfield Industries
Shipped from: **ONTARIO**

Toe Link
Vendor: Allfield Industries
Shipped from: **ONTARIO**

Cradle
Vendor: Martinrea Hopkinsville
Shipped from: **KENTUCKY**

Rear Differential Asm
Vendor: Getrag
Shipped from: **NORTH CAROLINA**

Trailing Blade Bracket
Vendor: Hydroform Solutions
Shipped from: **ONTARIO**

LH/RH E-brake Cable
Vendor: Hi-Lex
Shipped from: **MICHIGAN**

MARTINREA

Figure 4.5: Constructing a Part of a North American Car

GENERAL MOTORS THETA PROGRAM – CHEVY EQUINOX / PONTIAC TORRENT
(Assembled by Martinrea in London Ontario and Shipped to Cami Automotive in Ingersoll Ontario)

Source: Cited in Stephen Blank, "Building Autos: How North America Works & Why Canadian Studies Should be Interested," *American Review of Canadian Studies,* November 27, 2010.

➤ The Market for Energy and Climate Change

Thirty years ago, energy was a "sacred cow," untouchable in Mexico and Canada. Any hint of interest by U.S. oil companies in either country's reserves would cause both Canadians and Mexicans to reach for their guns. Since then, Canada opened its energy sector to competition, but Mexico has barely changed its approach. Only in October 2008 did the Mexican Congress begin a serious debate on whether to reorganize PEMEX, the national oil company, and permit foreign investment in the oil industry.

Joseph Dukert, an analyst of energy in North America, concluded that North America "is the world's largest and most successful regional energy market." The region produces almost 25 percent of all the energy on earth and 30 percent of the world's electricity. It also consumes about one-third more than it produces. From 1978 to 1990, U.S. imports of petroleum from Canada and Mexico more than doubled, and they doubled again by 2005. During the same period, continental electricity trade tripled. Two-way natural gas trade increased five-fold between 1978 to 2004.[45]

One third of all the energy imported by the United States comes from its two neighbors. When its tar sands are included, Canada has the second largest petroleum deposits after Saudi Arabia and the largest in the western hemisphere. Since 2000, it has more than doubled its production of oil from tar sands to 1.3 million barrels of oil a day in 2008. The expansion of tar sands production has raised increasing concern about climate change. These two interests—to expand production in energy while reducing carbon emissions—collide on the tar sands of Alberta, posing a major test for North America. Transforming the tar sands into oil requires huge amounts of natural gas and water and results in large quantities of waste material and carbon dioxide. The cost of production and the negative effect on the environment are so high that when the price of gasoline fell in 2009, more than 70 percent of the proposed projects were postponed.[46] Critics call it the dirtiest of fuels, and thus, it poses the classic trade-off between energy security and environmental sustainability.

In a very close vote on June 30, 2009, the U.S. House of Representatives passed the Waxman-Markey American Clean Energy and Security Act (ACESA) that aimed to reduce greenhouse gas emissions by 17 percent from 2005 to 2020. The bill established performance criteria and a cap-and-trade system to conserve fuel. With this system, Canada would either have to accept the same stringent regulatory requirements on fuel emissions as the United States, or it would have to pay a tariff on its exports of tar sands or other energy to the United States at a level that would equalize or offset the regulatory requirements. The bill also prohibited the U.S. government, including the Pentagon, from buying "dirty" fuels like tar sands. Canada protested the bill, which did not pass in the Senate.

The one country of the North American energy market that has the most restrictive policies is Mexico. Its constitution has given PEMEX a monopoly on energy production and distribution, and without competition and capital and technology from foreign investment, it has sunk into an abyss of inefficiency and corruption. Since the government relies on 30–40 percent of its budget revenues from PEMEX's profits, PEMEX does not have enough funds to explore for new sources of oil, and the constitution prevents any foreign company investment.[47]

The Cantarell oilfield, which was discovered in 1971 by a peasant of the same name, proved to be a bonanza at a time when Mexicans feared they were running out of oil. By 2004, at its peak, Cantarell accounted for 63 percent of Mexico's crude oil production. By 2008, when President Calderon sent a reform bill to his Congress, Cantarell was producing just 43 percent of Mexico's oil. Geologists predict that Cantarell will be exhausted by 2015, and Mexico will have to import oil. That news and the fact that Mexico already imports refined gasoline and about 25 percent of its natural gas from the United States woke up the Mexican political elite. It should also wake up the United States since Mexican oil constitutes the second largest source of its oil imports.

Mexico's national dialogue on energy in 2008 yielded a new law that reorganized the way that PEMEX would be governed, and it permitted PEMEX to negotiate performance-based contracts. Whether major oil companies with deep-sea technology will consider these contracts remains to be seen, but as Georgina Kessel, Mexico's secretary of energy, told me: "Oil is an extremely sensitive issue in Mexico. The best thing that the United States and its oil companies could do [to encourage investment in Mexican energy] is to say and do nothing."[48] The debate is not over. It just began.

Since the Arab OPEC oil embargo of 1973, every U.S. president has identified "energy security" as a vital American interest. As energy exporters, Canada and Mexico see this issue as an opportunity, not a problem, provided that the United States accepts their sovereign limits. But a new issue—climate change—makes the North American energy problem harder to solve. The region needs to decide how to fuel its economies at a time of reduced capacity and increasing global emissions, but there is no consensus on this within all three countries let alone among them.

➤ Illicit Markets

The expansion of a legitimate North American market coincided with the enlargement of illicit markets—most prominently, human trafficking and drug trafficking. These criminal "businesses" were not new, but they grew and became more dangerous as the North American market deepened.

Like the formal market, the illegal markets rely on supply and demand. The three governments enforce the rules of the game for formal markets. They cannot compel the drug traffickers to accept the rules, but they can raise the price of doing illegal business, and they do. When the U.S. government enforces the law on undocumented migration, poor Mexicans seeking work in the United States have to pay higher fees to "coyotes" (people smugglers) to get across the border. The prices range from $1,800 to $4,000 depending on whether they want to go through the desert or walk into the United States with a forged visa.[49] The profits are higher in the drug trade, and thus the competition among rival gangs is more treacherous. The drug traffickers intimidate people and the press by terrorism, and they corrupt officials by giving them the choice between being murdered or bribed (*plomo o plata*). This much is known.

Less recognized is that the United States and Canada are not just destinations for the drugs but also suppliers. The U.S. Department of Justice National Drug Intelligence Center estimated that the growth of marijuana production in the United States doubled since 2004. There is also two-way trade in marijuana between the United States and Canada, and most of MDMA ("ecstasy") shipped into the United States comes from Canada.[50] In addition, Mexicans are producers of marijuana, opium, and synthetic pills as well as the conveyor belt for cocaine coming from the Andes. They are also consumers.

As for corruption, Mexico faces a formidable task given the low wages of the police and the extravagant profits of the drug cartels, estimated by the Department of Homeland Security as between $19–29 billion.[51] Still, Mexico hardly has a monopoly on corruption. The Departments of Justice and Homeland Security have identified numerous cases of corruption by border agents and U.S. embassy personnel.[52]

The violence by the drug cartels generated widespread fear throughout Mexico, and it caused U.S. border state governors to request the National Guard, leading to a militarization of the border not seen since Pancho Villa massacred sixteen people in New Mexico in 1916. From Calderon's inauguration in December 2006, when he declared war against the cartels, through December 2010, more than 34,000 people died in drug-related violence. Despite the deployment of more than 40,000 soldiers to assist law enforcement authorities, the number of murders has risen each year since he took office. By 2009, there were more drug-related murders in Mexico than there were casualties in Iraq and Afghanistan.[53]

Most of the murders were by rival gangs against other drug traffickers, and most of the violence was concentrated in a few cities, mostly on the border.[54] Still, the gruesome nature of so many of the crimes and the kidnappings left the country reeling and America uneasy. The Joint Forces Command of the Defense Department asked whether Mexico had become a "failed state,"[55] and in September 2010, Secretary of State Hillary Clinton compared the struggle in Mexico to the insurgency in Colombia, though President Obama corrected her on that point the next day.[56]

The level and nature of the violence has risen, but it is not new, and it is also not unique to Mexico. El Salvador and Honduras have homicide rates of 71 and 67 per 100,000, which dwarfs Mexico's rate of 14.[57] What disturbs Americans is that the violence is closer to home. But then, the United States has experienced similar bouts of violence, for example during the Prohibition era, and cities like New York and Chicago have had, at different times, higher homicide rates than Mexico has today.

What makes the current struggle with drug traffickers different from the past? Modern technology and weaponry, more ghastly violence that sometimes targets innocent civilians, and a North American market. Whereas a few smugglers would move back-and-forth across the border two decades ago, today the traffic is heavy; the people are more familiar with both sides of the border; their operations are more sophisticated, and the market yields much higher returns and thus invites greater risks. The mafia cartels today build submarines, recruit armies, launder enough money to run banks, terrorize the people and the police with car bombings and atrocities, and have subsidiary offices across the United States. The illegal streams often merge into a single multinational company.

Mexico's Drug Trafficking Organizations (DTOs) have systematically squeezed the Colombian, Dominican, and Cuban DTOs. The Mexicans now employ approximately 900,000 criminally active gang members in 20,000 groups for retail drug distribution in more than 2,500 U.S. towns and cities. They represent the criminal equivalent of Wal-Mart in terms of the extensiveness of its impact in the United States and Mexico.[58] And they work both sides of the border. They kidnap poor victims in Zacatecas and demand ransom from their relatives in the United States.[59]

In June 2010, the Department of Justice announced an operation that led to 2,266 narcotics-related arrests in sixteen states and the seizure of seventy-four tons of illegal drugs and hundreds of firearms. These were the retail outlets of the Mexican DTOs, and it was the first significant joint operation between U.S. and Mexican legal officials on both sides of the border that paralleled the full operations of the multinational cartel.[60]

The operation was part of a broader effort that President Obama initiated in the spring of 2009. He reaffirmed his predecessor's "Merida Initiative" and pledged to expedite and increase the three-year $1.2 billion aid package of equipment, technology, training, and assistance against the cartels and in support of judicial reform. Mexico contributes $4.3 billion to combat drug trafficking.[61]

Never before had the United States and Mexico agreed to such a large aid program that also included judicial reform, a rebuilding of the Mexican police, and joint intelligence operations. Mexico, however, insisted this would differ from other U.S. aid programs in a fundamental way: instead of setting conditions on the use of aid, the United States needed to recognize a partnership. This proved quite difficult for the U.S. Congress to accept, but in July 2008, Congress led by Senator Christopher Dodd, who had long experience in Latin America, approved it.

In some ways, cooperation between Mexico and the United States improved. Mexico extradited more senior cartel leaders to the United States, and the U.S. government began to share more intelligence information with the Mexicans, making possible the joint operation to shut down retail facilities in the United States while arresting mafia leaders in Mexico. In other ways, the imbalance in the relationship shaped behavior in unhelpful ways. The U.S. government deported thousands of young gang members to the border without informing the Mexican government. The cartels recruited them. The United States blamed Mexico for the delays in transferring military equipment though the problem was often due to U.S. bureaucratic procedures.

On the issue of the sales of weapons from U.S. gun shops and gun shows to the cartels, President Obama gave the issue higher priority than his predecessor. From December 2006 until February 2010, Mexican law enforcement authorities seized about 80,000 firearms and 5 million rounds of ammunition from the cartels. The Mexican government gave the serial numbers of most of these to the U.S. Bureau of Alcohol, Tobacco, and Firearms (ATF), and 80 percent of those had come from the United States. Most of the arms were semi-automatic assault weapons, which were more lethal than the weapons carried by Mexican police. The Obama administration sent 100 ATF officials to investigate, and in 2009, they revoked the licenses of eleven U.S. gun shops—out of 6,700—near the border.[62]

Criminal organizations, like international businesses, have used the North American market to expand their activities. The governments have reacted to the criminal activities and violence, but the situation has not improved. The Mexican and U.S. governments have begun to cooperate, but they have not yet found the formula to defeat the cartels, nor have they found a way to involve Canada.

A clue to a more successful approach might be found in Mexico's most violent city, Juarez, across from El Paso, Texas. Juarez witnessed extraordinary growth in the 1990s due to the expansion of trade and the maquiladora sector. In the first decade of the twenty-first century, however, Chinese competition in textiles and lower-valued manufacturing hit the Juarez maquiladoras particularly hard. Unemployment surged and drug trafficking picked up the slack. There are other, perhaps more important reasons that Juarez has taken the brunt of the violence, including that it remains one of the main drug-trafficking corridors with a brutal war between the Sinaloa and Juarez cartels, but the failure by the city's business elite to join with North American firms to attract higher-valued manufacturing might be a piece of that puzzle. To defeat the drug cartels, law enforcement and businesses have to collaborate across the border better than the cartels.

➤ The Virtual Border

Just a few decades ago, barriers at the border were low. People could transit without too much difficulty. A few businesses worked both sides of the border. In the mid-1980s, trade began to grow, and NAFTA accelerated the trend. Then, 9/11 interrupted, and the borders are more like fortresses than turnstiles.

Still, the overflowing North American market renders the borders more a costly nuisance than an impermeable barrier. Those who prefer to avoid the harassment at the border stay connected with the Internet. These contacts, however, mask a more profound transformation. Today, on both sides of the Mexican-U.S. border, many of the people look Mexican while the economy looks American—and this is true not just along the border: it's becoming true in both countries. An east-west cleavage is also quite important. As one travels from the Gulf of Mexico in the east to the Pacific, the people and communities on both sides of the border grow more affluent. The violence has actually brought the people in the paired border cities—Brownsville and Matamoros, Laredo and Nuevo Laredo, the two Nogales, San Diego and Tijuana—closer together as friends and relatives look after each other.

On the northern border, Vancouver and Seattle are more alike than San Francisco and Los Angeles, and Windsor and Detroit have more in common than New York and Boston. The U.S. border states and Canadian provinces trade more with each other than they do with other states and provinces.[63] Observing these cross-border regions, Paul Krugman observed: "Canada is essentially closer to the United States than it is to itself."[64] Arizona's former Governor Janet Napolitano made a similar point in acknowledging that she worked more with the governor of Sonora than with the governor of New Mexico. Many who live near the southern and northern borders share a wish that the borders would be flatter and that their country's leaders would either fix border and bilateral relations or let them do it.

While the North American market raises issues in need of continental solutions, Washington is seized with the security-related issues. Ottawa and Mexico City want to shrink the border to permit more commerce and travel, but Canada does not want to work with Mexico on these issues. Therefore, the issues are handled on a dual-bilateral basis (U.S.-Mexico and U.S.-Canada) not as North America's problems, or they are addressed on a more limited scale at the state or local levels by border communities or civil society organizations. A few international organizations and fewer North American institutions are involved, but none very deeply. Stephen Clarkson surveyed the terrain and found governance at the North American level absent or inadequate.[65]

The three governments have two bilateral boundary and water commissions that were established at roughly the same time at the beginning of the twentieth century. Both have worked well because their mandate is specific and technical. At the time of NAFTA, the three governments established four sets of commissions: (a) the North American Free Trade Commission, composed of the senior trade representatives to review any trade problems; (b) the dispute-settlement mechanisms on trade and investment issues; (c) NAFTA's Commission for Labor Cooperation (NACLC) and the North American Commission for Environmental Cooperation (CEC), which were established by the two side agreements; and (d) The North American Development Bank, whose principal mission is to fund environmental and infrastructural projects on the border. Most of these mechanisms have performed adequately but have received neither the funds nor the mandate to have any significant effect on the region or its problems.

More important than these thin institutions has been the efforts by states, provinces, and civil society to construct "continentalism from below," to use Clarkson's phrase. Several clusters of states and provinces have built formidable networks focused on improving their immediate neighborhood. Perhaps the strongest institution is the Pacific Northwest Economic Region (PNWER), whose membership includes state legislators, governors, counties, and civil society organizations. PNWER has lobbied federal officials on ways to improve the border, e.g., by building additional lanes, and they do the most systematic research of border-related issues. In the northeast, the Canadian-American Border Trade Alliance, based in Lewiston, Maine, has worked with the Canadian Chamber of Commerce and business associations.

In the southwest, the Border Trade Alliance, based in Phoenix, has worked with the Southwest Governors' Association. Arizona State University's North American Center for Transborder Studies, the University of San Diego's Transborder Institute, the University of California/San Diego's Center on U.S.-Mexican Studies, and the University of Texas, Austin—all have programs across the border with El Colegio de la Frontera and Tec de Monterrey. The exchange of students and faculty, while still low by comparative international standards, is gradually increasing.

Civil society organizations, representing environmentalists, Native Americans, consumers, and all manner of professional associations have sprouted and bring collective pressure on the governments to address particular issues, whether it is the price of medicines or the availability of bilingual education. Business associations and labor unions also contest one another not only within each country but among the three.

All of these cross-border connections reflect and affect a widening but flawed market. This market has been assembled because of the logic of efficiency, but families on both sides of the borders and subnational organizations have also played important roles. At the same time, the security imperatives of fighting cartels and terrorists and the protectionist pressures of fearful firms and "cultural" xenophobes have created barriers. These two countervailing pressures—to create a seamless market or to construct barriers to impede transit—have led to a North America that is stuck between two worlds. A North American space is emerging, but it is imperfect and chaotic.

It used to be said that all things came together at the border, or they came apart. Nowadays, they can and often do both. We have seen how they have come together. In the next chapter, we will see how they have come apart.

5

Speed Bumps, Potholes, and Roadblocks on the North American Superhighway

On my third crossing of the border between Tijuana and San Ysidro, which is south of San Diego, in that many days, the Feds finally caught me. I had been waiting on line with Hector Vindiola, a Mexican, who was public affairs officer with the U.S. Consulate in Tijuana. Hector had arranged my lecture at El Colegio de la Frontera and an interview on the day before with Joseph Misenhelter, the assistant port director in San Ysidro of the U.S. Department of Homeland Security (DHS).

Hector and I waited on line for nearly two hours in the blazing heat, but we were so focused on talking about immigration-related issues that I had not realized that I was finally at the front of the line. Unlike those in the line, the DHS inspector was not accustomed to waiting, and his query mixed sarcasm with a barely concealed threat: "Are you interested in coming to the United States?"

"Yes, sir," I said with respect and brevity. "You have my undivided attention." The inspector then took about five minutes to review carefully every leaf of my passport. "You've been to Yemen. Other places in the Middle East? What for?"

"Yes," I said, "I was managing a State Department project to explore the prospects for democratization." I observed his face, and soon realized that bureaucratic battles can be as important as the real ones, and from DHS's perspective, a State Department project was only marginally better than getting a scholarship from Osama Bin Laden.

The border official sent me to "secondary." The equivalent card in *Monopoly* is "Do not pass go. Do not collect $200." "Secondary" is a lane of suspicion. It allows inspectors to ask more questions and check a name against an extensive "watch list." "Secondary" means waiting in two more lines, or if the individual looks dangerous or is uncooperative, he or she gets a "time-out" in a prison cell with rubber mats on the wall.

The next inspector took my passport and a yellow paper that included the suspicions of the first inspector. He stared at me, and then sent the papers to a third inspector who asked again: "When did you first go and when did you last go to the Middle East?"

I responded, and then he said: "Were you ever scared?" For a moment, I wondered whether this was a trick question, or whether he was simply curious. I said that I wasn't. After about five minutes of punching information into his computer, he finally looked up and said: "O.K., you can go."

The interrogation was aimless, but at least it was painless. Some others have not been so lucky. Dozens of people—mostly Muslim or from the Middle East—have been arrested by the United States and subject to long periods of detention, and some have been tortured. Benamar Benatta, an Algerian living in the United States, was detained at the Canadian border on September 5, 2001, and turned over to U.S. authorities for five years of detention. He was never charged with any crime. After being released, he returned to Canada but continues to suffer nightmares: "They ruined my whole life."[1] A more horrific case was that of Maher Arar, a Syrian-born Canadian citizen, who was transiting New York when U.S. officials were informed by Canadian officials that he was a possible security risk. When the Canadians said that Arar would not be permitted to enter Canada, the United States deported him to Syria where he was tortured. Eventually, Canadian officials acknowledged their mistake and apologized, but the United States was not as candid or generous.

The day before my experience in "secondary," Misenhelter, the twenty-one-year veteran customs' officer, warned me that the first mission of DHS was to stop terrorism. He then acknowledged that since 9/11, DHS officers on California's border had not arrested a single person coming from Mexico for being suspected of terrorism. This, I discovered, was not for want of trying, and it also wasn't because few people cross the border. Since 9/11, the California border has been legally crossed from the south more than 500 million times—on average, about 85 million per year.[2]

This was also true of the Canadian border. There, DHS officers were more evasive in answering the questions about arrests of people at the border for suspicion of terrorism, usually mentioning that a "terrorist incident" had occurred.

When one asks for specifics, they refer to the "millennium" bomber, but he was arrested by a border guard in Washington State in 1999—nearly two years before 9/11.

The costs and consequences of creating a mountain of restrictions since 9/11 have been exorbitant for the hundreds of millions of people who cross the Mexican and Canadian borders each year, but because most of these costs are not widely known, we suffer them quietly. The problem, as we learned in the last chapter, is that within North America, businesses are not just selling products, they are increasingly making products together and doing things together. These joint efforts need a "flat" terrain. Security restrictions are like speed bumps; they disrupt traffic and add to the cost of doing business. No one would question their utility if they stopped terrorists, but there is little evidence of that. This is not to suggest that we should open the borders and let everyone pass, but we should raise questions as to the effectiveness of the post-9/11 strategy and open our minds to the possibility of alternatives.

What we have done since 9/11 has created problems on our borders and in our relationships with our neighbors; but the real problem is what we have *not* done. As trade tripled, and about 80 percent of that is carried by trucks, we have not filled in the potholes. We have not maintained the infrastructure or built new highways. We have not planned or invested in transportation and infrastructure for all of North America.

And yet, paradoxically, at the very moment when highways and new corridors are needed to connect the North American market, a movement emerged in the United States to stop construction on a mythical twelve-lane superhighway from Mexico to Canada. The groups, which include a resurgent John Birch Society, identify themselves as opponents of the North American Union—also an illusory target. They fear that the highway aims to undermine the sovereignty of the United States and facilitate migration. The fact that no such highway is either being built or even contemplated has not deterred these groups. Indeed, their hysterical videos seem to grow in number and intensity.

While their fears of a highway are surreal, their concerns about illegal migration are shared by a broader constituency. Indeed, when Congress reviewed the immigration issue in 2006, the only part of a very complicated bill that was approved was to construct a wall. Instead of eliminating the speed bumps and filling in the potholes or approving comprehensive immigration reform, the United States Congress funded a wall across 670 miles of its border with Mexico. The declared purpose was to stop terrorists, undocumented workers, and drug traffickers.

Of course, a wall will not stop all illegal transactions. About 40 percent of undocumented workers—including the 9/11 terrorists—enter the United States legally with visas, but then overstay. Drug traffickers are very adept at finding new routes. A wall can reduce illegal migration and crime, but usually only at a few places on the border. The problem with the wall was it sent a message to Mexico and to Mexicans in the United States that we view them as the problem. On the northern border, the added restrictions are an annoyance, a serious cost to commerce, and a signal that the United States really does not trust Canadians to look after shared security concerns.

North America's problems are *speed bumps* (the new 9/11 restrictions); *potholes* (the failure to maintain or build roads and infrastructure); *roadblocks* (policies that prevent trucks from transiting the border or picking up return shipments); and *hidden tolls* (concealed taxes, including divergent regulations, that encourage inefficiency). Together, these problems have hobbled North America, insulted our neighbors, and been so costly as to have turned the North American advantage into a disadvantage.

➤ Inevitable and Irreversible, But That Could Change

"Economic integration within North America is not only inevitable; it is also irreversible," insisted Thomas D'Aquino, one of Canada's most effective and relentless advocates for trade and investment in North America.[3] D'Aquino began as a special assistant to then-Prime Minister Pierre Trudeau but made his mark as the chief executive officer (CEO) of a group of the 150 top CEOs in Canada. He is a voluble, irrepressible, one-person business roundtable. For nearly thirty years, he represented the largest businesses in Canada with assets exceeding $3.5 trillion. In that role, he tried to shape the country's business environment and improve its competitiveness.

Regarding his point about the inevitability of interdependence, however, D'Aquino was asserting his wish, not a fact. The truth is that interdependence is neither inevitable nor irreversible; indeed, it stalled mainly because of 9/11 and has been declining. "Security trumps trade," former U.S. Ambassador Paul Cellucci said, and he is closer to the truth.

On the morning of September 11, 2001, nineteen individuals not only struck terror into the mind and body of America, but they also slammed on the brakes of the North American experiment. Just a few days before, President Bush hosted Mexican President Vicente Fox for a state visit. It was a moment of high expectations, and Fox delivered a full set of proposals on immigration and economic integration. Soon after Fox returned to Mexico, Al-Qaeda struck—two planes went into the World Trade Center, one into the Pentagon, and the fourth would have hit either the Capitol or the White House if its heroic passengers had not forced it down. At 10:00 A.M. that morning, just three minutes before the fourth crash, the Acting Commisioner of Customs Chuck Winwood and the new Commissioner of Immigration Jim Ziglar ordered officials at all 300 land, sea, and air ports-of-entry in the United States to a "level one threat status," which meant complete examination of everything approaching the border. This order reached all the ports of entry within one hour and virtually shut down the border.[4] At 3:15 P.M., President Bush convened a secure video teleconference with his National Security Council. He opened the meeting by declaring: "We're at war," though it wasn't clear against whom. The secretary of defense directed the nation's armed forces to DefCon 3, an increased state of readiness, and for the first time in history, grounded all non-emergency civilian aircraft in the United States. No flights were permitted to enter U.S. airspace.[5]

The United States did not need to inform Canada and Mexico what happened because the whole world saw the attack on television, but Canadians and Mexicans would have appreciated being consulted or even just informed of the decision to close the borders. Both countries immediately felt the consequences. The impact of shutting the two borders was equivalent to damming two huge, raging rivers. The water backed up, turning our neighbors into instant reservoirs.

Within two days, the lines of trucks waiting to cross Windsor Bridge into Detroit stretched for twenty miles. By then, Ford, which used its Windsor plants to supply parts for eight of its fifteen U.S. plants, was forced to shut down five of its assembly lines and one of its plants. Chrysler shut all of its plants. Toyota cancelled shifts in its Kentucky plants. In San Diego, traffic stalled for eight hours. President Fox later described the economic aftermath in Mexico as "cataclysmic." Canadians expressed sympathy, not anger, and dutifully cared for all the international air travelers who were stranded for three days until the United States reopened air travel.[6]

When governments cannot locate a policy to respond to a crisis of the magnitude of 9/11, they tend to choose one of two "default options": they go to war or reorganize the government. The Bush administration did both. Bush went to war against the Taliban in Afghanistan, and soon overthrew the regime. Establishing a stable government to replace the Taliban proved to be a lot harder.

The job of reorganizing the U.S. government seemed more mundane, but in the long term, it might prove even more consequential. The president signed into law in November 2002 a law establishing the Department of Homeland Security (DHS) by assembling twenty-two existing agencies with 200,000 employees. It was the second largest reorganization in American history after the establishment of the Department of Defense (DOD) in 1947. As with the case of DOD, the implications of the decision to set up DHS will reverberate in the United States and the world for decades.

It was expected that the merging of so many autonomous agencies would become a bureaucratic nightmare. The more important issue—how would the new bureaucracy redefine America?—was never really debated because the administration was in a hurry to show it was doing something to prevent the next attack. Winston Churchill once remarked that men build institutions and then institutions define men. From its beginning, with some regrettable lapses, the United States has been a welcoming nation to the world and a relaxed neighbor. DHS and its leaders changed that.

Granted, the Immigration and Naturalization Service had an ambivalent mission: to turn immigrants into citizens while preventing entry by those without the proper documents. With DHS, the ambivalence dissolved. The mission of the new bureaucracy was simple and repeated as a mantra by every DHS official: "Close the door and shoot the terrorists!" In a politically correct age, targeting potential suspects is viewed as "profiling," and to avoid being "politically incorrect," DHS targeted everyone. It discarded the welcome mat and harassed everyone trying to enter the country legally. Those deemed suspicious or without adequate documents hit a roadblock.

Canada and Mexico were just gearing up to partner with the United States to create "the most efficient border in the world" when they realized that they had been transformed from policy makers to policy takers.[7] The United States was focused on dealing with its security concerns by itself, and so Canada and Mexico were left with no alternative but to try to relate to its neighbor by establishing counterparts of DHS. Border efficiency had been replaced by border security, and Canada and Mexico were on the other side of a new fortified border.

➤ Speed Bumps

In the millennium year 2000, which turned out to be the high point of North American integration, inspectors at all U.S. ports of entry counted 534 million people entering the United States. Of those, 437 million entered the United

States overland legally from Mexico and Canada. (See Figure 5.1) After September 11, 2001, the numbers declined each year until they reached 250 million people in 2009. This was not due to economic recession because the numbers declined even when the economy improved. It was not due to a problem in Mexico because the numbers declined from Canada even more. It was not due to global restrictions because the numbers arriving by sea and air remained steady. It was due to a "thickening" of both borders—the result of increasing restrictions.

Almost all of the people who entered came for short periods. A substantial number were commuters, living on one side of the border and working on the other, whether branch managers living in Arizona or nurses from Windsor crossing to work in hospitals in Detroit. Roughly one million a year came as permanent residents with the intent of immigrating permanently to the United States. Standing on the bridge overlooking the Tijuana-San Ysidro crossing and looking south toward Mexico, one sees a swirling, chaotic flood of people, cars, buses, and bureaucrats. For pedestrians and cars, this is the most traveled border crossing in the world with approximately 65 million people crossing each year. As one gazes more intently to the left, ones sees twenty-five lanes of traffic and a huge facility crammed with pedestrians, who have already waited in long lines for hours. The cars are going north, but most of the time, it seems like they are parked, and the people are standing still. The waiting time for

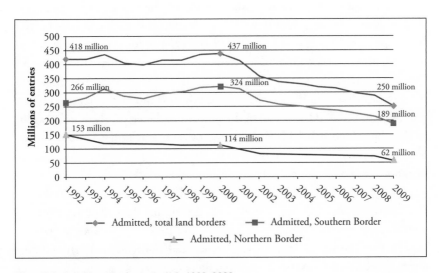

Figure 5.1: Legal Land Entries to the U.S.,1992–2009

Sources: U.S. Department of Homeland Security, *Immigration Statistics*, PAS G-22 1 FY 1992–2006; Operational Management Report 2007–2008; Bureau of Transportation Statistics, 2009.

pedestrians and cars varies, but in the three times that I crossed in October 2008, it never took less than one hour, and once, it took three hours.

To the right, one sees only five lanes going south to Mexico—one-fifth of the number of the lanes going north, and every lane is moving very quickly—like 50 miles per hour. Now, how could that be? Is everyone coming into the United States? Is no one returning to Mexico? No one knows for sure because neither government keeps records of those leaving the United States. When I walked into Mexico, not one official from either country stopped to ask me a single question or look at my passport.

Beyond the obvious point that the United States is more concerned about Mexicans entering their country than Mexico is bothered by the arrival of American tourists, there is a logic to stopping people in only one direction. The vast majority of the travelers are commuters. If they were delayed in both directions, there wouldn't be enough time in the day to work. Trade would shrink, and the border would shrivel. In 2008, the U.S. government proved this point when it stopped cars going to Mexico to search for weapons. The effort hurt the border economies and yielded just 70 firearms. In August 2009, following President Obama's pledge to stop the arms flow to Mexico, the U.S. government repeated this mistaken strategy. Joining with Mexico, DHS stopped southern-bound cars and trucks to look for weapons. The delays were comparable to the northern traffic flows, and the border communities felt the air escape from their economies.[8]

Leaving aside the guns, drugs, and commerce, the U.S. government's main preoccupation on the border is people. The legal entries each year have ranged from 240–437 million people each year, but the real focus are those who enter the United States without documents or remain after their visas expire. In the 1980s, when Americans perceived a crisis in undocumented migration and passed a law to stop it, the average annual flow was 160,000. (Figure 5.2) That number doubled in the first half of the 1990s, and then it nearly doubled again during the second half. This was a period of economic growth in the United States, and the number of visas for low-skilled labor was 5,000 while the annual flow of undocumented migrants exceeded 600,000.[9]

The biggest surprise was the increase in undocumented migrants in the period after 9/11. Between 2000 and 2005, the annual flow of undocumented workers rose to about 850,000 each year—five times the number of two decades before. From 2005–07, as Congress debated immigration, Bush strengthened enforcement, and the average numbers declined to about 550,000 per year. With the onset of the recession in 2007, the numbers dropped further to 300,000 per year.[10]

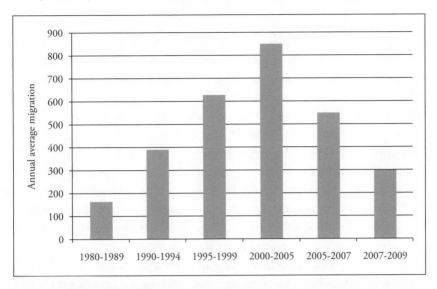

Figure 5.2: Undocumented Migration Flows to the United States, 1980–2008 (hundreds of thousands).
Sources: Jeffrey Passel and D'Vera Cohn, "U.S. Unauthorized Immigration Flows Are Down Sharply Since Mid-Decade," Pew Hispanic Center, 2010; Jeffrey S. Passel, "Unauthorized Immigration: Measurement, Methods, and Data Sources," Immigration Data Users' Seminar, Washington, D.C., October 16, 2008. (Available online: www.prb.org/presentations/passel.ppt) 2000 to 2009, year beginning in March.

Let us pause for a moment and try to understand why total legal entries declined in the four years after 9/11 while illegal entries leaped upwards. Since every illegal entry was a potential terrorist, one would have expected that the North American governments would have concentrated their resources in stopping them. Raul Benitez, a Mexican professor and advisor to CISEN, the Mexican intelligence agency, offered an interesting explanation. He said that after 9/11, Mexican intelligence infiltrated and paid the "coyotes" on the border to report any non-Spanish speaking illegal migrant, particularly those who looked like they were from the Middle East. At the same time, the Mexican officials turned a blind eye on Mexican and Central American illegal immigration.[11] On the other side, the Bush administration focused on finding terrorists at the border facilities and airports. The administration was not inclined to punish employers for hiring undocumented workers, and as enforcement declined, job opportunities increased. As a result, the number of undocumented migrants entering the United States after 9/11 each year was almost as large as the numbers with permanent resident visas.

The administration ratcheted up its war against terrorism without referring to illegal workers for another reason. Tom Ridge, the first secretary of Homeland Security, acknowledged in his memoir that it was not a coincidence that the threat level was raised before the 2004 election and lowered afterwards. The Bush White House judged that the administration and the Republican party benefited politically by playing on people's fears, and they were right.[12]

In a press conference on October 23, 2008, DHS Secretary Michael Chertoff cited estimates by the Pew Research Center that more than 800,000 illegal migrants entered the country each year from 2000–05, but he then noted the reduction to 550,000 in the following two years and saw this as a sign that enforcement "at the border has begun to turn the tide on illegal migration." Of course, allowing the illegal entry of a half of a million people each year is not exactly a success story. During the Bush years, the total illegal population in the United States increased 40 percent, from 8.4 million in 2000 to 12 million in 2007. In 2009, because of the recession and more enforcement, the number fell to 11.1 million,[13] but it rose again to 11.2 million in 2010.

To prevent people from overstaying their visas, as the 9/11 terrorists did, Tom Ridge announced in 2002 an automated entry-exit program. DHS officers captured the fingerprints of 90 million visitors entering the country, but the exit part of the program proved unworkable, and Chertoff, Ridge's successor, suspended it.

The two land borders have not moved or grown longer since 450 officers patrolled them in the 1920s, but today, there are many more inspectors.[14] (See Figure 5.3) That is because there are many more immigrants, and the government's tasks have grown more numerous and complex. They inspect cars, people, and trucks. They verify cargo, tax goods, and try to stop terrorists, illegal drugs, tainted produce, and viruses. From 1986 to 2001, the number of customs agents on the southern border tripled to nearly 9,000. In comparison, there were only 300 border officials and 1,500 customs agents on the 5,525 mile Canadian border. After 9/11, President Bush doubled the number of border agents on the southern border again, and the overall numbers grew to over 20,000 in 2009—five times as many as in 1992.

The expansion in personnel coincided with a proliferation of programs—each with its own acronym. It wasn't long before the bureaucrats had enough acronyms to design a new game of North American Scrabble. The U.S. government began by creating a Terrorist Screening Database (TSDB), which was itself a compilation of the following programs: CLASS (Consular Lookout and Support System) and TIPOFF from the Department of State; IBIS (Interagency Border and Inspection System) from the Department of Homeland Security; the No-Fly and Select Lists from the TSA (Transportation Security Administration); NAILS (National Automated Immigration Lookout System); IDENT (Automated Biometric Identification System) from the former INS (Immigration and

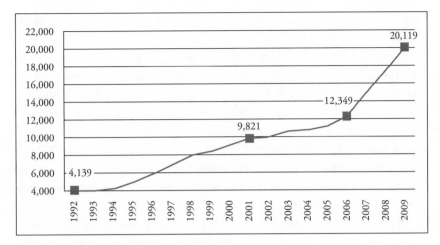

Figure 5.3: U.S. Border Patrol Agents, 1992–2009
Source: Customs and Border Protection database, data sent on request, October 2010.

Naturalization Service); VGTOF (Violent Gang and Terrorist Organization File) and IAFIS (Integrated Automated Fingerprint Identification System) from the FBI; and the Interpol Terrorism Watch List.[15] We're just beginning.

Citizens traveling frequently across the U.S.-Canadian border need as many as five separate credentials: (1) NEXUS, a biometric, photo ID card, to allow fast travel across the border; (2) FAST for their commercial vehicle; (3) TWIC for transportation workers; (4) a passport; and (5) PASS, an e-passport in order to be compliant with the Western Hemisphere Travel Initiative (WHTI). Each requires a lengthy and expensive application process, and if someone also wanted to cross the U.S.-Mexican border, they would need an equal number but different set of cards, each with different acronyms. Instead of NEXUS across the Canadian border, for example, you need a SENTRI card (Secure Electronic Network for Travelers Rapid Inspection Lines) to get into the fast-lane to cross into the United States from Mexico. Interestingly, if you only have an American passport, and you want to return home to the United States, your government will not allow you to use the SENTRI fast-lane.

Part of the frustration of people who cross the border regularly is that they spend substantial money and time to acquire NEXUS or SENTRI, and then, they discover that those lanes may be slower than the others. NEXUS is the one card used by both Canadians and Americans. Both countries check the background of the applicant, and each has the right to reject. However, neither country accepts the card as bi-national. By May 2010, 400,000 had been approved for a NEXUS card, and by September 2008, 175,000 had a SENTRI card.[16] These numbers are a faint shadow of the 250 million who entered the United States in 2009.

The requirements for truckers are even more complicated, expensive, and duplicative. In addition to needing the cards listed above, truckers have to be accredited to C-TPAT (U.S. Customs Trade Partnership against Terrorism), PIP (Canadian Partnership in Protection), and CSA (U.S. Customs Self-Assessment Program). These are supposed to facilitate rapid review of their cargos, but truckers also need to file their customs forms electronically with the U.S. Automated Commercial Electronic (ACE) and Canadian Automated Commercial Information (ACI). The North American Scrabble game is not only alive; it is procreating.

Louise Yako, vice president of the British Columbia Trucking Association, complained about the restrictions, the duplication, and the rising costs, and feared that many of the small trucking companies would go out of business. "They," she said referring to the Department of Homeland Security, "promised to consolidate the various programs and make them easier, but the requirements have multiplied and are far more costly." She estimated that the added cost to a large carrier (fleet size of 400 trucks) amounted to $2.4 million.[17] Another study by the Canadian Chamber of Commerce estimated that small trucking companies paid about $100,000 in fees and preparation over a two-year period to be certified, and one company complained that the rate of inspections increased by 30 percent after being certified.[18]

Yako's fears that the fees would drive small truckers out of business proved true. Bradbury and Turbeville found that the number of personal vehicles traveling from Canada to the United States declined by 24 percent and trucks by 6 percent from 9/11 to 2009. The western part of Canada suffered a 17 percent decline in trade since 9/11 because most trucking was by small firms that could not pay the additional costs and also because of the U.S. ban on meat imports from Canada between 2003 and 2005.[19] The ban was due to the discovery of a "mad cow" at a farm in Alberta. This led the United States to require that all commercial trucks, railway cars, and airline passengers pay an additional APHIS (Animal and Plant Health Inspection Services) fee to the U.S. Department of Agriculture, and that each cow have a health certificate number from a veterinarian. One food exporter estimated this would cost about $700,000 annually. The Canadians retaliated by insisting on the same procedures for U.S. exporters of food and poultry.[20]

The Canadian government analyzed the effect of security restrictions on trade and found a clear downward trend in transport and insurance costs in the five and one-half years prior to September 2001 and a sharp upward trend after that, increasing by 12.4 percent after 9/11.[21] Another study commissioned by the Canadian government estimated that the total border costs and fees paid by the trucking industry was about $10 billion.[22] Numerous studies since 9/11 have assessed the length and cause of delays and the cost to commerce and the nations, and they all point in the same negative direction. Dr. Hart Hodges at Western Washington University examined border crossings between the United States and Canada over a fifteen-year period and concluded that trade was reduced because of the costs and delays due to 9/11, not exchange rates.[23] Steven Globerman and Paul Storer took a different approach to the subject, but arrived at a similar conclusion: "Both U.S. exports to and imports from Canada were lower than they would otherwise have been in the post-9/11 period given traditional determinants of bilateral trade."[24] A study by KPMG for Canadian truckers in May–June 2002 found an average 20 percent increase in border delays going south to the United States and a 12 percent increase in delays northbound as compared to the previous year.[25]

In perhaps the most extensive study of the costs of delays on the U.S.-Canada border, financed by the U.S. Department of Transportation, John Taylor and Douglas Robideaux of Grand Valley State University and George C. Jackson of Wayne State University calculated that the border management system was costing both the United States and Canadian economies about $10.3 billion per year. This was equivalent to about 2.7 percent of merchandise trade in 2001,[26] which is higher than the average U.S. tariff before NAFTA.[27] This is a tax, however concealed. If it advanced security, it would be worth the cost, but there is little evidence of that.

The new administrative costs were heavier in certain sectors, such as in steel, where delays averaged about 5–6 hours on the border, adding $300–600 million to annual cost.[28] To assemble a North American car, auto parts, on average, have to cross the border seven times. The auto industry estimated that their "speed bump"—the total costs of the additional restrictions due to 9/11—added $800 to the price of each car.[29] This is quite a conclusion, and it might help to explain why the North American auto industry collapsed in 2009.

There are fewer studies on the U.S.-Mexican border, but their conclusions are consistent with those on the northern border. The most comprehensive report was done by El Colegio de la Frontera Norte in Tijuana based on an extensive survey of 15,600 north-bound cars and commercial vehicles and 1,248 pedestrians at every U.S.-Mexican border crossing. The study found an average delay for north-bound traffic of 150–180 minutes in Nogales, Ciudad Juarez, and Nuevo Laredo and 280 minutes at Tijuana. They assumed conservatively an hourly cost of $50, and computed total costs due to delays of $436 million per year, or $1.8 million per day. In addition, they estimated the cost to the local community of delays, added pollution, and job loss, and concluded that they suffered $7.5 billion in lost production, nearly 300,000 jobs lost, and $1.4 billion in lost salaries. They also found a significant decline in the number of commercial trucks approaching the border after 9/11 because of delays due to added security measures.[30]

The evidence, in brief, is substantial and incontrovertible. Delays have increased—about 20 percent for Canadians going south, 12 percent for Americans going to Canada according to one of the best non-government analyses. From Mexico, the delays increased 2.5–4.5 hours. The vast increase in border personnel has not facilitated legitimate travel or commerce, but it has added to the administrative costs. Although the estimates of the total costs vary based on different assumptions, all agree that they are high and have had a demonstrable effect on trade and the three economies. One of the estimates is that the added restrictions, applications, and filing fees amount to a 2.7 percent tax on commerce, which in 2008, with total trade of nearly $1 trillion, would amount to $27 billion. The costs of transferring cargo to other trucks on the U.S.-Mexico border are estimated at $436 million, but the spillover effects on the environment, the economies, and jobs added $8.9 billion to the total cost.[31] The added costs to individual sectors like steel and autos made them more vulnerable to other macroeconomic shocks like the recession. The direct cost to the taxpayer also soared. From 2001 to 2009, the U.S. Border Patrol budget alone tripled from $1.1 billion to $3.5 billion while the entire budget of Customs and Border Protection (CBP) grew from $3 billion to $10 billion. (See Figure 5.4).

U.S. Senator George Voinovich asked the General Accountability Office to assess whether the additional officials helped in reducing delays on the U.S.-Canadian border and whether the FAST program to expedite low-risk commercial trucking was working. The response was astonishing. The GAO could not reach any conclusion because CBP collected wait-times data "using inconsistent methods and are unreliable," and thus were of no use. With respect to the other program, CBP "lacks the data needed to determine whether the FAST program is effective."[32] Neither the GAO nor the CBP considered consulting or coordinating with Canada, which was unfortunate because Canada had been collecting wait-times at all their border posts since November 2001 and, more recently, posted them online and on Twitter.[33]

The Conference Board of Canada reported: "If crossing the border becomes too costly or uncertain, or is even perceived to be so, the advantages

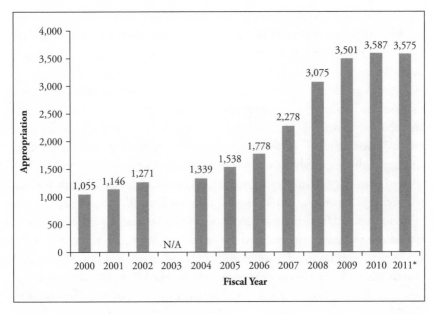

Figure 5.4: U.S. Border Patrol Budget, 2000–2011

Source: Chad C. Haddal, "Border Security," Congressional Research Service, August 2010, p. 11. Available at: http://www.fas.org/sgp/crs/homesec/RL32562.pdf.

of locating production in the smaller market [Canada] to serve the larger one [U.S.] disappears." Canadians feared that "just-in-time" was being replaced by "just-in-case" production, and the result would be less investment in Canada and fewer jobs.[34] Mexico faces the same challenge, but it has an even heavier burden because its trucks are not permitted into the United States.

It is hard to imagine a conservative administration in the United States mandating so many costly regulations on business. Of course, the Bush administration's decisions were based on security concerns, and in the atmosphere of a war on terror, few asked whether the additional restrictions enhanced security and thus were worth the price. Americans, Canadians, and Mexicans have viewed the security threat very differently, partly because the United States is the principal target for terrorism, but also because the fear of terrorism varies inversely with the distance—physical and temporal—from the 9/11 attacks. The further away from the attacks, the less fear people have. The more time passes without another attack, the less people fear terrorism. This formula applies within the three countries and among them. In February 2003, when asked "how likely" their country would suffer a terrorist attack in the next year, 56 percent of Americans and 12 percent of Canadians thought it very likely.

During the next two years, both groups' fears of such an attack declined quite sharply—down to 28 percent of Americans and 6 percent of Canadians. Mexicans were less fearful of foreign terrorism—though more concerned about public security—than Canadians.[35]

Canada and Mexico were initially sympathetic to the U.S. need to create a more secure border, but they were also wary of new barriers to trade. Canadians repackaged many of the initiatives that had been broached over the years into a "smart borders" agreement in December 2001 that increased border security without unduly harming commerce. The Mexican Foreign Minister tried to convince Canada to negotiate the agreement trilaterally, but Canada rejected that approach, and so Mexico replicated it with a similar agreement in March 2002. Despite those agreements, intrusive restrictions proliferated. Canadians and Mexicans resented the restrictions as well as the way that the U.S. government imposed them. A poll of Canadians in the fall of 2008 found two-thirds critical of the tougher restrictions on the U.S. border. Fifty-five percent called them "unreasonable," and two-thirds thought that they harmed Canadian exports.[36]

In the U.S. Consulate in Vancouver, the Consul General acknowledged that Canadians view U.S. border guards as rude and question whether the United States really trusts them to cooperate against threats. All Canadians—even well-known leaders—have border stories. Bill Sauder, a timber magnate, who had just given $20 million to build the University of British Columbia Business School, has a home in Palm Springs and a NEXUS card to facilitate entry to the United States. But when he received a new drivers' license, his NEXUS card was confiscated at a border crossing. "When you pull a Bill Sauder off the NEXUS list," the consul general admitted, "we have serious problems."

At the conclusion of Calderon's state visit to Washington in May 2010, he joined with President Obama to announce an agreement to build a "Twenty-First Century Border." On February 4, 2011, Obama met with Prime Minister Stephen Harper, and they made a similar pledge to improve the borders. Both promises were echoes of the two "smart borders' agreements" signed by their predecessors a decade before. The governments were no closer to that goal.

In summary, the U.S. decision to fortify its borders has reduced trade, investment, tourism, and jobs while irritating or angering its neighbors. The investment in border security was substantial, but there is no evidence that it has provided more security. The problem is not just the thickening of the border; it is the way the United States redefined itself. Of thirty employees in the U.S. Consulate in Vancouver, half are from seven different U.S. law enforcement agencies. This isn't Berlin during the Cold War or Yemen in 2010.

This is in Vancouver, the Canadian partner of Starbucks city. When half of all U.S. government employees stationed in one of the world's most tranquil and friendly cities are police or security officers, then that might be a sign that America has lost its way. "The core question that Canadians keep asking me," the U.S. consul in Vancouver declared with some frustration, "is: Can't the U.S. trust us?" If not Canada, then whom? If not now, then when?

➤ Potholes

If trucks and pedestrians only had to drive over several speed bumps, they could manage, but in the next stage of their journey to the heart of North America, the highway is ravaged with potholes, some so deep that they would immobilize any vehicle. These potholes come in many forms. Some are the old-fashioned kind caused by governments that do not maintain roads, bridges, railroads, ports, communications, and border facilities. In those cases, vehicles break down, and there are more accidents.

Another pothole has strange names, drayage and cabotage. Both raise the cost of trade by protecting markets rather than promoting competition. "Drayage" literally means "the cost of carrying wagon," but it actually means that many trucks are needed to do a job that one truck could do if there were free trade. "Cabotage" literally means the transport of cargo between two domestic points by a foreign carrier, but in reality, cabotage restricts foreign trucks, planes, trains, ships from carrying shipments between cities within a foreign country. After Canadian trucks, for example, deliver their load in Chicago, cabotage prevents them from picking up other shipments to deliver to another U.S. city, and often they have to return to Canada empty, thereby doubling the transportation cost for consumers.

The United States and Canada have gradually expanded cabotage rights so that some truckers can return to their country with freight, but there are still limits to picking up and dropping off cargo in the other country.[37] If progress has been slow on the northern border, the United States and Mexico have moved backward. NAFTA was supposed to permit Mexican trucks to cross the border by 1995, but as of 2010, they were still denied access to the United States. Drayage rules. Here is how it works:

Great volumes of all vegetables and fruits consumed in the United States are grown in Mexico, most in the state of Sonora bordering Arizona. In the case of large firms, U.S. Department of Agriculture (USDA) officials inspect the crops at the farm. Bell peppers, tomatoes, and other crops are then packed in boxes and stacked on large freight trucks. They journey north to a warehouse a few miles before the border at Nogales where workers unload all the boxes. On the Mexican side of the border, U.S. Department of Agriculture officials inspect the boxes again and stamp a certificate on each. Then a short-haul truck picks up the boxes and takes them to the border where Mexican customs officials usually observe them. Then, the trucks cross the border and pass through X-ray tunnels where U.S. customs officials inspect the boxes again while looking for drugs or undocumented workers. They are then permitted to travel a couple of miles before stopping at another warehouse where they unload the crates so that still another truck can take them to a supermarket somewhere in the United States.

At least three and often as many as seven trucks are involved in the transfer.[38] The Mexican government estimated that the additional "border transfer" cost of drayage was about 15 percent of the volume of trade—or about $616 million for 2008.[39]

Why would governments committed to free trade with each other tolerate drayage and cabotage? Most, though hardly all, trucking companies, shippers, and railroads declare their support for free trade, but the truth is that some of the companies fear competition and seek protection. Ship and plane manufacturers use "national security" arguments to justify protecting their industry from foreign competition. The Jones Act of 1920 is one of the oldest examples of cabotage in the United States. Its purpose is to protect and maintain the U.S. maritime industry by preventing foreign ships from picking up cargo in the United States and delivering it to another city in the country. The U.S. International Trade Commission estimated that the cost to the U.S. economy— the "concealed tax"—of the Jones Act was $656 million in 1999.[40]

Free trade agreements are intended to help governments stand up to these kinds of protectionist pressures from firms and unions, and NAFTA explicitly (articles 1202 and 1203) removes barriers to transportation in North America so that trucks from each nation could travel from the northern border of Canada to the southern border of Mexico. Those provisions were supposed to have been fully implemented in 1995, but President Clinton chose not to do so, and Presidents Bush and Obama continued to violate the agreement. What explains this failure to comply? President Clinton cited concerns about the safety of Mexican trucks, a complaint voiced by the International Brotherhood of Teamsters, even though the United States sets and enforces rules on safety and pollution.

Mexico finally took the case to a NAFTA arbitration panel, and in February 2001, the panel unanimously found that the United States had violated the agreement. It gave Mexico permission to retaliate by raising tariffs on products with a total value of $2.4 billion. Four months later, President Bush promised to comply, but a U.S. nongovernmental organization immediately challenged his decision in court on the grounds that an environmental assessment was required. In June 2004, the U.S. Supreme Court unanimously ruled against the need for such an assessment. Still, the U.S. dithered.

In December 2006, I interviewed Pedro Ciresola, the outgoing Mexican secretary of communications and transport. He said he doubted whether the borders would open to trucks because, as he said: "Our trucking companies and unions and yours do not want it opened. They want to protect their markets." I wondered whether he represented the trucking companies or the entire nation, but he was not alone. The governments had abdicated their responsibilities to the trucking companies and the unions.

In April 2007, after numerous rejections in court, U.S. Secretary of Transportation Mary Peters announced a one-year "demonstration program" that would permit U.S. and Mexican trucks to operate in the other country subject to being certified according to a safety and environmental protocol. The Teamsters, Public Citizen, Sierra Club, and others lobbied Congress to undo the program, and they filed suit in court. The U.S. Court of Appeals denied the motion for a stay of execution on August 31, 2007, and the program began on September 6, 2007.

However, Congress overwhelmingly passed an appropriations bill on December 26, 2007, prohibiting funds for the pilot program. Since the program did not involve any additional appropriations, Bush ignored the amendment and went ahead with the program for up to 100 trucking companies from each country. The trucking companies, however, were reluctant to invest the time and resources, including insurance, in the program or in their trucks with such strong Congressional opposition. As a result, by the end of the one-year program, only 27 Mexican trucking companies with a total of 107 trucks and 10 U.S. carriers with 55 trucks were participating in the Pilot Program. This represented about 8 percent of the potential companies that bring produce to the border, and a trivial percentage of the total trucks—about 11,000—that approach the border each day. In early September 2008, the Federal Motor Carrier Safety Administrator John H. Hill announced a two-year extension of the program to "reassure trucking companies that they will have sufficient time to realize a return on their investment."[41]

Trucks coming from Tijuana that are part of this project enter a California inspection station one-half mile after crossing the border and another one a few miles after that. Those that do not pass the tests have to return to Mexico.

This was not acceptable to the trucking lobby, and they inserted a provision in an omnibus spending bill, signed by President Obama in mid-March 2009, that cut off all funding for the pilot project. Mexico lost its patience, and on March 18, it exercised its right under the NAFTA ruling and slapped tariffs on 89 U.S. products with an export value of $2.4 billion. Mexico was as concerned with the lack of compliance with the original agreement as it was with the prohibition on its trucks. In 2002, the United States brought a case against Mexico for permitting the former state monopoly Telefonos de Mexico (Telmex) to set the terms and conditions for the termination of all international calls. In April 2004, the tribunal ruled in favor of the United States, and Mexico promptly revised its laws to comply. The Mexican government naturally expected that the United States would also comply with the decision on trucking, and it decided to provide an added incentive by retaliating. A group of 141 U.S. companies wrote to President Obama that the tariffs put 26,000 jobs at risk, and the U.S. Department of Transportation estimated that Americans paid an additional $400 million per year for Mexican imports because of the drayage system.[42] Two years after promising to solve the problem, Obama met Calderon on March 3, 2011, and announced he had found a "clear path to resolving the dispute." Calderon pledged to remove the tariffs when the plan was accepted by Congress and implemented.[43]

If the trucks are ever able to cross the continent, they will find real potholes—not just the political-bureaucratic kinds, in the roads, bridges, and infrastructure. In a report to the Canadian-U.S. Inter-Parliamentary Group, Val Meredith, a member of Parliament, wrote: "While continental trade has skyrocketed, the physical infrastructure enabling the movement of these goods has not."[44] The report was issued in 2000, and she warned that if nothing was done, the situation would be chaotic by the year 2005. Nothing was done, and she was right.

There were other signs. On August 14, 2003, a few trees fell on power lines in Ohio and within hours, a power outage affected 50 million people, including one-third of the population of Canada. Bill Richardson, who had been secretary of energy, said the essence of the problem was that the United States was "a superpower with a third world electricity grid." As Canada is connected to the grid, they could not have been happy to learn that.[45] Three years later, a bridge near Montreal collapsed, killing five people, and the next year, August 2007, a Minneapolis bridge that is part of the interstate highway system dropped into the Mississippi River.

The collapse of the bridges raised awareness of the declining state of North America's infrastructure. The U.S. Department of Transportation reported that one-fourth of America's nearly 600,000 bridges needed significant repairs. The Federal Highway administration reported that one-third of the country's major roads were in substandard condition, and that was a "significant factor" in 43,000 traffic fatalities each year. The Texas Transportation Institute estimated that commuters wasted 4 billion hours each year and nearly 3 billion gallons of gasoline in traffic jams. The U.S. system is bad and deteriorating, but the World Economic Forum judged that infrastructure in Canada and Mexico was even worse.[46]

The debt crisis of the mid-1980s compelled the Mexican government to reduce its spending for infrastructure—from about 8 percent of GDP in 1981 to less than 2 percent in 2002.[47] By the latter date, the World Bank estimated that Mexico had a ten-year infrastructure deficit of $20 billion per year. (This was separate from the additional $10 billion that Mexico needed to invest annually in exploration and development of its natural gas and oil fields.)[48] Canada, like Mexico, reduced significantly its investments in infrastructure in order to close its fiscal deficit. By 2005, the Western Transport Ministers reported that total government spending for infrastructure as a proportion of GDP dropped by more than half—from 2.9 percent in 1991 to 1.4 percent in 2002–03. Just as the demand for infrastructure was growing, the funds were evaporating.[49]

As the three countries became aware of the infrastructure deficit, the governments approved some funds. The United States acted first with three major highway bills beginning in the 1990s with the U.S. Intermodal Surface Transportation Efficiency Act (ISTEA) and continuing through a bill signed by President George W. Bush on August 10, 2005. These bills aimed to support local roads. They had modest funds for border infrastructure, but nothing aimed to facilitate trade throughout North America.

In his first State of the Nation Report on September 2, 2007, Calderon proposed a six-year, $25 billion National Infrastructure Program (2007–12) aimed at building highways, ports, airports, and multimodal corridors.[50] Canada followed one month later with a seven-year plan called "Building Canada."[51]

Guy Stanley of McGill University analyzed these plans as well as twelve reports on North American transportation and infrastructure and found a consensus on the nature and magnitude of the challenge and the importance of large-scale public investment to improve and expand the infrastructure. But he also found little interest and resources devoted to connect the three countries' infrastructure. "The supporting transportation infrastructure is now inadequate to handle the projected volume growth of North American supply chains freight flows," he concluded. "Longer term, the system is incapable of improving without substantial changes in governance." By that, he meant cooperation among the three governments.[52]

The U.S. financial crisis that began in the fall of 2008 compelled both the Bush and Obama administrations to seek a recovery package that included funds for infrastructure. On January 12, 2009, just before his inauguration, Obama told Mexican President Felipe Calderon that some of those funds would be used for border infrastructure, but the amount was trivial as compared to the growth in trade and the need to connect the three economies. In summary, there was a growing recognition of the importance of infrastructure in all three countries, but the resources did not match the need, and each tended to use local plans rather than develop national or continental plans.

There is one area that witnessed some breakthroughs in North American transportation—railroads—and that was mostly because the governments cleared the way to allow the private sector to integrate the system. In the mid-1990s, several of the largest American railroad companies merged. Burlington Northern combined with Santa Fe, Union Pacific absorbed Southern Pacific, and CSX and Norfolk Southern divided up Conrail. At about the same time, the Canadian and Mexican governments privatized their railroads. Two U.S. railroads bought Mexican railroads, and the newly privatized Canadian National acquired assets in the United States and made arrangements with other railroads. The result was that the railroads became more continental. Their ultimate success, however, will depend on their connecting with other transport systems—ports, roads, and airports.

China's surge of exports to all three North American countries stretched the carrying capacity of west coast ports to their limit. America's largest ports are Los Angeles and Long Beach, and by 2007, they were able to handle 15.7 million TEU (twenty-foot equivalent containers). Demand is estimated to double to 35 million TEU's by 2020, but neither port has the space for significant expansion, and the other Pacific ports are not large enough to assume the extra burden.

Mexico expanded its port at Lazaro Cardenas, but that also would not be sufficient so President Calderon developed an ambitious plan for Punta Colonet, which is 150 miles south of San Diego. The project would require billions of dollars to construct and connect it to the border with a railroad by 2015. To transport 6–8 million TEUs would require 20,000 trains a year or about 55 every day, and these would have to move across the border rapidly. The recession caused the government to postpone and scale back the project in 2010, but the larger problem is the lack of coordination with its neighbors. Canada is planning to expand Port Rupert for the same purpose. The United

States has to approve the permits to allow the railroads to transit the two borders, but that approval process could take as many as eight years, and it has not begun.[53]

➤ Roadblocks and Walls

With the expansion of commerce in North America over the last fifteen years, one would have expected that all the potholes would have been fixed and a NAFTA superhighway would have been built. Nothing of the sort happened. When I interviewed Pedro Ciresola, the former Mexican secretary of communications and transport, in December 2006, I asked him whether the U.S. and Mexican presidents and the Canadian prime minister had ever requested a continental transportation plan from their ministers. He responded that the leaders had never asked for such a plan. While the leaders have been silent, the people with the loudest voices on the issue have lobbied to stop any North American roads.

The United States is actually moving in reverse. Instead of planning for a North American highway, it invests in expensive walls to separate the countries. Congress moved with unusual speed to appropriate $2.1 billion for a 670-mile wall on the southern border, and President Bush waived environmental laws and ignored cost overruns to try to finish it by the end of his term. The wall wound through urban and rural areas, taking many shapes, including steel mesh fences to stop pedestrians, barriers to vehicles, and "virtual" fences of radar towers and ground sensors. The wall divided part of the campus of the University of Texas in Brownsville as well as some Texas farms. It made crossing both more difficult and dangerous, but in a survey of undocumented immigrants, Wayne Cornelius from the University of California in San Diego found that 97 percent of those who try to cross eventually succeed. They just have to try more times.[54]

➤ Hidden Tolls

North America's prosperity has been stunted not just by speed bumps, potholes, roadblocks and walls at its borders, but also by tolls that are concealed in the higher prices consumers have to pay for North American products. Unlike "drayage," which protects trucking firms, no one benefits from these concealed taxes. They are simply the unnecessary costs of doing business within the continent. These additional tolls fall into three categories: (1) "rules of origin," which impose unnecessary costs at the border in identifying the part of the product that is made in North America; (2) trivial differences in regulations that compel exporters to adapt their products to three different sets of regulations though the purpose of the rules is the same; and (3) taxes that encourage inefficiency.

Michael Hart, a Canadian trade negotiator and one of the foremost authorities of regulatory divergence in North America, defines these inefficiency taxes as "the sum of duplicative regulations, border administration delays, and other regulatory impediments."[55] The duplication occurs when truckers (and indirectly, consumers) have to pay for multiple credentials from at least two governments to cross the border in a theoretically expedited lane and fill out slightly different customs forms on both sides of both borders.

NAFTA eliminated tariffs among the three countries, but it allowed each country to set its external tariff to the rest of the world. In order to prevent one of the countries from allowing a fourth country—say China—from using one country's relatively lower tariffs as an entry point to swamp the other two markets, the three North American governments instituted "rules of origin" provisions.[56] Written in a 200-page annex to the agreement, these procedures require every exporter to fill out a "certificate of origin" describing the origin of each part in a product. The complicated administrative procedures and cumbersome paperwork created an entirely new intermediary operation conducted by brokers. Mexico required that all merchants use brokers. Danielle Goldfarb of the C.D. Howe Institute in Canada concluded that the procedures led to "more complicated border inspections, less predictability, lower levels of trade and investment, higher component prices for producers and higher prices for consumers."

Goldfarb measured these costs. Using a European Union formula, she estimated that the United States and Canada could save as much as $31 billion annually if the three countries agreed to a common external tariff (customs union).[57] Another study suggested Mexico could save as much as 2 percent of the value of its exports to the United States, which, in 2008, would amount to $4.7 billion.[58] For North America, the "rules of origin" cost sums to $35.7 billion. Using a general equilibrium analysis and examining the deeper effects of the procedures on the three economies, Alex Appiah estimated that the total cost of the "rules of origin" procedures amounted to about 2–3 percent of North America's GDP. With a GDP of $17 trillion in 2008, 2.5 percent would amount to $425 billion.[59] This constitutes a colossal tax that consumers and producers unknowingly pay in North America.

The European Union recognized this problem at the beginning of their integration process and dealt with it by negotiating a common external tariff. That eliminated the rules of origin provisions entirely and was a critical step to creating a continental market.

A second area where North Americans are paying taxes without getting benefits is the result of different rules. "Regulatory divergence" represents the next generation of issues that the three governments need to negotiate in order to improve market competitiveness. The logic of harmonization is clear-cut. All three governments have laws to protect the environment, ensure that food is safe, and guarantee good labor conditions. In those cases where the laws are very different, harmonization is not an option, but in many cases, the differences in the laws and regulations are trivial—say, on the size of a label. These increase the costs of production without benefit to society. In these cases, the three governments should negotiate a common standard.

These issues have become more important for three reasons. First, in a free trade area, the administration of regulations has replaced the collection of customs duties as one of the main responsibilities of border administration, and it adds considerably to the time needed to inspect commercial shipments. Secondly, in the last two decades, most countries have seen regulations multiply and extend to the full gamut of public concerns—food and car safety, environmental protection, labor rights, market failure. Canada's Fraser Institute estimated that the Canadian government approves more than 4,500 new or amended regulations every year, and the U.S. government approves about 4,000. Mexico also passes numerous regulations though not quite at that level.[60] Whether these regulations achieve their purpose is a question for each country. The question for North America is whether each country's regulations on the same products are sufficiently different to justify an additional cost for North American exporters, or whether the difference is not important, and the regulations function as a "concealed tax."

Soon after NAFTA came into effect, the three governments set to work to harmonize standards on the weight and length of trucks. To carry wheat from Alberta to Chicago, Canadian trucks have to meet standards in multiple jurisdictions. Indeed, each state and each province sets different standards for trucks. These are mostly designed to protect the local trucking industry from competition, although some of the standards are the product of different climate and road and bridge capacity. So the three governments convened a group—the NAFTA Land Transport Standards Subcommittee to harmonize the 64 different standards. In 1997, the Subcommittee gave up, saying "there is no prospect of developing a complete consensus within North America on a common set of truck weight and dimension limits."[61]

While difficult, it does not seem to be impossible for the leaders of the three countries to reach an understanding on standards for truck weights, particularly because the differences are trivial. As one example, the maximum width and height of a Mexican truck should be 8.5 feet and 13.9 feet; for a U.S. truck, 8.5 feet and 14 feet, and for a Canadian, 8.53 feet and 13.6 feet. What explains the failure to establish a single standard?

One explanation is bureaucratic inertia combined with an interest group that fears change. Secondly, people are not aware of the added cost. The formula for computing the added cost is straightforward. Identify the cost of moving freight from one site to another and returning full in the same country. The added cost is the difference between that and the actual cost of loading and unloading the freight to a new truck at every jurisdiction multiplied by about 11 million trucks a year. The governments should look after the public interest, but they spend more time seeking campaign contributions from those seeking protection from competition. This is just one example.

The third reason why regulatory divergence is the new frontier for North American integration is because of increased trade and expanded regulation. As trade and regulations grow, they affect each other more. The three North American governments estimated that the amount of their reciprocal trade affected by regulations was about $715 billion.[62] Some of the differences in regulations among the three governments are important. One country might want to maintain a higher quality standard for food or the environment. But over time, all three countries will want to maintain best practices and highest standards, and if they set that as a goal, finding a common approach might not be that difficult in concept, if not in politics.

The OECD estimated that divergent standards can add 2–10 percent to overall costs of production.[63] That plus the magnitude of trade within the European Community explains why Europe has worked so long and hard to reduce the trivial differences in standards. In 1968, on completing the Customs Union, the European Community embarked on a two-decade journey toward a Single European Act to develop a unified approach. The North American journey could be much easier because there are only three countries and languages as compared to twenty-seven countries and twenty-three languages in Europe. President George W. Bush pressed this agenda into the "Security and Prosperity Partnership Framework," which he proposed with the Mexican president and Canadian prime minister in March 2005, but the leaders invited only CEOs to help them, and that made all the opponents of NAFTA more suspicious. As Elizabeth May, a Canadian leader of the Green Party, said: "There's never been an effort at bilateral or trilateral cooperation that so excluded civil society while at the same time including corporate CEOs. It's held in deep secrecy, and that's not healthy." She noted that in her travels, Canadians vented their fears that the process would steal Canadian sovereignty and lead to the sale of Canadian fresh water.[64]

In the Guadalajara Summit in August 2009, Obama, Calderon, and Harper commended "the progress achieved on reducing regulatory differences," although they were unable to point to any examples. The "institutional" legacy of the Bush years—the CEO's North American Competitiveness Council and the Security and Prosperity Partnership—was discarded. Instead, they instructed their ministers to "continue this work."[65] Canada and the United States reached an equivalency agreement on labeling organic products, and the three governments negotiated an understanding on nutritional labeling and on common fuel-efficiency standards. At the conclusion of Calderon's state visit to Washington on May 19, 2010, Obama and Calderon created a High-Level Regulatory Council, and Obama designated a key aide, Cass Sunstein from the Office of Management and Budget, to oversee the process in the U.S. government. Eight months later, instead of making the process trilateral, Obama and Harper established a parallel organization, the U.S.-Canada Regulatory Cooperation Council.

In brief, the three governments are groping for ways to address the complexity of regulatory divergence, but it is also worth recalling that despite the high priority given to it by President Bush, Calderon, and Harper, the three governments failed to agree on jelly-bean regulations—an interest of Harper's—and cereal—an interest of then-Secretary of Commerce Carlos Gutierrez, a former CEO of Kellogg.

➤ The Third Law of Motion

Sir Isaac Newton posited that for every action, there is an equal and opposite reaction. This does not mean that an object that is moving forward is compelled to stop and go backwards. What Newton meant was that a boat had to push water backwards in order to move forwards, or to take a modern example, an airplane engine had to push air backwards through its engine to propel the plane forwards.

In the social and political domain, the Newtonian metaphor can be interpreted to mean that after a period of progress, a country needs time to rest and consolidate. Arthur Schlesinger, Jr., and other historians wrote of cycles in American history between progressive change and consolidation. After the New Deal, the United States needed time under the Eisenhower administration for Republicans to adjust to its programs before America could extend the social reforms into health and education through the Great Society of Lyndon Johnson.

While NAFTA was a revolutionary act, it was fundamentally different from the New Deal or the Great Society. NAFTA enlarged the market and promoted competition and efficiency, but in the absence of measures to distribute the benefits of growth, it contributed to widening income disparities. That explains why labor unions and other progressive sectors in the United States were ambivalent or opposed.

The changes within and between the three countries are still not widely understood. Mexico, the poorest and most stratified, experienced the most profound modernization and democratization, but those who were better off and in the north benefited more. Canada kept its fiscal house in order and thus experienced a positive economic jolt, but 9/11 confounded their manufacturing strategy and, together with the speed bumps and potholes described in this chapter, Canada found its entire economic trajectory at risk. Canada's dependence on the U.S. market deepened, but the United States treated the convergence of the two economies as if it had not happened.

The combined effect of increased dependence and a distracted neighbor was felt deeply in Canada and Mexico after 9/11, but that was merely a fever compared to the pneumonia that struck with the financial crisis of 2007–09. The auto industry, which had propelled the first wave of integration, suffered the most grievous collapse. U.S. imports from Canada of autos and auto parts declined by 21 percent from 2007 to 2008, and then plummeted by nearly 52 percent in the first half of 2009. A similar, though not as pronounced decline occurred with Mexico in autos, but the U.S. recession was the principal factor contributing to an economic decline of 6.5 percent in 2009.[66] Both Canada and Mexico sought more trade agreements to try to reduce their dependence on the United States, and these partly explain the reduction in integration. These agreements, however, did not lift the two economies, nor have they improved the region's competitiveness.

The groups in the United States that opposed NAFTA initially blamed it for the decline of manufacturing and the rise of immigration. These negative perceptions shaped the national debate and policy. The widening gap between the two major U.S. political parties exacerbated differences with its neighbors. The Democrats relied on labor unions, which opposed trade, and the Republicans depended on the Christian conservatives, who feared Mexican migration or a loss of sovereignty.

The inauguration of George W. Bush as president coincided with the arrival of Vicente Fox and true democratization in Mexico, and expectations for a new breakthrough rose. But Bush had no vision of a North American future, and 9/11 set back prospects for serious cooperation. At the same time, out of power, the Democrats became hyper-critical of NAFTA. The Bush strategy that led to the SPP and the collaboration with big business provoked deeper suspicions, and the result was an increasingly strident assault on the idea of North America.[67]

President Bush chose not to engage or even rebut these criticisms. At the same time, the two principal Democratic presidential candidates—Barack Obama and Hillary Clinton—expressed their opposition to NAFTA. The arguments for more integration could not be heard over the noise. When Obama took office, he retreated from his negative statements about NAFTA and sought to warm the two bilateral relationships, but his agenda was so full—with two wars, a deep recession, health insurance—that he could not devote the time or political capital to refashion the North American relationship.

This is the political context that explains why the three governments failed to take any steps to flatten the speed bumps, fill the potholes, eliminate the roadblocks, tear down the walls, and stop extracting tolls in the absence of roads. Real integration stalled and went into reverse. The costs of doing business among the three countries increased. In the second decade of the twenty-first century, the United States and Mexico were focused on the violence of the drug war, and Canadians focused on their bilateral relationship with Washington.

The promise of North America was eclipsed. To lift the three countries out of their dual-bilateralism into a continent competing with Europe and Asia requires a new vision of the trilateral relationship and a blueprint for achieving that vision. That is the purpose of the next two chapters.

Part III: The North American Advantage

*Make no little plans. They have no magic to stir
man's blood and probably . . . will not be realized.
Make big plans . . . remembering that a noble,
logical diagram once recorded will never die,
but long after we are gone will be a living thing,
asserting itself with ever-growing insistency.*
  —Daniel Burnham, Chicago Architect
  (1864–1912)

6

A North American Community: A Vision

My grandfather galloped down from Ohio and found his American dream in Guanajuato.

—Vicente Fox Quesada, President of Mexico (2000–2006)

So much of North America's history has focused on the differences between the three countries that few people on the continent realize how much they have in common. One leader who does is Vicente Fox Quesada, the first person chosen president in a genuinely free election in modern Mexico. His grandfather, he told me, was a gringo and an evangelical Christian, who never learned Spanish, but came to love Mexico and marry a devout Catholic Mexican woman.[1]

Before he entered politics, Fox was president of Coca-Cola de Mexico, and he still tries to promote public policy like he was marketing the *Real Coke*. He can explain to Americans that his grandfather found his American dream in Mexico, and he tells Mexicans that there is nothing wrong with those who seek their dream in the United States. Indeed, he views them as part of Mexico, and he understands, as few leaders in the three countries do, that you can be Mexican and North American at the same time. He tried to sell his inclusive vision of North America to U.S. President George W. Bush and Canadian Prime Minister Jean Chretien, but neither could grasp it. Three decades ago, however, Ronald Reagan captured the essence of the North American Idea when he told his fellow Americans that we should stop treating our neighbors as "foreigners."

The next stage of North America's development is to forge a community of three sovereign states. The essence of the community is that each has a stake in the success of the other, and each will pay a price if one fails. Why is a North American Community necessary? The contemporary agenda—drugs, violence, economic progress, immigration, border security, trade problems—cannot be effectively addressed by one or two countries. All three need to work together and fashion new and creative responses.

The only way that the three countries will entertain a new relationship is if the public is convinced of a spacious vision of North America's potential. Leadership is essential to explain how each country could benefit and what each needs to contribute to achieve that goal. To inspire the people of North America to reach beyond their nations to their neighbors will require practical reasons but also a transcendental cause—a sense that their efforts will shape the world in the twenty-first century in fundamental and positive ways.

None of the many proposals that have been advanced for the region can be achieved without such a vision. Americans and Canadians will not provide funds to narrow the development gap with Mexico without a convincing vision of how Mexico's growth will benefit their countries. There is little prospect of reaching an agreement on labor mobility, an environmental agreement, a transportation plan, or most any proposal that would cost money or change the status quo unless there is a vision of a wider Community that could attract the support of the people and their legislatures.

➤ Short-Sighted or Far-Sighted?

George H. W. Bush was often criticized for being short on "the vision thing." Of course, like many American leaders, whether conservative or liberal, he viewed his pragmatism—of trying to solve one problem at a time—as a better asset than vision. Both have their virtues. A "vision" is an aspiration, a picture of a future that can cause people to want to work to attain it. When Winston Churchill and Franklin D. Roosevelt met at sea off the coast of Canada in August 1941, they called for "the final destruction of Nazi tyranny," but their joint statement looked beyond the conflict to describe a vision of a new world without colonialism and with self-determination, and a peace that would allow all peoples "freedom from fear and want." A different mission—a victory by one alliance against another—might have mobilized soldiers to win the war, but it would not have been sufficient to build a peace around the United Nations and the Universal Declaration of Human Rights. A vision can motivate people to win a war or solve a problem, but its true purpose is to inspire nations to redefine themselves and imagine a different future.

Similarly, in North America, the United States and its neighbors can continue to approach one problem at a time, but that has not been productive because so many of the issues are connected and the contests are unequal— usually between a potent constituency and a foreign government. It will be a rare politician who will side with a neighboring country against a home group—whether a business or a labor union, whether in the lumber or trucking industries—that can deliver votes or campaign contributions.

There is another reason why these issues cannot be solved alone or by two nations. The major issues that confront the three nations of North America are more domestic than foreign. That is why each nation has addressed these issues—drugs, violence, immigration, regulations, trade, environment—by itself in the past and why they are reluctant to "share" decision making today. But the old approach is not working. The market and its problems have expanded across all of North America, and for the policy to be effective, many actors should help forge and execute the policy.

A compelling vision of a North American Community can contribute some balance and insight to the debate. If an American congressmen and his constituents believed in a North American Community, where our nearest neighbors were not treated as foreigners, they would be more inclined to apply the same regulations—for example, on the safety of trucks—to Mexico that are applied to Americans.

In a war, it is easier to apply the same logic to one's allies. To defeat Hitler, the U.S. Congress readily approved billions of dollars of "lend-lease" for the Soviet Union, and it was willing to give aid and support to dictatorships that sided with the United States in the Cold War. In the absence of a security threat, it is harder to marshal funds or to face down domestic interests. That is precisely why a "vision" is so essential.

The vision of a North America Community begins with three sets of principles—interdependence not dependence; reciprocity not unilateralism; and a negotiating style based on a community of interests not a quid pro quo.

First, *interdependence*. If one nation prospers, all benefit. If one nation declines, all three will be adversely affected. When a neighbor's house burns or is vandalized, then all the houses in the community are in danger. When the value of a neighbor's house rises, this lifts the value of the other homes. These are the two sides of a vision of a North American Community. Increasing interdependence offers additional benefits and costs. To expand the benefits and reduce the costs of a more integrated and less regulated market requires a new consciousness among both leaders and people—a new way of thinking about our neighbors. And it needs continental plans and institutions.

The second principle is *reciprocity*, and it means that each nation should aim to treat the others as it wants to be treated. The golden rule applies to international as well as to human relations. In an asymmetrical relationship, the strongest nation can insist that its way is the only way, but that approach cannot build a community. All members—particularly the strongest—should be willing to learn and apply lessons from the others.

Canadians and Mexicans follow American legislation and often adapt it, but the United States has shown little interest in learning from its neighbors. Two examples. The United States spends about 15 percent of its GDP on health care. "Canada," according to Gary Hufbauer from the International Institute of Economics, "spends about half that, and health care is just as good if not better in Canada."[2] And yet during a lengthy debate in Congress, there were few legislators who inquired as to whether we can learn from Canada. Indeed, Canada's health care system was often vilified as "socialist" without giving Canadians an opportunity to explain it. Similarly, in twelve years, from 1988–2000, Mexico's electoral system went from the most fraudulent in the Americas to one of the most professional and sophisticated. In an analysis of the three electoral systems in North America, the United States came in third on almost every indicator, and yet no one in Congress thought they could learn from America's neighbors.[3] Reciprocity means taking your neighbors seriously.

On the issue of harmonizing regulations, it would be very tempting for the United States to insist that its rules should be the standard, and it is possible that technocrats in Canada and Mexico might accept that because the U.S. market is the largest. However, if the United States is going to behave as a twenty-first-century leader, it needs to demonstrate that it is prepared to follow, not just lead, and to be fair, not arrogant.

The third principle is a *community of interests*, and it means that all three governments share responsibility for problems, and that the most effective solution is one in which all three decide what each can contribute to solving the problem. To confront the drug-trafficking issue in North America, one country cannot impose conditions on aid or demand something for what it gives. This approach is the customary one, but in a region laden with a history of dominance by the major power, conditionality should be replaced by a different approach—one that defines the common interest and then divides responsibilities. In other words, if all three share a goal—e.g., narrowing the development gap with Mexico—then the richer countries should contribute without insisting on a quid pro quo from Mexico, and Mexico should contribute even more because it has the greatest stake in the project's success.

All three countries need to define a continental framework that is fair; aims to enhance the well-being of all its citizens; and makes all countries more secure, competitive, and just. The three peoples should not deny national pride, but that should be supplemented with a feeling of North American-ness. The goal is not to replace a national with a continental identity or fortress, but rather to bolster neighborly connections to compete more effectively in the world and to serve as a model for other regional groups.

These basic principles—interdependence, reciprocity, and community—seem obvious. Indeed, leaders often refer to these concepts, but few, if any, act on these principles. The usual approach is that the strongest nation insists, and the weaker ones resist or accommodate. In the negotiations on trucking standards, each country argued that their way was the only way. When the richer countries changed from being empires to just donors, they moved a short distance from giving instructions to the developing countries to insisting on conditions. In other words, these three principles, which almost sound like clichés, are actually quite revolutionary when countries move from words to actions.

The vision of a North American Community goes beyond the rhetoric of good relations that every leader deploys. Rather it means consigning a widening circle of domestic issues to trilateral consultation, which over time, could lead to coordination, and perhaps even unified policies.

Because the European Community became the European Union, some confuse the two terms and fear that a similar evolution might occur in North America. Some political economists also suggest that there is a logic of integration that proceeds from a free trade area to a customs union (common external tariff) and from there to a common market (free movement of labor), a monetary union (a single currency), and a unified multinational state. Each step reduces transaction costs and leads to greater economies of scale, and thus the logic of good public policy moves countries down that road.

North America is not Europe, and it will not emulate the European Union. Indeed, the larger problem is that the desire to be different from Europe might lead policy makers to ignore the mistakes as well as the successes of Europe. The wise course would be to learn from Europe's experience and to avoid the experiments that failed and adapt those that hold promise for North America.

European integration has been driven by two devastating wars in the twentieth century, and by a belief that unification could prevent a new war. North American integration was driven by the market and a belief that the standard of living of its people would be improved if barriers to trade and investment were removed. These different motives explain why the direction and pace of integration in North America bear little resemblance to Europe's.

To return to the definition, a North American Community is decidedly *not* a North American Union, which is a unified state with a central government. Instead, a North American Community is a region in which its principal units are three independent countries. A North American Community is also *not* a common market where labor can move freely. At some point, the United States and Canada might want to negotiate an agreement that would allow freer movement of labor between the two countries because the difference in the standard of living is not wide enough to generate a significant population shift. Of course, this is not the case with Mexico, and, while freer movement should be permitted for individual categories of professionals or "guest workers" among all three countries, a common market is out of the question until the income gap narrows significantly.

However, it is in the interest of all three countries to move to the next stage of a free trade area, which would involve the negotiation of a single common external tariff, commonly described as a "customs union." That would remove an inefficient but exorbitant tax on all North Americans that was estimated as high as $510 billion in 2008. That "rules of origin" tax is paid by consumers and producers. It hinders trade, but no one benefits. A region with a common external tariff is called a "customs union," but that is not a common market or a union.

A North American Community should be more than a free trade area or a simple partnership. It means a common vision and joint efforts to address shared problems. The word *community* refers to a group in which the members feel an affinity and desire to collaborate to solve problems and build something larger than the sum of their parts. Community seems especially appropriate for North America because it is a flexible concept; it does not have a fixed definition. It leaves space for all three countries to define it. The vision guides the decision makers, but the community can be as limited or expansive as its members choose, and it can change over time as the countries change and the region's personality develops. Like the people and states of North America, the term community is eminently pragmatic. North Americans will choose their future based on their best judgment of what is likely to work. If one policy does not achieve the goal, they will seek another.

➤ Why Has a North American Community Been Elusive?

The logic of a community—where all benefit from each one's success—is the rhetoric of politicians, and yet policies rarely reflect that promise. Why not? The answer is that the most important political units in North America are three nation-states. Their leaders respond mostly to interests within—not outside—their nations. This fact of political life—that democratic leaders pay attention to their constituents rather than to friendly neighbors—has special significance in North America because of the new agenda and the old way in which the three governments dealt with each other.

As the market enlarged to the size of the continent, the three countries of North America found themselves facing an agenda that is both domestic and continental, while the institutions charged with dealing with the issues are local or national. The immigration issue is shaped by people in small towns in Mexico in search of a better life and people in small towns in the United States worried about their jobs and culture. The trucking issue is driven by the U.S. Teamsters Union, but it too has consequences for Mexico and the credibility of the U.S. government. The "buy American" issue is driven by America's fear of the growing strength of China, but it affects Canada and Mexico more. In the arena where the key decisions are made, these problems are weighted to favor the domestic rather than the North American interest. As the three economies and societies integrate, there will be many decisions like these, but the U.S. government is not organized to make these decisions in a way that could foster a North American Community.

The issues that the three leaders discuss are the same ones that are debated in their legislatures—the financial crisis, illicit drugs, environmental regulation, labor conditions, and immigration. But the discussion at the continental level is more symbolic than substantive, more bilateral than continental, and more frustrating because real agreements are rarely achieved or implemented.

Since NAFTA came into effect in January 1994, all three governments have settled back into the relationship that had existed before, which was a dual-bilateral relationship—the United States and Canada and the United States and Mexico. The third leg of the triangle—the relationship between Mexico and Canada—is quite new. Indeed, relations between the two governments were only established in 1944, and trade was negligible until NAFTA. Since then, trade has grown rapidly but from a very low base. The Mexican-Canadian leg of the triangle remains weak and over-shadowed by the other two legs.

It is a puzzle why the three governments prefer their two dysfunctional relationships rather than a more equal trilateral relationship. For Canada and Mexico, dual-bilateralism accentuates their weakness and reinforces the imbalance in power. Asymmetry means that the United States can, and usually does, impose its will or ignores its neighbors. It means that the United States can avoid the hard trade-offs that so many of the transnational issues require. The Canadian prime minister raised the issue of U.S. duties on its soft-wood lumber exports at virtually every meeting for nearly a decade, as the Mexican president did with issues like trucking or sugar. The U.S. president's response was nearly always the same: "We will look into it." And the United States did look into it before deciding not to solve it. The U.S. president did not want to antagonize America's lumber industry, the Teamsters, or sugar growers, and so he dodged the issues. In a region of growing interdependence, the power to delay is often as consequential as making a decision.

Some Americans believe it is in U.S. interests to dominate weaker states rather than to submit to international institutions that apply rules equally to all states. When Fox proposed the establishment of a North American Commission, Bush rejected the idea because of his antipathy to international institutions that could constrain him. Bush reflected one side of America that has preferred a unilateral approach without restraint. But there is another side of America, where the pertinent distinction is not between whether the United States should pursue its interests, but rather whether its interests should be narrowly construed or longer-term. The United States can acquiesce as the Teamsters Union sabotages an international agreement, or it can try to build a community. The sad irony is that the United States would be far better off economically if safe trucks from all three nations were free to transit the entire continent. If the United States pursued a community, it would help itself overcome a bad policy while demonstrating respect both for its neighbors and the agreement it signed.

"I am sympathetic to the idea of North America," Michael Ignatieff, the leader of Canada's Liberal Party, told me, "but the problem is the lack of compliance with the existing agreement by the United States. The United States does not want to adhere to agreements, and so the issue for us is how to manage U.S. unilateralism."[4] If Canada and Mexico perceive the United States as the problem, and resistance as the solution, then solving the region's problems become secondary. And if the United States invests its energy in maintaining the status quo, then it will compromise its role as a global leader and undermine its firms' capacity to compete. So a bilateral approach might yield satisfaction for a particular U.S. interest at the cost of the long-term interest of building a community.

At the end of the Second World War, the United States was, for all intents and purposes, the only winner. Except for the surprise attack on Pearl Harbor, an overseas territory, the United States was the only major power that escaped the ravages of war, and in building an arsenal for its allies, it created an industrial structure that produced almost half of the world's wealth by 1945. At that moment, with Europe and Asia flattened, the United States could have seized all of the colonies of the defeated nations and even from some of its allies. It could have chosen to provide aid to its allies only if each accommodated itself to U.S. interests.

The United States chose a path that no other great power had ever contemplated, let alone executed.[5] The United States forged a United Nations and ended colonialism. Instead of pursuing a classic "divide-and-rule" strategy, the United States promoted European unification, though that strategy created a formidable competitor. The United States provided aid to Western Europe, including its former enemies, and insisted on only one condition— that the nations present a common program for recovery. Instead of using its officials and agencies to manage the international trade and monetary systems, the United States designed international institutions—the International Monetary Fund, the World Bank, GATT—to do that. It would have been in the short-term interests of the United States to pursue its goals bilaterally, but presidents Roosevelt and Truman chose a long-term approach and shaped a new world.

In contrast to the far-sighted policies in the period just after the Second World War, U.S. policy toward its neighbors has been short-sighted. Rhetoric notwithstanding, the U.S. government has opted for the status quo over its long-term interests. The strongest North American state has been the most defensive, parochial, and fearful of losing its sovereignty to its weaker neighbors. But the United States is hardly the only reason why North America is stuck. The United States has not had to divide Canada and Mexico; they have divided themselves.

The strategies of Canada and Mexico have been even more puzzling than America's. Canada—a world leader in multilateralism and humanism—has been uninterested in creating multilateral institutions in North America and selfish and condescending with its poorest neighbor. Mexico—the weakest of the three—has been the boldest in proposing continental initiatives even when they would pay the highest price if the proposals were accepted. How are we to explain the three puzzles?

The Canadian Puzzle. Canada has justly earned the reputation of a committed multilateralist everywhere except in North America. Its soldiers have been pioneers of UN peacekeeping; its diplomats have staffed the United Nations and the international courts; its leaders have articulated global strategies of "human security" and the "right to protect"; its government has negotiated treaties on the International Criminal Court and on land mines. Despite these achievements, Canada has *not* proposed a single multilateral initiative in the one region—North America—that matters most to it. Worst of all, it has rejected virtually every North American initiative.

While Canada deserves credit for starting the North American engine, albeit for defensive reasons, it also deserves most of the blame for stopping that train and steering it to bilateral tracks. Jim Kolbe, former Republican Congressman from Arizona, described one instance: "I chaired the U.S.-Mexican Inter-Parliamentary Group for years, and I tried to get Canadians to join us, but the Canadians always opposed the idea." Raul Rodriguez, the former president of the North American Development Bank, said that Mexican President Vicente Fox asked Jean Chretien to join the NADBank in 2004, but he rejected the idea.[6] Soon after the 9/11 attacks on the United States, Jorge Castañeda, Mexico's foreign minister, approached his Canadian counterpart, John Manley, to propose a North American "smart border" agreement, but again, Canada declined in favor of a bilateral agreement with the United States.[7]

Canada is also very generous, providing $4.7 billion in aid in 2008 or roughly twice as much of its gross national income as the U.S. provides. Canada focuses its aid on twenty countries, but Mexico is not one of them. Indeed, Canada gave $5 million to Mexico in 2007, one-third of what it provided to Ukraine.[8] When Canadians refer to North America, they almost always omit Mexico.

What explains this gap between multilateralism globally and bilateralism in North America? Some have suggested that Canadians fear being tainted by association with Mexico and its drug-trafficking, violence and immigration problems. Others believe that its "special relationship" with the United States gives it an advantage that it would lose if it allied with Mexico.[9] A third explanation is psychological—a kind of sibling rivalry between Canada and Mexico that plays itself out at the beginning of a U.S. administration when each tries to be the first one through the door to meet the new U.S. president. It is unseemly but persistent. Still, others, like Thomas D'Aquino, the former CEO of Canadian Chief Executives, believe that a trilateral approach would simply slow down negotiations: "Three can talk; two can do," he likes to say.[10]

If effectiveness were the criterion, Canada's bilateral strategy has not done well. If two can walk faster than three, how long did it take for the United States to reach agreement on soft-wood lumber? And that agreement was neither fair to Canada nor durable. Working by itself, Canada failed on soft-wood lumber, national labeling, the auto industry, and it made no discernable progress in managing the border with the United States. Indeed, Canadians felt insulted when Janet Napolitano, the Secretary of Homeland Security, suggested at the Brookings Institution in March 2009 that the United States wanted to treat its two neighbors and its two borders on the basis of equality. Canada expected preferential treatment. It was undoubtedly disappointed when the United States announced in May 2010 that it would proceed with two major initiatives—on the border and on regulatory harmonization—with Mexico, without mentioning Canada.

The answer to the puzzle is that Canada thought its "special relationship" with the United States would serve its interests. It was wrong. It betrayed its multilateralist reputation for a bilateral strategy that never worked.

The Mexican Puzzle. In the early years of NAFTA, soon after the first genuinely democratic election for president, Mexico's new President Vicente Fox offered a flurry of new proposals, including a customs union, freer movement of labor, a Cohesion Fund, and a North American Commission. His counterparts in the United States and Canada rejected all of these proposals in favor of an alphabet soup of vacuous bureaucratic initiatives. The more interesting question was why Fox proposed ideas that would have been far more difficult and costly for Mexico to implement than for the United States and Canada. Notably, a customs union would have meant that Mexico would have had to reduce its tariffs, which were the highest in North America, to the lowest level. Mexican firms would have suffered deeply from the competition.

The answer is that Mexicans were in a hurry to join the club of advanced countries, and its technocratic leadership understood that the best way to develop the country was to open the economy to global competition. Beginning in the mid-1980s, Mexico embarked on a comprehensive set of reforms that shook the old economy to its roots but permitted it to shift from a sharp dependence on oil to one that relied on manufacturing exports. By the late 1990s, when a second generation of reforms—fiscal, labor, energy, education—were needed, Mexico was undergoing an even more profound transition toward a democratic system.

In 1997, the governing party—the PRI—lost its majority in Congress for the first time in its history, and in the year 2000, it lost the presidency. The president and the elite understood the reforms that were needed, but a more fragmented political system made them harder to achieve. Elected by a very slim margin in 2006, President Felipe Calderon did not revive Fox's grand proposals on North America, perhaps because of the difficulty of persuading his Congress, or perhaps because he realized that his two neighbors had no appetite for such proposals.

The answer to Mexico's puzzle is that it remains eager to join the first world and ready to pay the price, but it needs its neighbors to commit themselves to help. That support, however, should be offered in a way that gives the Mexican president the leverage to gain the requisite domestic support. If the United States and Canada set *conditions* on aid as the way to compel Mexico to change its policies, that approach would give the gift of nationalism to the Mexican president's opponents and probably preclude passage of the reforms.

The United States Puzzle. The most perplexing puzzle of all is the United States, a country that blends the cosmopolitan and the parochial in ways that are hard to understand even for Americans. The United States has more foreign-born residents than the entire population of Canada, and more troops stationed in more countries throughout the world than all other countries combined. And yet the United States is also very insular. One would have expected, for example, that given the depth of American interests in the world, an important criterion for choosing the President and Vice President would be their international experience, and yet that was barely considered in 2008 when it became known that the vice presidential nominee of the Republican Party had applied for her first passport just one year before the nomination.[11]

After fading away as an issue in the mid-1990s, NAFTA reemerged during the presidency of George W. Bush when he proposed a rather innocuous interbureaucratic mechanism called the Security and Prosperity Partnership. Led by two conservative cable channel anchors, Lou Dobbs of CNN and Bill O'Reilly of Fox News, the new assault on NAFTA came from an unexpected direction with a startling argument—that Bush was abandoning American sovereign rights by surreptitiously creating a North American Union.

This fear of being controlled by international forces did not take its advocates to a new isolationism but rather to an old unilateralism, and its neighbors in North America intensely felt this shift. In an analysis of the weak institutions in North America, Professor Kim Richard Nossal of Queen's University concludes: "American enthusiasm for such institutions is very much linked to the degree to which the US is able to control these institutions. And when that control begins to slip, we see an annoyance creep into US policy." While President George W. Bush's policy represented an acute case of unilateralism,

Nossal did not see Bush as aberrant. There is a "deep reluctance by the US to allow institutions that it cannot control."[12]

Why would the world's sole superpower fear domination by its two weaker neighbors? The puzzle is even harder to unscramble because surveys suggest that public opinion favors more cooperation within North America. Instead of being angry or frightened by its neighbors, Americans view both Mexicans and Canadians very positively. The explanation is that the voices of the majority were drowned out by the 15–20 percent of the public who feel a loss of control as the forces of globalization or regionalization grow stronger, and their jobs are threatened by outsourcing, trade, and immigration. These concerns rise when the economy declines. In the American political system, "single interest" groups with an intense constituency base or substantial funds can skew policy. This conservative critique did not convince President Bush and Congress, but it did inhibit them from considering new ways to collaborate with Mexico and Canada.

But Stephen Clarkson, a Canadian skeptic of NAFTA, was not convinced that the Dobbs effect would last: "The persistence of this nationalist, sometimes xenophobic sentiment does not negate the possibility of a North American Community emerging."[13] With the election of Barack Obama, who was more sympathetic to multilateralism, Clarkson seemed to have been vindicated. Obama articulated the theme of "shared responsibility" and met often with Calderon and Harper, but his attention was limited by an overflowing global and domestic agenda, and his policy to Mexico was driven by the drug and violence issues. Obama showed little interest in the North American dimension. Indeed, he deepened the dual-bilateral approach by agreeing to parallel structures on border and regulatory issues.

So the answer to the American puzzle was that the conservative critique of a North American Union and the tendency toward crisis-management inhibited the U.S. government—under both Bush and Obama—from proposing any grand initiative for the region.

The three puzzles—of Canada as a bilateralist, Mexico as a bold but discouraged partner, and the United States as a country fearful of losing its sovereignty—are symptoms of a larger problem. Every movement forward toward integration unleashes opposite forces that stall or reverse integration. That is often the rhythm of change. There are ways to alter that pattern by a new consciousness and institutions, but these take time to create.

Without a vision, the governments are compelled to spend their time on crises. They take the agenda rather than make it, and in the contemporary period, the agenda is drugs, violence, immigration, and borders. This is an important agenda, but the dual-bilateral, incremental approach will not succeed. The agenda that should draw the attention of the leaders follows from the three challenges described above. The most important is the development gap between Mexico and its northern neighbors. The second is the need for lean, flexible North American institutions driven by a vision of a North American Community, and the third is a different American style—one in which the United States listens, learns, and adapts to its neighbors as much as it offers its views. If the three governments grasp this new agenda, they will find it much easier to solve or manage the urgent crises.

➤ What's In It for Us?

For the three states to recognize that they are a part of a wider North America is no mean feat. Because pragmatism sits at the core of North America's genetic code, we must begin by demonstrating that a change from dual-bilateralism to a North American Community will benefit each of the three countries as well as all of them together. We need, in brief, to answer satisfactorily the popular question, well-rooted in self-interest: "What is in it for us—as a person, a nation, a region?"

We have seen that Canada's efforts to dissociate itself from Mexico in order to use its "special relationship" with the United States to advance its interests have failed in persuading Washington, though it succeeded in disturbing Mexico. Canada would be more successful if it worked with Mexico on a joint approach that focused on fairness and rules and therefore would not be perceived by Washington as if its neighbors were ganging up against it.

In the spring of 2009, twelve senior members of the Canadian House of Commons Committee on International Trade lobbied U.S. congressmen and executive-branch officials without success on any of the issues they raised. The issues were the proliferation of "Buy American" provisions in different state and federal laws, the "country-of-origin labeling (COOL)" provisions that function as a nontariff barrier to Canadian beef, the Western Hemisphere Travel Initiative, and the "black liquor" tax credit that discriminates against the Canadian wood industry.[14]

Some of these issues affect Mexico; others are similar enough to merit a trilateral conversation. Congress legislates with a high interest in assuaging the concerns of a particular interest group and with almost no attention as to how that might affect its two neighbors. To help Congress understand this effect, Canada should join with Mexico to explain that U.S. credibility depends on fulfilling its agreements. Second, by introducing a third party, Canada could evaluate an issue at a generic rather than a particular level. For example, the fundamental issue underlying the soft-wood lumber dispute is not the value of government subsidies in Canada, which was the U.S. complaint, but rather that each of the three governments has different policies managing their natural resources. As trade and integration increases, the three governments have a greater incentive to negotiate common standards if not policies. But the major reason that Canada should approach Mexico is because the latter has two advantages in Washington that Canada lacks: crises and constituents.

Virtually all of the world's crises are deposited at both ends of Pennsylvania Avenue—the Capitol and the White House—and therefore, neither has much time for routine issues. In this context, Mexico's liabilities also happen to be its assets. Drug-related violence is a crisis for both Mexico and the U.S., and the Mexican ambassador has few problems getting the attention of Washington. Canada does not have crises and even if it did, it instinctively would try to downplay them, and that is one reason that its embassy has a problem in gaining attention. Canada's predicament in gaining attention is captured in the title of the excellent memoir by former Canadian Ambassador Allan Gottlieb, *I'll Be With You In A Minute, Mr. Ambassador*.[15]

The second asset that Mexico has and Canada lacks is constituents. By 2015, there will be more Mexicans living in the United States than Canadians living in Canada. They are represented by an expanding number of leaders. The number of Hispanics in the U.S. Congress leaped from six in 1980 to twenty-six in the 112th Congress (2011–2013); two-thirds are of Mexican origin.[16] This is a formidable block that has not adopted North American issues in part because neither the Mexican nor the Canadian ambassador has encouraged them to think of their problems as "North American."

Ottawa is more likely to succeed in advancing its interests in Washington if it collaborates with Mexico City than if it continues to lobby an inattentive U.S. Congress by itself. The "Buy American" laws in the stimulus package of 2009 are a harbinger of other laws or rules to assist U.S. businesses by creating new barriers to foreign trade or investment. These provisions will have a disproportionately adverse effect on Canada. If Canada were to alter its strategy of trying to gain "a Canadian exemption" in favor of a "North American exemption," its chances would improve substantially. If Canada and Mexico were to develop a generic proposal for dealing with the pricing of products that are publicly subsidized—e.g., soft-wood lumber, medicines, and agriculture— a solution might be easier to locate. If Canada were to join with Mexico on border management issues—like consolidating ID requirements and customs forms and expediting the construction of FAST lanes—some breakthroughs might be possible.

Moreover, if Canada were to decide to accept its "North American challenge" and apply the skills it has refined in the multilateral arena to designing North American institutions, it would find an eager partner in Mexico. Given its global burdens, the United States is unlikely to take the initiative, but the Obama administration is likely to be open to a joint effort by its neighbors. Republicans are more skeptical of multilateral institutions, but if a broad segment of the business community were supportive, that could swing the decision in favor of a North American exception.

Canada could start by addressing the question of how to assure compliance with international agreements, such as NAFTA. Two of the more prominent cases have been soft-wood lumber and trucking. In both cases, the existing dispute-settlement mechanism was inadequate to the task. One solution might be to replace this ad hoc mechanism with a permanent tribunal on trade and investment disputes. The judges on the court would serve ten-year terms, and the court would have greater power to fine a country that rejected compliance. Other ideas for new institutions or for reforming existing ones are discussed in the next chapter, but the point is that Canada ought to seize as its particular mission the task of designing a modern set of institutions for trilateral cooperation.

Mexico's challenge is to blaze a path to the first world. Like Canada's challenge to build an institutional architecture, Mexico cannot accomplish its goals on development on its own. It will need support and a coordinated approach with the United States and Canada, though most of the actions will need to be done independently by each country in pursuit of a "community of interests."

Mexico has succeeded in dramatically expanding its manufacturing exports and attracting substantial foreign investment. After two serious downturns—in 1982 and 1994—Mexico was able to reign in inflation to under 5 percent while increasing productivity by about 80 percent in manufacturing. On the negative side of the ledger, Mexico has sustained low levels of domestic investment—around 19 percent of GDP, half that of China—and job growth has remained weak with wages stagnant except in the export-oriented economy. The country is increasingly divided with the north growing at a rapid clip, and the south falling behind. The causes of slow growth include poor infrastructure, lack of credit, poverty, low levels of public investment, a weak educational system, and uncompetitive sectors, especially in energy and telecommunications. Despite the increasingly constructive role played by the Central Bank, Mexico's macroeconomy remains quite vulnerable to external shocks. The OECD gave Mexico its lowest ranking among its members in terms of energy efficiency with prices of natural gas, electricity, and fuel oil among the highest in the world, and telecommunications prices amongst the highest in Latin America.[17]

The problem has not been NAFTA, according to Robert Blecker and Gerardo Esquivel, but "the fact that NAFTA was never supplemented by deeper forms of regional integration, social policies, or economic coopera-tion [and these] probably limited the benefits and exacerbated the costs."[18] There is an emerging consensus among policy analysts that fundamental eco-nomic reforms are essential to kick start Mexico's economy, and there is also agreement on the kinds of reforms.

Of central importance is a combined reform of both fiscal policy and the energy sector. PEMEX, the energy monopoly, is inefficient, but the Mexican government relies on its revenues for 30–40 percent of its budget. As a result, in 2004, Mexico's tax receipts as a percentage of its GDP was 12 percent—the lowest of any OECD country and one-third that of Brazil—while PEMEX oil production is declining rapidly because it does not have enough funds to ex-plore for new oil.[19] Mexico would profit if PEMEX had competition as well as private investment and technology from foreign energy companies. The fiscal system needs to be reformed to obtain more revenues for infrastructure and education.

Institutional reforms are needed to strengthen the rule of law, enhance the capabilities of regulatory institutions (particularly the Competition Commis-sion and the media), make the legislature more accountable by permitting re-election, and strengthen the independence and integrity of the judiciary. Some past reforms on pensions and privatization are incomplete or need more work.

Thus far, President Calderon proposed some reforms, but his Congress has sliced and diced each one to the point that they have not had much of an effect. His problem in undertaking the reforms identified above is mostly political. Like Obama, he faces a legislature that has stalemated or blocked his proposals. If a North American effort were properly designed to assist Mexico on its long-term development plans, that might provide critical support for Calderon to achieve these reforms.

America's challenge is to design a new style of global leadership as creative as FDR's and Truman's after the Second World War but one adapted to the twenty-first century. To achieve the goal of being a new kind of leader in the world, the president needs also to find ways to inspire Americans to participate in a new mission. The path to success internationally must begin by demonstrating genuine respect for neighbors. Like the other two challenges, this one will require a new spirit of collaboration.

The new leadership defines goals in collaboration with our neighbors and identifies the contributions each must make to achieve those goals. To accomplish this, the U.S. government needs to reorganize the way it relates to its neighbors because the current way is not working; it is so decentralized as to be dysfunctional. John Dickson, a career U.S. foreign service officer, served at the State Department and as the deputy chief of the U.S. embassy in both Mexico and Canada. After years of negotiating these issues with both countries, he concluded: "The hardest negotiations on North America are within our governments rather than between them."[20]

Both Canada and Mexico have organized their entire governments to deal with the United States. They have little choice given the weight of their neighbor on their economy and society, but it is precisely because the weight of Canada and Mexico—particularly when they act alone—is so light on its shoulders that the U.S. government has never organized itself to deal with its neighbors. Indeed, until 1996, the U.S. Department of State dealt with Canadian issues in the European Bureau and Mexico in the Latin American Bureau.

Outside of the Department of State, U.S. domestic agencies handle their part of the North American relationship as if it were only a domestic concern, which means that Canadian or Mexican interests are given short shrift. Also, the government is not structured to give the president a clear choice between complying with an international agreement or siding with a particular corporate or bureaucratic interest.

It is not possible to build a North American Community unless the U.S. government establishes a high-level mechanism to address the full gamut of issues. There are many ways to organize the U.S. government to approach North American issues, but given the importance of domestic issues and politics, the policy needs to be coordinated at the White House, preferably under the auspices of a senior official, like the vice president or the national security advisor working with the director of the National Economic Council.[21] A special advisor to the president for North American Affairs would coordinate the operation and report to the president through either the vice president or the NSC. The advisor should chair a deputies-level North America committee that prepares options for NSC meetings to be chaired by the president.

Only the president can make the decisions needed to organize the government to give him the advice to upgrade the relationship, and only he can signal to the domestic departments that issues of concern to our North American neighbors should take precedence. As president, Jimmy Carter instructed his cabinet to give priority to Mexico, and he established a coordinator in the Department of State to manage the process. Although the coordinator, Robert Krueger, had been a Texas congressman and was knowledgeable of the bureaucracy, his position at the State Department made it difficult to influence the domestic agencies, and being called an ambassador confused many about his role vis-à-vis the U.S. ambassador in Mexico. By moving the office to the White House and by embracing both Canadian as well as Mexican issues, the special advisor to the president for North American affairs could avoid these mistakes.

Because of the conservative criticism of the North American Union, President George W. Bush instructed his cabinet to continue working on North American issues but to do so "under the radar screen" and without resources or legislation.[22] This approach failed. To build a North American Community, the legislatures should be incorporated into the process. The two Inter-Parliamentary Committees dealing with Canada and Mexico should be merged into an Inter-Parliamentary Committee on North America, and the special advisor should meet with the group regularly to discuss legislation. Public opinion surveys suggest that the American and Canadian public are tired of incremental muddling and favor a more comprehensive approach.[23] A bold vision of a North American Community cannot be translated into real policies unless the president reorganizes the executive branch and connects those officials with the Inter-Parliamentary Committee.

None of the three challenges can be achieved by a single country, working on its own, and that is the real message of the North American Community. Mexico cannot lift itself from poverty without the help of its neighbors. Canada can design North American institutions, but it cannot implement them without the agreement of its neighbors. U.S. leadership depends on Canadian and Mexican cooperation and a new mechanism to organize the government and relate to its neighbors.

These are the three core challenges for North America, and yet these challenges are not even on the agenda of the three leaders. The reason is that the leaders have not begun to think continentally, and as long as they focus on bilateral relationships, they will be blind to the promise and the problems of the entire region. Once they visualize "North America" and decide to approach their problems from a continental perspective, solutions will appear that were previously invisible. Only then will they understand that what is in it for each can only be attained when they pursue what is in it for all.

➤ From a Bilateral to a Continental Agenda

In meetings that U.S. President Barack Obama had with Mexican President
Felipe Calderon on January 12, 2009, and with Prime Minister Stephen Harper
on February 19, 2009, the three leaders sketched two agendas that were quite
similar. The issues were the economy, energy and climate change, pandemics,
and security. Instead of pursuing this dual-bilateral agenda or merging the two
agendas into a single North American one, the three governments are each
making its own policies separately. Thus, on the economy, each government
submitted its "stimulus" package to its legislature without consulting with
each other. On energy and climate change, each of the three leaders is negotiating its proposal with their legislatures with little, if any, consultation across
the borders. Only on pandemics like H1N1 (swine flu) has there been coordination among the three health networks.

On security and border management, the United States and Mexico have
announced a forum for addressing the issue, and Canada is expected to join
it, but all three governments would be wise to review the implementation

Figure 6.1: Mexican President Carlos Salinas de Gortari, U.S. President George H. W. Bush, and Canadian Prime Minister Brian Mulroney witness the initialing of the framework for the North American Free
Trade Agreement on October 7, 1992 in San Antonio, Texas by their trade ministers, Mexican Secretary
of Commerce Jaime Serra Puche, U.S. Trade Representative Carla Hills, and Canadian International
Trade Minister Michael Wilson.

Source: George Bush Presidential Library and Museum.

Figure 6.2: President George W. Bush walks with Mexico President Vicente Fox, left, and Canadian Prime Minister Paul Martin upon their arrival. Wednesday, March 23, 2005, Waco, Texas.

Source: Photo by Krisanne Johnson, courtesy of the George W. Bush Presidential Library.

Figure 6.3: President Barack Obama, Canada's Prime Minister Stephen Harper, left, and Mexico's President Felipe Calderon, center, sit down for a working dinner at the North American Leaders' Summit in Guadalajara, Mexico, on Aug. 10, 2009.

Source: Official White House Photo by Pete Souza.

of the "smart borders agreements" before reinventing the wheel. One of the most concrete elements of the U.S.-Canadian Smart Borders Agreement of December 2002 was a pilot project for "land preclearance" or "shared border management." In order to facilitate commerce across the border while assuring security, both countries were supposed to relocate their border inspection operations to the other side of the border. Trucks going to Buffalo, New York would clear the U.S. side in Fort Erie, Ontario, and the Canadian operation would move to the U.S. side. After intensive negotiations beginning in 2005, the United States officially ended the talks in April 2007. The next year, the U.S. Government Accountability Office (GAO) was asked by Congress to explain the failure.

In an incisive report, the GAO explained that the United States and Canada could not reach agreement on five issues: arrest authority; the right of individuals to withdraw an application to enter the United States while at the land preclearance site in Canada; fingerprinting processes; how information collected by the United States would be shared; and assurances that Canadian courts would not interpret their Charter of Rights and Freedoms in a manner that would affect adversely U.S. officials.[24] As one reads through the issues, it is clear that the problem was that each side would not budge from its own procedures, and the leadership on both sides failed to provide a vision of what a common approach should look like. After nine years of bilateral discussions, the U.S.-Canadian border is not managed any better than it was before 9/11, and there is substantial evidence that it is much worse. This case offers a compelling illustration as to the futility of the bilateral approach and the need to try a North American approach.

The truth is that both borders are dysfunctional for similar reasons—inadequate infrastructure; additional security requirements imposed by the U.S. government; and a fragmented approach by agencies within and between the three governments. The question is whether a single North American negotiation is more likely to succeed in designing a common approach with similar rules and requirements and jointly trained personnel to manage the borders. It could not do worse.

What is needed is leadership at the top defining a vision of North America based on reciprocity and "best practices." None of the three governments has a monopoly on wisdom in finding the best way to manage the border, and all three have a shared interest in both security and facilitation of commerce. Of course, each government has developed procedures over time that are different from each other, and the question is whether an honest exchange among senior officials could not find a formula in each of those five areas that would satisfy the combined needs of all three countries. It should not be so hard. The failure until now is that the leaders have not led, and the bureaucrats have not moved. Adding a third country to the table might make it easier to see which country has "best practices."

A trilateral approach would help on the other issues as well. To narrow the development gap between Mexico and its northern neighbors, all three should design a plan and then decide what each would contribute. A trilateral approach would mean more resources. If it were just bilateral, the donor would likely demand a quid pro quo, which would make it harder—if not impossible—for Mexico to accept. While Mexico would benefit the most from the North American Investment Fund, its growth would translate into increased imports from the United States and Canada.

To address the dual problems of energy security and climate change, a global carbon tax or cap-and-trade system would be optimal but unlikely. If the three governments of North America found a formula for undertaking and testing such a system at a regional level, the international community could learn from that experience.

A dual-bilateral approach has not yielded any progress on transportation or infrastructure—the most obvious preconditions to further growth in trade—nor on education. Beyond the dividends derived from more effective policies on each issue, a trilateral approach yields broader benefits because it is more likely to yield an outcome based on fairness and rules than one based on the balance—or rather the imbalance—of power. As such, Canada and Mexico are more likely to feel as if they have a stake in the region's future.

As they forge continental answers to shared problems, the three governments will find themselves constructing a community that is greater than the sum of the individual policies. An important tool for facilitating this transition is to exchange senior personnel and incorporate them at high levels of the bureaucracy. These exchanges could generate new ideas and nurture a sensitivity of each national perspective that could permit the emergence of a North American Community.

On the eve of a meeting among the foreign ministers of the three countries on July 16, 2009, in Washington, Canada imposed a visa on Mexicans wanting to travel to Canada. The reason was to try to reduce the numbers of Mexicans seeking asylum. Mexico viewed this decision as insulting, particularly because of the timing. If Canada had been sensitive to Mexico's perspective, or had consulted the United States, the government would have realized that it had a commonality, not a conflict, of interests with the Mexican government. To apply for refugee status, the applicant needs to prove that he or she has a "well-founded fear of persecution" based on race, religion, or political beliefs. This is insulting to Mexico because while its democracy might be imperfect, it is genuine. The problem could have been easily solved, and the insult never hurled, by incorporating the Mexican perspective before announcing the policy. Over time, one hopes that the three countries will begin to think more systematically about the future they want to share.

The pragmatists in the three countries often ask: "What's in it for us if we were to move to a North American Community?" We have just reviewed how bilateral talks have failed and how a North American approach could yield benefits on the full agenda for each of the three countries.

The most compelling reason, however, to embark on a journey toward a North American Community is to create a new model for the twenty-first century. The world in the twenty-first century faces a new set of challenges different from, but no less consequential than the ones it faced in the twentieth. The challenges span social, economic, and environmental problems and issues of peace and health. The effective management and solution of these problems depends on vision and governance within countries and among them.

The paramount challenge of our time is to lift the poorest countries to the middle class and the middle-income countries to the first world. That is why Mexico joined NAFTA, but what we have learned is that free trade is necessary but insufficient to achieve sustainable development. If the three countries of North America can design a program to narrow the gap, then that would give hope to the majority of countries in the world.

Canada's challenge is to design and construct a new set of twenty-first century institutions for three countries of unequal power and wealth on a wider set of issues than has been done before. The U.S. challenge is to fashion a new style of leadership that corresponds to the new agenda and the changes in the international system.

A shared vision of a community is a critical point of departure. The next step is to reorganize governments and establish new institutions. From there, if all three governments work together on the three challenges, a community will take shape. If North America succeeds, many lessons can be drawn and applied to the wider world.

It all begins with the North American Idea. Once that is grasped and internalized, many new policies become possible. In the next chapter, we will develop a detailed blueprint composed of those new policies.

7

New Policies for North America's Twenty-First Century: A Blueprint

Few ideas are in themselves practical. It is for want of imagination in applying them that they fail. The creative process does not end with an idea—it only starts with an idea.

—John Arnold

Old, stale arguments about NAFTA can still be heard, but the real debate is over. NAFTA is complete. Today, the three countries of North America face a much more complex twenty-first century agenda, and they find themselves midway between domestic constituencies and continental interests, between national governments and an unregulated North American market.

The most serious problems that have emerged in North America since 1994 are either unrelated to NAFTA or they are the consequence of NAFTA's success in spawning an enlarged market. Today's problems are the result of the three governments' failure to govern the North American space. The leaders of the three governments have chosen not to offer grand proposals like a customs union or a fund to narrow the development gap because they thought their people were not ready for such a leap. Instead, they have decided to work privately and incrementally, pursuing small steps, like pre-clearance facilities between New York and Ontario or harmonizing regulations on jelly beans. But these incremental steps have also failed. Boldness has not been tried. This book suggests a third way, one that begins with the North American Idea— the idea that the three nations can only achieve their goals if they find a new way to relate to each other. Without a vision of a future North America, minor incremental reforms are not worth the energy, and bolder proposals will not be taken seriously.

In this chapter, we will offer a blueprint of twenty proposals that could be the building blocks of a North American Community. They are grouped into four broad areas dealing with (1) the North American economy; (2) national and public security; (3) transnational issues, like immigration and climate change; and (4) institutions.

Many of these ideas will be dismissed as politically impractical, particularly in a time of legislative stalemate and austerity budgets, when most leaders are looking backward to see where the people are, and few are looking forward to where we should go. This chapter is not aimed at the contemporary debate; it is aimed at the next generation and the discussion that is needed.

At the beginning of the twentieth century, the American government slowly awoke to the realization that a national market had emerged because of railroads and electricity. Innovative leaders like Theodore Roosevelt and Woodrow Wilson responded by creating national institutions like the Anti-Trust Commission and the Federal Reserve Bank—the first to prevent a concentration of economic power in the hands of a few industrialists, and the second to manage the currency and the boom-and-bust swings of the economy. These new institutions and many others helped lift the United States to become the most powerful economy in the world.

By the dawn of the twenty-first century, national economies and the nature of international competition had been transformed. The outline of a new North American market became visible while the European Union expanded and integrated, and East Asia blossomed. New challenges required new ways to relate to one's neighbors.

➤ The North American Economy

Businesses and entrepreneurs have done much of the heavy lifting to create a North American market, but there is not enough magic in the marketplace to fill in the potholes, invigorate the three economies, and share its benefits with those workers who have lost jobs due to increasing competition. The three governments have not done their share. They have five tasks to strengthen and energize the North American economy so that it can compete against Asia and Europe in the twenty-first century.

The paramount challenge in North America is to close the development gap separating Mexico from the two more advanced economies. Secondly, the three governments need to negotiate and implement a North American plan for transportation and infrastructure, which will be the platform for a modern, continent-wide economy. Third, while the three economies are increasingly synchronized, economic policies are not. The governments need to create a consultative web to coordinate policies. Fourth, to awaken the region from its stupor and foster deeper economic integration, the governments need to negotiate a customs union. Fifth, the three governments should commit to new methods to address the new frontier of integration—regulatory convergence.

1. CLOSING THE INCOME GAP

Notwithstanding the rhetoric, North America will never be a true partnership until the development gap separating Mexico from its northern neighbors begins to close. The gap explains why the war on drugs looks so different in Mexico than in the United States and why the enforcement strategy led by Mexico's police and military is inadequate to the task. The development gap, the supply of unskilled labor in Mexico, and the demand for cheap labor in the United States are the main reasons for the growing numbers of illegal immigrants.[1] An effective U.S. immigration policy can reduce the flow of undocumented migration on the margin, but in the long-term, the only way that immigration can stabilize is if Mexico grows faster than the United States and, by doing so, begins to close the income gap.

Increased trade modernized parts of Mexico's economy, but it also exacerbated inequalities between the urban and the rural areas, between the export and the domestic economies, and most of all, between the north and the south. Average wages in Mexico showed little or no improvement under NAFTA, but if one disaggregated the data, one would find that the north—connected to North America—has grown at ten times the rate of the south.[2] The fact that the north advanced explains the success of NAFTA; the decline of the south is due to the lack of a development strategy.

Theories of economic convergence predict that the gap in incomes between richer and poorer states in a free trade area will narrow because capital will invest and technology will deploy where it can gain greater returns. The closing of the gap between the northern and southern states after the Civil War is proof of the theory. With free movement of labor, a mammoth migration of 6 million African-Americans north, and a common currency, the gap began to close between the north and south. The only problem is that it took more than a century.

In contrast, the European Union significantly closed its income gap between the richest and the poorest countries in just twenty years, but it didn't succeed because of free trade. It was due to a major restructuring of the recipient economies and the transfer of resources on a scale that made the Marshall Plan modest in comparison. Since its founding, Europe contributed about € 650 billion (approximately $850 billion) through various programs, including cohesion funds, to narrow the income gap within as well as between the rich and poor countries. One of the motives was to preclude large-scale migration from the poorer southern European countries, and the strategy succeeded in preventing that.[3] The per capita income in Portugal and Spain as a percent of Europe's nearly doubled, and Ireland climbed from the second poorest to the second richest country in Europe—before the 2008 recession—with 164 percent of the European average income. In contrast, between 1980 and 2008, the income gap between Mexico and the North American average did not narrow.[4] (See Figure 7.1)

There is no question that Europe's cohesion funds contributed to reducing the gap, though some scholars debate the extent. There is also a consensus that the most productive use of the funds was for transportation, infrastructure, education, and communications in the poor countries that helped connect them to the richer markets.

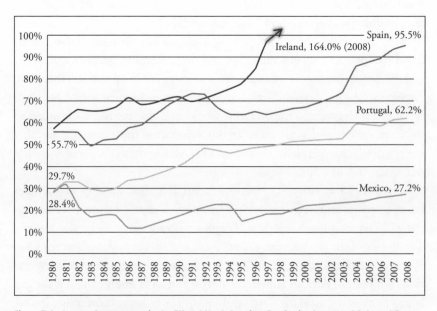

Figure 7.1: Income Convergence in the EU and North America: Per Capita Average of Selected Countries in Each Region, 1980–2008

Note: EU average reflects accessions.

Source: World Bank, World Development Indicators, accessed in 2010.

For third world countries like Mexico to move ahead, trade is not enough. Substantial aid together with incentives to make hard decisions on economic policies are essential. Aid without reforms would reinforce dependency, and reforms without aid would not generate enough revenue to pay for the needed public infrastructure. If one can find the formula for Mexico it could be a model for other middle-income countries.

With several colleagues, I directed a research project sponsored by the North American Development Bank that proposed a North American Investment Fund to close the gap. Using a dynamic Computable General Equilibrium Model (CGE) and asking how much and what kind of investment would generate an annual growth rate of 6 percent in Mexico, we estimated that $20 billion per year would be needed for a decade, and that should be invested mostly in infrastructure with a smaller amount in education. If the United States and Canada each grew by 3 percent during that time, Mexico would close the income gap separating itself from the United States by 22 percent in a decade.[5] In a separate report, the World Bank also estimated that Mexico needed $20 billion per year for a decade to close the infrastructure gap.[6]

Learning from both the mistakes and the success of the EU model, the North American Investment Fund should place 90 percent of the funds in infrastructure to connect the south of Mexico to the United States and Canada, and 10 percent in post-secondary education. Rather than create another institution, it would be more efficient to use the World Bank as the administrator of the fund. Mexico should pay half through increased tax revenues; the United States, 40 percent, and Canada, 10 percent.

The EU's grants were effective in part because the recipient countries had undertaken serious economic reforms. Mexican leaders understand the kinds of reforms that are needed, and Mexican President Felipe Calderon pressed Congress to approve them, but the Congress moved slowly and inadequately. The fiscal reform raised taxes, but not nearly enough to permit PEMEX to invest in exploration or the government to invest in infrastructure. Judicial reform will take years to be implemented. The energy reform narrowly opened contracts for international corporations to transfer technology and assist in exploration, but not enough to reverse the decline in Mexican oil production.

Normally, the United States provides aid with strict conditions. That is why Mexico rejected the Alliance for Progress. It refused to be told by the United States what it should do, and there is an additional reason beyond nationalist pride why the North American Investment Fund should be approached with

a different mindset. If the leaders want to establish a new model of cooperation, they should replace the conventional quid pro quo with the idea of a
"community of interests" in solving a shared problem. They should agree on a
strategy to close the income gap and the contribution each of the three countries should make to achieve that.

If Mexico can grow faster than its neighbors, their imports from the United
States and Canada would increase. Indeed, the best destination for U.S. businesses to double their exports by 2014, as President Obama pledged, is in
the neighborhood. Also, when Mexicans can see that their economy is doing
better than its neighbors, their calculations as to whether to immigrate may
change. The three governments could have had a head start in developing the
Fund when they appropriated stimulus packages for infrastructure and other
purposes, but without a North American Idea, the problem of the development gap did not occur to them.

2. TRANSPORTATION AND INFRASTRUCTURE

Markets usually begin alongside roads when farmers bring their produce to
sell to people who are coming or going. Then, a small store opens, and then
others. Roads and ports are essential for a market to begin and to thrive, and
governments are needed to build this infrastructure. Markets can only facilitate the production of goods and services at competitive prices if governments plan ahead. In the case of North America, the governments have fallen
behind.

The good news is that the three governments began the twenty-first century recognizing the deficiency of their infrastructure and, largely because of
the economic crisis, appropriated funds for maintenance and new construction. The bad news is that the magnitude of the funds needed to construct a
state-of-the-art transportation system for North America greatly exceeds the
authorized amounts. Moreover, in all three countries, the projects are designed
and driven at the local or state levels. There are no national plans let alone a
North American plan. Even worse, transportation regulations are balkanized
in the United States and Canada and largely unenforced in Mexico.

So what is to be done? The three leaders should begin by instructing their
Ministers of Transportation to work together to develop a plan for North
American Infrastructure and Transportation for the year 2020. This plan
should be comprehensive and ambitious, but the schedule for implementation
would depend on the amount of funds that the three governments would allo-
cate. Each of the plans should be multi-modal, connecting high-speed trains,

roads, ports, and airports, and include new trade corridors from Canada to Mexico.[7] The North American Investment Fund would provide part of the funding. Separate but related to these plans, the leaders should designate a senior person from each of the governments to co-chair a task force to negotiate unified regulatory standards for trucks and other modes of transportation.

The North American Plan for Transportation and Infrastructure has several goals. First, it would relieve transportation congestion, reduce transit costs, and encourage more trade. Second, the plan would connect southern Mexico to markets in the United States and Canada and thus contribute to reducing the disparities between the poorer and richer countries. Its third goal would be to improve border infrastructure. About $13.4 billion is estimated to be needed on the northern border and $11 billion in the south.[8]

It is important to emphasize that border improvements are a small part of the North American Transportation Plan. One of the reasons that undocumented migration has grown worse is because the border industrialization program has been a magnet attracting labor from south Mexico to the north and then to the United States. The main objective of the plan would be to encourage workers to remain in the south and center of Mexico by promoting investment and building roads that reach there.

The model for the new North American highway could be the Pan-American Highway which extends from the northern reaches of Alaska to the southern tip of Argentina. It was conceived at the first Inter-American Conference in 1889 and was constructed between 1923 and 1950. The Pan-American vision propelled that project just as one hopes the North American Idea would propel a new high-speed corridor from northern Canada to Chiapas.

The Security and Prosperity Partnership aimed to harmonize transportation regulations—a critical component of the entire effort—and limited progress was made. For example, they were able to develop compatible standards for driver age, language, and medical requirements. They developed a common format for recording drivers' hours of service, and they adopted compatible regulations for transporting hazardous materials. At the same time, however, the most difficult issues were not resolved. These included immigration restrictions on transportation workers, the harmonization of vehicle weights and sizes, cabotage, and allowing Mexican trucks into the United States.[9]

In brief, what is needed is a continental plan for transportation and infrastructure, long-term commitments of funds, and an empowered task force to harmonize rules on transportation. These steps would go a long distance to creating the platform for a North American Community.

3. ECONOMIC POLICY

When Mexico succumbed to a debt crisis in 1982 and to a foreign exchange crisis in 1994, the United States recognized that it could not insulate itself from the economic consequences, and it offered substantial funds to stabilize Mexico's economy. When the United States was buffeted by its own economic crisis in 2008, both Canada and Mexico had solid fiscal and trade balances and relatively secure financial systems, and yet their dependence on the U.S. market was such that they could not protect their economies from the U.S. downturn. "In fact, no major country in the world," writes Earl Fry, a leading scholar of Canada, "is as dependent for its economic well-being on another nation as Canada is dependent on the United States."[10] Actually, there is one other country, Mexico. The United States is, of course, not as dependent, but still one-third of its global trade is with its neighbors.

The markets have connected, and the business cycles are increasingly synchronized, and yet, the governments have not modified their policy making to take this into account. Real cooperation across a wide economic front is necessary to promote integration and prevent or mitigate crises. The Central Bank presidents and the Treasury ministers of all three governments should meet regularly to exchange information on each economy and to develop plans to address any upcoming problems. These meetings would generate confidence and help the public understand the importance of North America.

Other groups like the U.S. Auto Industry Task Force and the Steel Group should collaborate routinely with counterparts in Canada and Mexico. More effective consultation could lead eventually to greater coordination on financial issues, including coordination among regulators of the securities and stock markets.

4. CUSTOMIZING THE FREE TRADE AREA

NAFTA created a free trade area, but since all three governments maintain different tariffs to the world, they use complex "rules of origin" procedures to ensure that other countries would not slip their products into the area through the country with the lowest tariff. That is the ostensible purpose; the actual reason for the "rules of origin" is to protect firms from fourth country competition and encourage foreign investors to locate in North America. The procedures are so cumbersome that exporters often have to hire brokers. Some exporters prefer to use the most-favored nation (MFN) tariffs—the standard for all members of the World Trade Organization—but of course, that defeats the very purpose of a free trade regime. The costs are not only at the border but in the distortions they introduce into the three economies, which is why the total cost is estimated at 2–3 percent of North America's GDP or $510 billion in 2008.[11] That constitutes a super-size tax on North American consumers with no corresponding benefit. Free trade is not supposed to work like that. Brokers are needed in poor, corrupt developing countries to "expedite" trade; they have no place in a modern free trade area.

In 2005, under the Security and Prosperity Partnership, the three North American governments decided to remove rules-of-origin provisions on selected products. After several years, the negotiators had removed provisions on $30 billion worth of goods. This might seem like a lot, but it is actually less than the average annual growth of trade among the three countries. At that rate, they would never eliminate rules of origin.

The most efficient way to eliminate this tax would be to set up a Customs Union with a "common external tariff." External tariffs in the three countries would have to be fixed at either the MFN level or the lowest level of the three. These products could then cross the border without duties and "certificates of origin," and inspectors could concentrate their energies and time on illicit drugs, undocumented migrants, and terrorists. There are other impediments to trade that could be reduced as the three countries move to a common external tariff. Customs procedures could be harmonized so that exporters would fill out just one form for all three countries. The three agencies responsible for border administration—the Mexican Customs Agency, the Canadian Border Services Agency, and the U.S. Customs and Border Patrol—could develop a unified system, and their officials could be trained and serve together.

There will be some difficult obstacles to overcome in negotiating a customs union, beginning with reducing tariffs on sensitive goods, like peanuts, tobacco, textiles, clothing, and footwear in the United States; and dairy products, poultry, textiles and clothing in Canada.[12] The United States also has separate agreements on agriculture with Mexico and Canada, and these would have to be reconciled. In addition, all three countries have free-trade agreements with other countries. Mexico has the most agreements, including with the European Union and Japan. Without some adjustments in the other agreements, a customs union in North America would mean that these countries would have freer access to the U.S. market than the United States would have to theirs.

Canada and Mexico trade with Cuba while the United States maintains an embargo. One way to reconcile this difference would be for the United States to remove the embargo, but that is unlikely in the near future for political reasons. Alternatively, Mexico and Canada could prevent transshipment of Cuban goods.

In a customs union, the tariff revenues should be shared. The European Union transfers the revenues to the central budget. North America might consider using the revenue for the North American Investment Fund or to assist workers adjusting to international competition. In addition, as all three countries would have adopted the same external trade policy, they might negotiate future trade agreements together, and they could, for example, join in approaching China to revalue its currency.

A customs union is the most logical path toward deeper and more efficient integration in North America. It would be difficult to negotiate and even harder to secure the approval of the U.S. Congress, but it would not be as hard as NAFTA.[13] With a clear vision of its importance to a North American Community and a full understanding of the costs of maintaining the status quo, it becomes feasible.

5. REGULATORY CONVERGENCE

Manufacturers have to make sure that their products meet the standards of the country to which they export. The United States and Canada, for example, have different standards for the same cereals. Even if the difference is trivial, as is the case with most foods, some firms need to use a separate factory just to adapt the product to a slightly different standard. The OECD estimates that divergent standards can add 2–10 percent to overall production costs.[14] "For companies exporting to multiple markets," Michael Hart writes, "the promise of 'one standard, one test, accepted everywhere' has become increasingly attractive."[15] Reducing regulatory divergence is the frontier of trade, and that should be the goal for the next stage for North America.

There are several ways to promote regulatory convergence. Each country could share its proposed regulations with the others and seek their comments. The three countries have begun to do this in limited ways. This has the advantage of leaving the responsibility for making rules in the hands of each government, but it has a disadvantage in that Canada and Mexico are often left with the choice of adopting or rejecting the U.S. standard.

With the increased importance of trade in agriculture and concerns for food safety, the three governments might want to focus first on seeking harmonization or mutual recognition of different standards in food health and safety (sanitary and phyto-sanitary measures). To facilitate this procedure, the agencies in the three countries could exchange personnel for two-year assignments. Alternatively, the three governments could explore establishing a North American Food and Drug Agency, modeled on the United States and Canadian agencies, and including scientists from all three countries. This could serve as a model for connecting other regulatory agencies that deal with different functions. The legislatures should be involved to ensure that the proposed regulation is consistent with the original statute or order.

Still, another area where the three governments could promote efficiencies in transnational businesses would be to certify hospitals in Mexico for Americans and Canadians and allow retirees to spend their Medicare or health insurance there. Many medicines require a prescription in Canada and the United States but not in Mexico, and some people have argued that would make certification impossible. But if Mexico understood that a more professional policy on prescriptions would yield an expanding business with its North American partners while improving medical safety for Mexicans, that is likely to be sufficient incentive to harmonize.[16] The certification process for professionals—whether nurses, real estate agents, contractors, teachers— would also benefit from harmonization and could facilitate the growth of tri-national business.

Conclusion: The five proposals to lift the North American economy are complementary. The North American Investment Fund could be the Mexican part of a new Plan for North American Transportation and Infrastructure. A Customs Union combined with the elimination of drayage (allowing Mexican trucks in the United States) and cabotage would make the continental market as efficient as the national markets. Regulatory convergence would generate new efficiencies to make business far more competitive. Finally, a new framework for coordinating economic policies would tie together and oversee all these threads.

➤ National and Public Security

The first decade of the twenty-first century transformed the national and public security landscape of North America. Previously, there was hardly any cooperation between the United States and Mexico and Mexico and Canada, and cooperation between the United States and Canada was through formal institutions. Since 2001, North America has been terrorized by Al-Qaeda and the drug cartels, but not in the same way or degree, and the degree of cooperation has increased, but not enough to make a difference. Let us explore how a North American Idea might translate into a deeper form of collaboration in each of the following areas—public security, counter-terrorism and joint border management, natural disasters and pandemics, and national and North American security and foreign policy.

1. PUBLIC SECURITY AND DRUG TRAFFICKING

Like two blind and suspicious people, Mexico and the United States have groped for the best way to deal with drug traffickers and with each other. During the past four decades, the United States, at times, shut the border to express its displeasure with the lack of commitment by Mexico to stop drug trafficking. Mexico found ways to remind its northern neighbor of the importance of respecting its sovereignty. This unconstructive pattern changed in the first years of the twenty-first century as a result of three new factors: NAFTA, which brought the two countries together; democracy, which made the Mexican government more accountable to its people but also fractured the cozy relationship between the ruling party and the drug-trafficking organizations (DTOs); and the transformation of the DTOs from conveyor belts for Colombian gangs to formidable multinational entities with enough firepower to make war on one another and society.

By the time that Felipe Calderon was inaugurated in 2006, the level of violence and kidnappings was so high that Mexicans labeled "public security" their principal concern, and he reached out to the United States at a meeting in Merida with President Bush for a new partnership that was as radical as NAFTA had been. For the first time, the full gamut of law enforcement and military agencies in both countries began working together, and the United States provided more than $1 billion because of its "shared responsibility" on the drug scene and without the kinds of conditions that had long characterized U.S. aid policy.

In making the case in Congress for the Merida aid package, the Bush administration called the crisis urgent, but by the time Bush left office, almost none of the funds had been spent. By July 2010, the Government Accountability Office reported that less than half of the funds had been obligated and only 9 percent spent. The GAO report was devastating in its criticism of the capability of the U.S. government to devise or implement a strategy on drugs and violence. It described an administration changing goals, but only marginally, and creating new coordinating mechanisms that multiplied the letters in the North American Scrabble Game. But the U.S. government failed to devise measures to assess performance or timelines for achieving the goals.

One measure of state incapability—of the United States, not Mexico—is that each of three bureaus in the Department of State responsible for managing one slice of U.S. funds "has a different method for tracking. Each uses different budgeting terms [and] . . . spreadsheets. . . .. And [the] State [Department] currently has no consolidated database for these funds." At the same time, the United States blamed Mexico for not filling out the requisition forms properly![17]

The unsettling truth is that three years after the agreement, the violence was worse and the supply and consumption of drugs in the United States was unchanged. The absence of performance targets may have been a reflection of the U.S. government's awareness that it shared the responsibility not just for the problem but also for the failure to reduce the violence or affect the demand or supply of drugs.

What lessons can be drawn from decades of failure? Can the North American Idea help? Drug trafficking is the classic transnational issue. Like immigration, drug trafficking responds to both demand and supply, and no effective approach is possible that is not comprehensive. Thus far, the issue has been addressed in a bilateral setting, and there are many dangers lurking on that front. The sensational and deadly aspects of drug trafficking together with heightened concerns about undocumented workers have skewed U.S. attention to look at Mexico through a law enforcement lens. This has led some to see that a border wall is the solution and that the National Guard is an essential line of defense. It leads others to conclude that we have the answers, and Mexico is the problem. This approach disturbs the Mexicans, and it causes both sides to overlook the promise of the economic and social relationship.

The first lesson is to view the issues from the perspective of "shared responsibility" for both the problem and the solution. The Obama administration has grasped the principle, but the execution is the hard part. The second lesson is to find a way to involve Canada in all facets of the problem. While Canada does not have a direct stake in the current problem in Mexico, the consequences are felt as far afield as British Columbia and Ontario, and Canada's experience in the treatment of drug-related problems—from a health and enforcement perspective—could be valuable. For that reason, and to relieve the U.S.-Mexican strategy of the burdens of asymmetry, it would be desirable for all three countries to address the crisis together. The Royal Canadian Mounted Police began a small project with the Mexican police. This should be expanded.

A group of Latin American leaders, led by three distinguished former presidents of Brazil, Colombia, and Mexico wrote a report in 2009 that accepted the failure of "prohibitionist polices based on the eradication of production and on the disruption of drug flows as well as on the criminalization of consumption." As presidents, each had dealt unsuccessfully with the problem. They asked the United States and Europe to develop a plan to reduce demand, and they proposed three points that should govern a new policy: (a) drug users should be handled as a problem of public health; (b) drug consumption should be reduced by information, education, and prevention; and (c) forceful strategies should aim at organized crime. They also called for a public health evaluation of cannabis.[18] If all three governments can commit to a broader strategy on drug trafficking and violence, the new relationship could be extended to a wider security agenda that includes more systematic coordination against terrorism and management of the border, and new opportunities for collaboration on international peacekeeping.

Obama's Director of the White House Office of Drug Control Policy Gil Kerlikowske was right when he criticized the phrase "war on drugs." As long as there is a supply of illicit drugs and a demand for it, we cannot declare victory, and we cannot wish the problem away. "De-criminalization" of one drug—like cannabis—might make a part of the problem manageable, though Kerlikoske opposed this, and permit more effective utilization of scarce resources in the judicial and enforcement areas, but efforts to de-criminalize other more potent drugs are unlikely. Kerlikowske added a second important dimension by giving greater emphasis to the demand-side of health and education.[19] More should be done to treat addicts in a public health system.

Obama also pledged to stop the flow of guns and money from the United States. President George W. Bush had promised to do the same and sent his attorney general in May 2001 to Mexico to address the firearms issue,[20] but the Merida Initiative did not include any dedicated funding to stop the flow of firearms, and a General Accountability Office Report acknowledged that prior to a June 2009 Report from the Office of National Drug Control Policy, "the U.S. government did not have a strategy that explicitly addressed arms trafficking to Mexico."[21] Furthermore, by allowing the ban on assault weapons to expire in 2004, Bush made a bad problem worse.

The Obama administration's strategy of monitoring the sales of gun shops within fifty miles of the border and inspecting traffic and trains going south has not been effective, and as we have seen, stopping traffic will create more problems than it would solve. A better strategy would be for the United States to renew the ban on the sale of assault weapons; close gun shows, which allow people to purchase weapons without background checks; and shut down gun shops within fifty miles of the border. Only a concerted North American strategy would permit a U.S. president to implement such an approach and overcome the resistance of the National Rifle Association (NRA).[22] If Americans were being killed by guns coming in from Mexican gun shops near the border, the U.S. Congress would insist on nothing less.

2. COUNTER-TERRORISM AND JOINT BORDER MANAGEMENT

Few statements by American leaders rile Canadians more than the assertion that the 9/11 terrorists entered the United States from Canada. Canadian ambassadors quickly correct the mistake, but there are two larger truths that are undeniable. First, all three countries of North America are vulnerable to threats and terrorism. Even if one country is attacked, the other two will experience the insecurity and the economic aftershocks. Secondly, the United States is the mostly likely target of international terrorism, and it has a history of acting without consulting its neighbors or taking account of their interests. It is conceivable that the United States might alter its historical behavior if its leaders internalized a vision of a North American Community and bound the country to procedures and institutions that ensured that a response to terror would be North American, not just American.

The legacy of 9/11 is a "thicker" border that has added costs to the economies with little or no security dividend. All three countries have recognized this problem, but they have chosen to address it in an ineffectual dual-bilateral way. The time has come to consider a trilateral approach based on the principle of reciprocity.

The three governments should negotiate a unified border action plan that utilizes those practices that have worked most effectively. One such program is the Integrated Border Enforcement Teams (IBET) of Canadian and American law enforcement officers that work on both sides of the border. This program began as a pilot project in 1996 in the northwest, but after 9/11, it was expanded to cover fifteen regions and twenty-three strategic locations on the border. IBETs consist of officials from two Canadian and three American law enforcement agencies focusing on transnational crime. A parallel operation involves the intelligence agencies of both countries targeting national security threats.[23] This model of interagency and international cooperation should probably be extended to other functions and to Mexico. Such teams, for example, should jointly inspect container traffic entering North American ports.[24]

A coordinated North American effort should share data about the exit and entry of foreign nationals, harmonize both entry screening and tracking procedures as well as exit and export tracking procedures, and to the extent possible, harmonize visa and asylum regulations. Instead of having as many as ten different credentials to facilitate rapid transit across the U.S.-Canadian border, at great cost, and almost as many on the U.S.-Mexican border, the three countries should replace all of them with a single North American border pass with biometric identifiers approved by all three governments. Only those who voluntarily pay the cost for a clearance would obtain the pass.[25] The pass could be "layered" by level of clearance so that government officials could use the same pass with a code that would permit them entrance to sensitive facilities.

A "North American Security Perimeter" was proposed after 9/11, and before any government could describe how it would work, the reaction was negative. Some in Canada feared it might extend the U.S. government's reach to all of Canada's borders while some in the United States interpreted it to mean that the United States would pay less attention to its own borders.[26] By 2006, public opinion swung in favor of the idea. A plurality of Canadians (47 percent in favor; 25 percent opposed) and Americans (49 percent in favor; 20 percent opposed) judged the idea worthwhile.[27]

Five years later, on February 4, 2011, Obama and Harper issued a statement calling for a more modern border. They mentioned the word "perimeter," though failed to develop the idea. They should invite Mexico and design a plan that would permit representatives of all three governments to work together at every port of entry into North America. A perimeter strategy could communicate to the world that all three governments are collaborating against terrorism, and that a terrorist would face an equally difficult time entering North America no matter which country he chooses.

3. NATURAL DISASTERS AND PANDEMICS

When Hurricane Katrina devastated New Orleans in August 2005, both Canada and Mexico offered assistance. The three governments also collaborated effectively when H1N1 (swine flu) struck Mexico in 2009. As part of the broader vision of North America, the three governments might want to work with civil society organizations of all three countries to develop an emergency framework to confront shared crises or diseases. Their efforts could supplement those of the three governments and infuse a sense of community in the three countries.

4. NATIONAL AND NORTH AMERICAN SECURITY

All three governments participate in two collective security organizations— the United Nations and the Organization of American States. In addition, the

United States and Canada are founding members of NATO and of the North American Aerospace Defense Command (NORAD), which was set up in 1957 as a joint command to monitor and defend North American airspace and warn of missile attacks. At the NORAD headquarters, the commander is an American, who reports through the chain of command to the U.S. president and the Canadian prime minister. The deputy is a Canadian. In NORAD's office in Canada, the commander is Canadian.

After 9/11, the United States established NORTHCOM, a coordinating mechanism for homeland defense, and then-Secretary of Defense Donald Rumsfeld invited Canada to join but gave the prime minister a thirty-day deadline. When Canada did not respond, the United States went ahead by itself, and in 2006, Canada created its own Canada Command, a mirror of NORTHCOM.

A commitment to a North American Idea, however, would logically lead the three governments to explore new areas to collaborate. They could re-constitute NORTHCOM as a North American operation that covers land, sea, as well as air defense, and includes senior Canadian and Mexican officers in the planning and execution of a continental defense system. NORTHCOM could also be transformed from a strategic unit focusing on the defense of the U.S. homeland to a defense of North America.

A more modest proposal would be to expand NORAD, which has functioned effectively between the Canadian and American Air Forces, to include joint command on land, the seas, and in the air. A Canadian-U.S. Joint Planning Group recommended that in a recent report, and they should invite Mexico to join.[28] For the first time, Mexico has begun to show some interest in NORAD.

All three governments have vibrant and independent foreign policies at three different levels of the international system. As the sole superpower, the United States plays a central role in almost every important issue. Canada has developed an effective voice as "a middle power," leading in the development of international conventions such as on land mines or the International Criminal Court, and as one of the most experienced in peacekeeping. Mexico is a leader in Latin America and the third world.

Mexico and Canada are viewed as independent of but not antagonistic toward the United States, and so it would *not* be helpful to contemplate a unified approach on all foreign policies—but that does not mean that the three governments could not find opportunities to collaborate. At their Summit Meeting in Guadalajara in August 2009, the three leaders spoke with one voice on the importance of supporting the restoration of the

Honduran president to power, and the three Foreign Ministers have cooperated on Haiti and Central America.

Another possible path might be North American peacekeeping operations. Mexico has been reluctant to participate in UN peacekeeping operations, but public opinion surveys in 2006 and 2008 in Mexico suggest that a significant change has occurred. Public support for participating in UN peacekeeping operations increased from 49 percent in 2006 to 60 percent in 2008. This reflects a general trend among the Mexican public that their country should assume greater international responsibilities. Ironically, at the same time that the public displayed greater support for UN peacekeeping operations, Mexico's leaders showed less support. In 2008, 59 percent of leaders said Mexico should not participate. It is possible that the leaders are stuck with an older position even as the military and the public are evolving.[29]

The shift in Mexican public opinion suggests, again, that proposals that seem infeasible may be open to change as leaders or the environment change. A North American peacekeeping force, which would have been impossible a decade ago, could happen in a decade. It would certainly offer a powerful statement that the three countries view their relationship and collaboration as important and worth expanding.

Areas that the three governments should address together are the Caribbean and Central America. Small and dependent on the North American market, these countries have benefited from the U.S.-Central American Free Trade Agreement, and they would benefit even more from a more direct association with all the countries of North America. The question is when and how to invite them. One of the EU's mistakes was widening to include more countries before it deepened enough to address the new agenda of integration. As a result, every stage of integration was a ferocious political battle, and Europe looked weaker even as it tried to get stronger.

The advantage of North America is that it is composed of only three countries. If these three can create strong institutions and begin advancing on the new agenda, and, most importantly, if Mexico can find a path to the first world, that would create a moment to invite and encourage Central America and the Caribbean to unite and adapt their laws to be compatible with NAFTA's. If North America cannot assist Mexico's transition, then its capacity to assist Central America and the Caribbean will remain limited. The same logic applies to the rest of Latin America. Both Presidents Clinton and Bush pursued a Free Trade Area of the Americas, but this initiative failed when several South American countries chose a different path. If North America succeeds and

Central America and the Caribbean join, the rest of Latin America might renew their interest in a wider free trade area.

➤ The Transnational Transformation

A substantial part of the future agenda of North America relates to the quality of life, including immigration, environmental sustainability, climate change, labor conditions, and education. There is no consensus on dealing with these issues in each country, and that offers an opportunity for the three countries to try to answer them together.

As we learned in the third chapter, the public is prepared to consider deeper forms of integration if convinced that their standard of living would improve and their culture would not be endangered. A majority of the public in all three countries also want their governments to collaborate in developing policies on the environment, border security, transportation, economic policy, and defense policy. Even on energy policy, 68 percent of Americans, 51 percent of Canadians, and 50 percent of Mexicans said they would prefer integrated to independent policies. The surveys also suggest that all three publics would prefer a coordinated, cooperative approach to immigration.

1. IMMIGRATION

What might a cooperative approach to immigration look like? First, at the most general level, all three governments could introduce a "North American preference" system, meaning that all three governments would revise their immigration polices to give preferential access to their neighbors. Secondly, they should pledge to treat all immigrants—whether legal or illegal—with fairness under the rule of law.

Immigration remains very controversial in the United States, particularly when the economy is doing poorly and people are losing jobs. Between 2005–2007, the United States began a debate on immigration that proved both poisonous and inconclusive. The good news was that Congress did not seriously consider reducing legal immigration. The focus was on how to stop illegal migration. This is a legitimate concern.

In 1986, when the Immigration Reform and Control Act legalized roughly 2.6 million people, Congress insisted that it would never repeat such an exercise. However, since then, about 11 million undocumented workers settled in the United States. This has generated substantial uneasiness around the country interspersed with pockets of rage. States and localities have tried to restrict illegal immigration. President Obama insists that immigration is a federal responsibility, and his administration and several leaders in Congress have proposed a comprehensive immigration bill. The principal elements include: (1) stronger enforcement at the border and in the workplace to prevent undocumented workers from getting jobs; (2) a biometric card to identify whether a job applicant is an American citizen or a permanent resident; (3) a path to legalization for the 11 million people who live in the United States illegally; (4) a temporary worker program for agricultural and low-skilled labor to be managed in accordance with the labor demands of the economy; and (5) acceptance of more immigrants with higher skills.

Republicans have tended to emphasize enforcement, encourage more temporary and skilled labor, and oppose legalization. Democrats favor different paths to legalization, although the specific path remains unclear. There has been very little debate on the biometric identification card, but such a card is essential to construct an effective enforcement system at the workplace. The irony is that the conservatives who are most opposed to illegal migration are also most hostile to a national ID. Absent a secure card, however, it will be hard to curb illegal migration.

One element that has been missing from the debate is how to prevent illegal migration in the long-term. There is only one way: the nations need to close the income gap. A possible instrument for accomplishing that would be a North American Investment Fund. The Fund sends a message similar to what Obama and Hillary Clinton sent to Mexico on drug trafficking. It says: "We share responsibility for the migration problem. We are the demand, and you are the supply. We understand that Mexicans want to remain and work in their country, and we are willing to contribute to helping them do that. That is the community we want to build."

The United States and Canada should also open a discussion on labor mobility—temporary and more permanent. This might include the harmonization of immigration and refugee policies. On refugee policies, both countries and Mexico should accept the international legal definition and standards for "refugees." On immigration policies, there has been a gradual convergence between the U.S. system, which has stressed family reunification, and the Canadian system, which has emphasized skills. The United States has increasingly moved toward the Canadian model, and Canada, toward the United States policy on family reunification; therefore, it should not be impossible to reconcile the two sets of policies.

2. CLIMATE CHANGE AND ENERGY SECURITY

With the inauguration of Barack Obama, all three governments accepted the need to curb carbon emissions in order to preclude cataclysmic changes in the climate. As they search for an effective way to reduce carbon emissions, the question is whether they will seek to coordinate their policies. A useful precedent was the decision by the United States to stop "acid rain"—sulfur dioxide—that was emitted from power plants in the Mid-West and was carried by winds to Canada. Complaints from Canada over the course of a decade finally led to amendments in 1990 to the Clean Air Act, which mandated a 50 percent reduction of emissions during the course of the decade. Those amendments were "considered by many to be the most successful domestic environmental legislation ever enacted."[30] Some believed that industries would not comply, but they did, and now, many look to the same cap-and-trade model to curb carbon emissions.

The need for a North American approach to reducing carbon emissions stems from a simple dilemma: If one country imposes a high price for carbon emissions, and its neighbors do not, companies that are carbon-intensive might relocate to the other countries. So the question is how to integrate the domestic decision-making processes of all three countries to ensure a comprehensive and unified approach.

Since Richard Nixon, American politicians have promised energy independence, but no one has come close to fulfilling the promise because it is neither realistic nor even necessary. It is possible for North America to be energy self-sufficient, but that would require both significant conservation and fundamental changes in Mexico where oil production and proven reserves are declining.

In a global market, where transportation costs matter, Mexico and Canada—as well as Venezuela—have an incentive to export to the United States. The issue is not "independence" but "security," and there are several ways to achieve that. The easiest path would be if Canada and Mexico increased production, but Canada's expansion would come at the cost of exacerbating climate change, and Mexico is still restricted by its constitution and by the lack of technology to do deep-sea drilling. The United States is also constrained by environmental considerations, particularly off its coasts and especially after the BP oil spill in 2010.

A second option is an underground oil reserve, but after thirty years of experience, it is clear that it is useful only during a brief national emergency. A third path involves cooperation on noncarbon energy sources from new technologies like solar, wind, ethanol, and biofuels, and old and important sources like hydroelectric power. Canada has been a significant exporter of hydroelectricity for many years, and while the electric grid has had its problems, the system has been upgraded and offers a reliable and efficient alternative to carbons.

A fourth path toward energy security is conservation, but that works best when the price of gasoline and other carbon products can be kept high for a long period. The three governments can achieve this goal by a cap-and-trade system, by raising the price of energy through a carbon tax, by imposing fuel-efficient standards on autos and plants that emit carbon, or by providing incentives for alternative, low carbon fuels. A carbon tax is the most efficient and effective policy, but also the most difficult politically.

At the North American Leaders' Summit in Guadalajara on August 10, 2009, Presidents Obama and Calderon and Prime Minister Harper agreed "to work collaboratively [and] . . . to combat climate change as a region." The United States set up a committee with Canada and one with Mexico to expand research and development on clean energy technologies and to undertake other tasks related to reducing the use of carbon, but the amount of funds devoted to this were limited. The Summit declaration hinted that the three would begin to work together, but it also suggested that each country would develop its own policy.[31]

The three nations of North America are at a crossroads of deciding whether to expand and integrate their energy sectors, conserve energy use, or do some combination. They must also decide whether they will proceed alone or together, or on a bilateral basis, or as part of a North American strategy. There is a North American energy market, but it is impeded by restrictions, weak national energy policies, and a lack of imagination.

While many scholars point to Mexico's sensitivity to foreign investment in the oil industry as the main "problem," all three countries have constraints, and there is no magic or easy formula to relax these constraints. If conservation succeeds, or there is a breakthrough in electric automobiles or renewable fuels, there would be less of a need to increase production of fossil fuels. But whenever petroleum prices rise, the public clamors for more production. Under those circumstances, and as the debate on energy in Mexico proceeds, it is not inconceivable to imagine a three-sided discussion on how to relax the constraints for production in all three countries while at the same time trying to reduce greenhouse gas emissions and investing in new energy technologies.

To facilitate these discussions and to undertake additional work on climate change, North America is fortunate to have one trilateral institution that has already undertaken good research and work, the North American Commission for Environmental Cooperation (CEC). The three governments should instruct the CEC to serve as a clearinghouse for monitoring, reporting, and verifying climate-change related data. To do that well, all three governments would need to standardize definitions of renewable energy and coordinate policies as they relate to cap-and-trade. They should also seek to harmonize emissions standards.[32]

The environmental issues of concern to North America extend considerably beyond the problem of climate change, but while civil society groups are working on these issues, including pollution and migratory and endangered species, the three governments have dropped the ball. As just one example, NAFTA required that the governments negotiate a Transboundary Environmental Impact Assessment Agreement within one year, but in 2010, they still had not completed it. The three governments ought to complete those negotiations and give the CEC authority to enforce violations of the side agreement. Some have proposed the use of trade sanctions to enforce standards, but monetary fines would be a better means of enforcement.

3. LABOR CONDITIONS

Critics of NAFTA argued that large corporations were the principal beneficiaries, and the costs of integration were borne by workers. It is true that jobs in manufacturing in the United States and to a lesser degree in Canada have been lost, particularly since 2001, and that wages of unskilled workers in the United States declined since the mid-1990s. Most economists attribute the loss in manufacturing to a restructuring of the economy and the increasing importance of technology, which made U.S. firms more productive even as the number of workers declined. The side agreement to NAFTA on labor negotiated by the Clinton administration did not help because it was more symbolic than substantive. It simply called on each government to enforce its own laws. During the presidential campaign, Obama promised to upgrade labor standards in the agreement, but since his inauguration, trade officials have talked about doing this outside the agreement, which is a better idea.[33]

All three governments have rigorous labor laws that adhere to the core labor provisions of the International Labor Organization (ILO), though two ironies are concealed within this pledge. First, the United States alone of the three has not ratified the eight core ILO conventions, though U.S. laws mandate the same standards.[34] Secondly, the World Bank has criticized Mexico's labor laws not for their low standards, but because they are too restrictive, making it hard for employers to hire and fire. The rigidity of the labor laws has the unintended consequence of encouraging small businesses to remain outside the formal economy so employees lack protection, and the firms avoid taxes. The Mexican government has tried to make its labor laws more flexible, but its Congress has resisted.

So what is to be done? The United States could negotiate a labor agreement with the other two governments, or they could seek a social charter that would identify the rights of workers in each country, set standards for all of North America, and adopt a plan of action for achieving those rights.[35] Such an agreement could improve the existing side agreement by allowing workers whose rights have been violated to bring a case against their employer or government using one of the dispute-settlement mechanisms. Workers who win would be compensated. The North American Commission for Labor Cooperation, which has been quite weak, could be strengthened to investigate allegations and research ways to reduce disparities in income and labor conditions.

There are many policies that could have a far more positive effect on the lives and standard of living of workers. These include national health insurance, a more progressive tax code, better job training, and enhanced adjustment assistance for those firms and workers adversely affected by trade. These policies could be national or continental. Canada has a more comprehensive safety net than the United States, but the three governments could agree to a minimum standard.

4. EDUCATION

Proximity has not generated curiosity. Canadians, Mexicans, and Americans feel they know each other so well that few have bothered to really study the other. Students in Mexico and Canada learn how different they are from Americans and each other, and Americans rarely learn anything about their neighbors. In an age when students are venturing farther afield for a semester or their entire undergraduate or graduate education, few students from the three countries study in the other two countries. Although Canada and Mexico are the first and second largest markets for U.S. goods, Canada ranks fifth and Mexico seventh in sending its students to the United States—much fewer than from China, India, Taiwan, and South Korea. About one thousand Mexicans study in Canada, and Americans study much less at universities in their two neighbors than in Europe or Asia.

What should be done? Textbooks would be a good place to start. Civics or history textbooks in all three countries should include a section on North

America and on the other two countries. To appreciate each other's countries, the three governments need to promote exchanges, research, and studies on North America. The governments should support the Consortium for North American Higher Education Collaboration (CONAHEC), directed by Francisco Marmolejo of the University of Arizona, and they should re-shape the Fund for the Improvement of Post-Secondary Education (FIPSE) to provide scholarships to study for a semester abroad in the other North American countries. That should be linked to a "language immersion" program to allow students to learn at least two and preferably all three of North America's official languages. There are other structural impediments to exchanges including requirements for university entrance, the annual schedule, and course credits, but the Europeans have resolved more difficult problems to create the Erasmus program, which facilitates student exchanges, and North Americans could as well. In addition, universities and the governments should promote North American music festivals, film and documentary awards, and sports events and competitions.[36]

The European Union spends, on average, about $10 million each year to finance EU Study Centers in universities in all three countries. In contrast, the three countries of North America spend nothing to support Centers for North American Studies. A small annual grant of about $5 million for 10–20 universities could be used to promote national competitions and thereby raise awareness of the region's importance. These grants could promote course preparation, lectures, conferences, research, and student and faculty exchanges. The Centers could function as hubs for a wider network to undertake research on continental challenges and inspire students to appreciate their neighbors. Education should be the foundation of building a North American Community.

➤ The Institutional Black Hole

Europe may have been mistaken in creating too many supranational institutions, but North America made the opposite mistake: it created almost no credible institutions. That is one of the reasons why the challenges addressed in this book have been handled so poorly. A shared vision is essential to guide the three countries to give priority to their community over particular interests, but unless the three governments organize themselves differently, empower existing North American organizations, and create new, lean and effective institutions, then the region is unlikely to make progress. Good institutions should help the leaders make the tough political decisions, persuade their legislatures and the public of the benefits of North America cooperation, and make sure that decisions are implemented and agreements are enforced.

The need for North American institutions is particularly acute because the agenda and the actors are as wide as the continent, and they are expanding. The debate on health care in the United States raised a question as to whether new U.S. hospitals built in Mexico can be certified as Medicare institutions. The expansion of trade in hazardous wastes among the three countries poses problems that none of the three countries are addressing.[37] The actors include a staggering number of local, state, and federal agencies, private and nongovernmental groups, and academic institutions. When the border governors from the southwest of the United States and the north of Mexico meet, as they do annually, they discuss many of the same issues as the presidents or the three legislatures, but there are no coordinating mechanisms to make sure that decisions are moved forward rather than sideways or in a circle.

Many institutional initiatives are needed to translate the vision into policies and a specific blueprint for cooperation. The three leaders could begin by reaching an agreement to hold annual summits. They should encourage the establishment of a North American Advisory Council or a Commission to prepare options for the summits, monitor decisions, and educate the three publics. A North American Inter-Parliamentary Committee is needed to keep the three legislatures deeply involved in the issues. In addition, they need to establish a Permanent Tribunal on Trade and Investment; a North American Competition Commission to protect consumers and dismantle cartels; and a North American Regulatory Commission to connect functional agencies and facilitate the convergence of regulations to uniform and higher standards.

1. SUMMITS

Since NAFTA, the three leaders began meeting from time to time as a group, and after the Waco Summit in March 2005 to establish the Security and Prosperity Partnership (SPP), the three leaders have met annually. At the North American Leaders Summit in Guadalajara in August 2009, President Obama promised to attend the next meeting in Canada, but there was no formal agreement to maintain the Summit on a routine, annual basis, and Canada decided not to host it in 2010. President Obama complained that he had to attend so many multilateral summit meetings—G-8, G-20, NATO, APEC, the Americas, and North America—that he had little time for serious work. His frustration was understandable.

The Summits follow an unproductive pattern whereby bureaucrats nego-tiate the fine points of a "Declaration" in which the details camouflage its vacuousness. Then, bureaucrats justify the Summits as necessary to keep the heads of state engaged and pushing the bureaucracies, but Obama was right. A cursory comparison of the Declaration at the North American Summit on August 9–10, 2009, with some of the proposals in this chapter proves the point.[38] That and previous Summits have been more photo-opportunities than substantive discussions.

North American summits are necessary but hardly sufficient to address the many-sided issues that constitute the continental agenda. The Summit should also be an opportunity for civil society to participate, but a North American institution is needed to prepare an agenda, develop options for addressing the items on the agenda, and ensure that all three leaders participate in all of the discussions.

2. NORTH AMERICAN ADVISORY COUNCIL

In the absence of a North American Idea, each government prepares its leader to discuss the dual-bilateral issues on their agenda. To grasp the full North American agenda, it is necessary to reach outside the government to a group of eminent persons and mandate them to prepare an agenda with options. That group could either be called a North American Advisory Council or a Commission. It would stand apart from the three governments but would be close enough to the leaders so that they would take their advice seriously. The Council should be composed of 30–45 people, reflective of civil society in all three countries, including representatives from the border states, businesses, unions, and academe.

However the group is constituted or named, it should be independent and a source of "creative energy," in the words of the Council on Foreign Relations Task Force,[39] pushing the envelope with new ideas, but without obligating the incumbent leaders to accept. The members should be committed to a broader vision of North America but should reflect different perspectives as to how best to achieve the vision.

After getting approval of an agenda from the three countries, the Council should commission papers with specific proposals for each issue. Each govern-ment would prepare its leaders to respond to the agenda. The second task of the Council would be to monitor implementation and help make the case for spe-cific policies to the public. The third task would be to sponsor research among scholars on issues that might be too sensitive for governments to undertake.

The fourth task for the Council would be to connect and nurture the many groups and individuals with a stake in improving relations among the three countries. Many groups in different regions are already engaged, and their voices should be amplified by the Council. In the southwest, The Border Trade Alliance, based in Phoenix, and in Seattle and Vancouver, the Pacific Northwest Economic Region (PNWER) play similarly important roles. Governors also have institutions that permit regular contact. The two most important are the Conference of New England Governors and Eastern Canadian Premiers and the Southwest Governor's Association. Although not supported by the federal governments, there are a number of university-based centers in the United States that not only teach about North America but endeavor to play an active role in the public debate—at Arizona State University, American University in Washington, D.C., Western Washington University, Texas A&M, and the University of Maine in the United States; and Monterrey Tech, ITAM, Universidad de las Americas in Mexico; and Carleton, Toronto, McGill, Alberta, Calgary, and Vancouver in Canada.

Finally, the fifth task is to educate the publics of all three countries to the challenges, the costs, and the benefits of a North American Community.

3. LEGISLATURES

Because so much of the agenda is domestic, the three legislatures need to be fully engaged in the process. The easiest way to do that would be to combine both the U.S.-Mexican Inter-Parliamentary Group and the U.S.-Canadian Inter-Parliamentary Group into a single *North American Parliamentary Group*. This combined group could designate an Executive Committee that could work with the Council and the governments in preparing the agenda and proposals. If the North American Parliamentary Group works well, it could be the decisive institution because ultimately most major initiatives will require Congressional approval. And if Congressional leaders become committed to the North American Idea and develop strong relationships with their counterparts in Canada and Mexico, they could facilitate convergence on a domestic and foreign policy agenda.

A Summit, an Advisory Council, and an Inter-Parliamentary Group— these are the core institutions of a new North America. Some Americans fear or simply dislike the European model, but at base, these and other institutions proposed below are very different from those in Europe. First of all, Europe has a directly elected Parliament whereas the North American Parliamentary Group are legislators elected in each of the three countries. Secondly, Europe has an Executive Branch—a Commission—that implements policies and laws—and all the leaders meet often. The North American Advisory Council has no authority; its job is merely to advise and raise public awareness.

4. STRENGTHENING EXISTING NAFTA INSTITUTIONS

Four existing institutions—the North American Free Trade Commission, the North American Commission for Environmental Cooperation (CEC), the North American Commission for Labor Cooperation, and the North American Development Bank—are in need of steroid injections just to stay awake. Today, the governments do not issue any reports on North America. Even during SPP, the government Web site was pathetically lean, defensive, and usually out-of-date. The first step to strengthen these institutions is to instruct them to publish annual reports summarizing what they have done, analyzing problems in their areas, and proposing recommendations.

The North American Trade Commission is composed of the three trade ministers. They decided at their first meeting to establish a Coordinating Secretariat, but they never implemented that decision.[40] The three governments should implement their original decision and charge the new office with issuing a single report summarizing and analyzing the progress and the problems regarding trade and investment in North America. They should also propose solutions to chronic or recurrent trade problems, e.g., on the pricing of natural resources. The Commission Secretariat could also propose steps to repeal subsidies or dismantle existing restrictions on trade in agriculture.

The North American Commission for Environmental Cooperation should be charged with negotiating a common position on carbon emissions and climate change. It also needs more funding to undertake the kind of research that is needed to understand the state of the environment in North America.

The North American Commission for Labor Cooperation needs to be taken out of the governments and made independent like the CEC. It could then play a role in "shaming" any government or business that is undermining the rights of workers. It could also shame unions if they are not protecting their workers' rights or defending their interests.

The North American Development Bank (NADBank) has funded environmental infrastructure projects near the border (expanding from 100 to 300 kilometers). To make the NADBank more effective, Canada should join and together with the United States and Mexico, they should expand the bank's mandate to include transportation projects, permit it to access domestic capital markets, and strengthen its technical assistance programs for good governance.[41]

5. CREATING NEW NORTH AMERICAN INSTITUTIONS

Permanent Tribunal for Trade and Investment Disputes. NAFTA established four distinct dispute-settlement mechanisms to deal with problems related to investments, trade remedies, finance, and higher-level trade issues. Chapter 11 of NAFTA provides assurances that a firm's investment would not be expropriated without prompt, adequate, and effective compensation. While it was mainly intended to reassure foreign investors in Mexico, it has been used against all three countries and in ways that no one had contemplated. The most controversial cases involved firms protesting new environmental rules that were judged "tantamount to expropriation." In subsequent free-trade agreements with Chile and Central America, the United States revised the wording so as to preclude any effect on environmental or health policies.[42] The three governments should sign a memorandum of agreement that would make NAFTA consistent on this matter with the newer agreements.

Chapter 19 was intended to prevent arbitrary, protectionist use of U.S. trade laws, and although it set a limit of 315 days for completion of panel proceedings, the average length has been nearly twice that, and the United States has been reluctant to accept any rulings against it. The most notorious case involved soft-wood lumber "where the United States stalled cases interminably and Canadians eventually were forced to pay $1 billion to settle legal cases they had won before bi-national panels and in U.S. courts."[43] That $1 billion went to lawyers' fees and nongovernmental organizations connected to the forestry companies and the George W. Bush administration. This has left a very bad taste in the mouths of Canadians.

The current ad hoc dispute-settlement mechanisms rely on temporary panelists that are increasingly likely to have a conflict of interest since many of the panelists have used their past experience to bring cases to the courts. Moreover, it is not possible to establish precedents or build any institutional memory if one uses an ad hoc mechanism. The three North American leaders should therefore establish a Permanent Tribunal for Trade and Investment Disputes and fold the other dispute mechanisms into it. A Permanent Tribunal should prevent the three governments from gaming the system and eroding the region's confidence in NAFTA. The World Trade Organization (WTO) has established such a permanent court, and it is functioning very effectively. It's time to apply it to North America.

North American Competition Commission. As the market expands to all of North America and as firms assemble products together, antitrust enforcement needs to be continental. Each country has its antitrust agency, but the market now suggests we should merge these agencies into a single

North American Competition Commission. There is a second reason for establishing this Commission. One of the remaining protectionist devices used by U.S. firms to resist competition from across the borders is to petition the U.S. Department of Commerce for "countervailing duties" or "anti-dumping" protection. The U.S. firm charges the foreign firm with either receiving government subsidies—thus warranting "countervailing duties"—or selling its product below cost. If the U.S. firm wins its case, then the foreign firm or government is compelled to pay the additional duties, but the procedure is often used as a threat to discourage exports.

Canada sought to eliminate these provisions during the NAFTA negotiations. The United States objected but permitted Canada a second review by the dispute-settlement mechanism. U.S. firms continue to use these remedies. As of October 2004, the United States had filed 351 cases worldwide, but only fifteen were against Canada and eleven were against Mexico.[44] A large firm uses predatory or subsidized pricing to capture a market and then raises prices. Antitrust commissions handle this problem within their borders. As the market extends to all of North America, the antitrust action should be commensurate in scope. A North American Competition Commission would be fairer and more effective in preventing predatory or subsidized pricing than countervailing duty and antidumping provisions.

North American Regulatory Commission. Although an important goal of the Security and Prosperity Partnership was to harmonize regulations, the governments made scant progress. Instead of trying to decide on one regulation at a time, a North American Commission could connect the agencies in all three countries with the same function—e.g., on food safety or environmental quality—and require a single North American standard. Or it could establish a single North American Commission with broad or functional responsibilities to regulate a sector.

➤ The Costs and Benefits of Action and Inaction

North Americans are a practical people. They want to know the costs and benefits of implementing such a strategy. Let us start by summarizing the estimated costs of inaction, of maintaining the status quo, that we developed in chapter 5:

- Annual cost of "rules of origin" procedures: $35.7 billion
- Annual cost of delays and border security restrictions: $27 billion (2.7 percent of trade, 2008)

- Annual cost of drayage (prohibiting trucks): $616 million
- Annual cost of cabotage (only Jones Act on shipping): $656 million
- Annual cost of divergent regulations (2–10 percent of production costs)
- Cost of building the wall on the southern border: $2.1 billion
- Total of above: $66.1 billion

This bill is paid annually by North American consumers and businesses. Most of the $66 billion in taxes are associated with inefficiencies such as rules of origin and excessive administrative restrictions on the border where North Americans do not derive any benefits. One scholar estimated that the distortions due to the "rules of origin" provision may cost the three economies as much as $510 billion, but these were not included in the numbers above because these costs were indirect. The costs of divergent regulations is estimated by the OECD as 2–10 percent of the overall costs of production, but a precise figure is not available, and so it is also not included in the overall costs. In sum, the annual bill of $66 billion each year is a very low estimate.

The annual payment of $1.3 billion for drayage and cabotage and the retaliatory tariffs on $2.4 billion of goods are spent to protect unions and inefficient companies from healthy competition. The administrative costs of approximately $27 billion and the $2.1 billion for the wall are supposed to provide added security. Of course, this represents a token amount of the money that the three governments have devoted to security since 9/11. The United States alone paid more than $1.1 trillion to fight wars in Afghanistan and Iraq.[45] The Department of Homeland Security tripled its annual budget since it was established in 2002—from $17 to $53 billion.[46]

The questions are whether the United States and its neighbors are more secure as a result of the activities identified above. There can be little doubt that some of the added security has been helpful, although a legitimate question can be asked as to whether the $1.1 trillion for the two wars strengthened or weakened the United States. The harder question is whether there was a less expensive way. Lt. General John R. Vines, who was in charge of reviewing the Defense Department's most sensitive programs for dealing with terrorists, acknowledged that "we can't effectively assess whether it is making us more safe." He was referring to the entire intelligence operation that was expanded after 9/11: so far the cost of the expanded intelligence operation has been $75 billion and involves 1,271 government organizations, 1,931 private companies, an estimated 854,000 people with top-secret security clearances, 33 building complexes occupying 17 million square feet, and the publication of 50,000 intelligence reports each year.[47]

There are additional costs to our relationships with our neighbors that are impossible to quantify, but that does not mean that they are inconsequential. As one steps back from 9/11, it seems clear that the United States overreacted and overspent. Given the magnitude of the trauma, this is understandable, but the question remains as to whether the restrictive measures that affect our neighbors provide additional security, and whether there are more effective alternatives that would cost less and provide the same security. The answer is that there are many alternative approaches that would provide as much security at less expense and with fewer impediments to legitimate travel and commerce. These range from a single biometric card for expedited travel to a combined customs operation.

Now, let us look at the costs of the proposals to help build the North American Community. The only new significant cost would be the contribution to the North American Investment Fund. Each year for ten years, Mexico would contribute $10 billion; the United States, $8 billion; and Canada, $2 billion. The U.S. contribution each year would be less than what the United States spent on average each month in Iraq in the years after the invasion in 2003. A contribution of $80 billion to a North American infrastructure project over ten years would amount to .08 percent of the funds obligated to bail out Fannie Mae, Freddie Mac, Bear Stearns, and AIG.

The benefit of the Fund is that it would permit Mexico to grow on a sustainable basis at twice the rate of the United States and Canada, providing its people a sense that their country has a future, and they don't need to leave. The contributions by the United States and Canada could also be used as leverage by the Mexican president to persuade his Congress to accept needed reforms. Growth would translate into significant additional imports from the United States, as Mexico already purchases more per capita of U.S. exports than any other country in the world except Canada. In 2010, Mexico recovered from the recession. The United Nations estimated that Mexico would grow by 5.3 percent in 2010 and increase its imports by $66 billion, two-thirds of which would come from the United States. That would add $44 billion to the $129 billion of U.S. merchandise exports to Mexico in 2009—a total of $173 billion. In comparison, in 2009, total U.S. exports to India amounted to $16 billion and to China $70 billion.[48] While the United States and Canada gaze at Asia, it turns out that the greatest opportunities for growing their economies—especially through exports—are at their doorstep.

The most enduring benefit of the Fund would be the construction of a path for Mexico to reach the first world. On its journey, a North American Community could emerge. The other costs of the strategy—creating new institutions, research centers, and scholarships—are minimal. From a strict cost-benefit analysis, the plans to develop North America would yield substantial economic and political benefits to all three countries while reducing costs to travel, trade, and transit.

➤ "With a shift of the mind's eye"

In a devastating critique of the state of North America after fifteen years of NAFTA, Stephen Clarkson, a professor at the University of Toronto, found that the three governments had failed to "address the social, environmental, and migratory problems generated by North American integration. The continental leaders' rhetorical affirmation of their commitment to the spirit of regional economic integration has been continually contradicted by the United States' propensity to take unilateral and protectionist action. Mexico's call for strengthening NAFTA's institutions along EU lines fell on deaf ears in both Washington and Ottawa." As a result, Clarkson concluded that North America is "economically precarious, politically unstable, and institutionally impotent."[49]

Clarkson is speaking of the new agenda that emerged as a result of NAFTA and of the failure of the three governments to address that agenda. This book confirms his conclusion, but NAFTA was not designed to address that agenda, and since then, only one leader—Vicente Fox of Mexico—of the three governments has shown any interest in it. Europe has spent decades searching for ways to strengthen their ties and deepen integration. North America's leaders have not yet decided where they want to go.

Here is the first question they need to answer: Should the three governments move from a beggar-thy-neighbor policy to an assist-your-neighbor approach in which all three seek to raise the living standards of all North Americans? If they choose the latter option, then they have a full menu of options to make the North American market work, to assure public and continental security, to address the social and environmental challenge, and to develop plans and projects in transportation, infrastructure, and education. Last, but hardly least, they need to strengthen existing institutions and establish some new ones to guide the region toward the next stage of integration.

If the leaders explain to the people how our individual countries will grow as we integrate a North American Community, then many things become possible. It needs to begin, as Albert Einstein noted, "with a shift of the mind's eye."

But we don't need to wait for the leaders. There is a growing segment of civil society at all levels who feel attached to a North American Idea. A network is ready to be connected and participate in defining a North American Community, which could begin to build from the bottom-up.

Amos Oz, one of Israel's greatest writers, recalled how a few people planted the seed for a tree of peace and watched it grow: "When my friends and I started advocating a two-state solution [Israel and Palestine] in 1967, there were so very few of us that we could conduct our national assembly inside a public telephone booth." Today, a majority of the public in both Israel and Palestine approve the idea.[50]

North America is still a new idea. Few people have thought much about it, and some are frightened that it might diminish their own nation. The opposite is more likely. If the three countries can view themselves as part of a region in which each has a challenge that requires cooperation to succeed, then North America becomes larger than the sum of its parts.

When will this occur? Some ideas take a long time from conception to realization. Amoz Oz's idea of a two-state solution to the Middle East conflict is a good example, and there are many more. William Wilberforce, a member of the British Parliament, undertook his campaign to abolish slavery in 1787. It took the British Empire forty-six years to implement Wilberforce's recommendation, and another three decades and a civil war before the United States followed. In 1848, a movement to grant women the right to vote was inaugurated in Seneca Falls, New York. It took 72 years before the movement achieved its goal. The idea of social security was first conceived in Germany in 1889. It spread to other European nations, but the United States only adopted it in 1935 during the Great Depression.

The end of slavery, the women's right to vote, and social security—these ideas seem self-evident today, but it took a long time for people to see what is so obvious with hindsight. The "North American Idea"—the construction of a new relationship among the three countries—is today a darkened room. Before too long, however, some leader will find the light switch and turn it on. After that, the North American Idea will seem as logical and obvious as those older ideas.

I can recall a visit to Spain in the mid-1990s where I encountered a Mexican and felt the kind of camaraderie that I had previously sensed decades before when I met other Americans in Europe. Within a half hour, we noticed that we were looking at Spain in similar ways, and that being from the United States and Mexico, we had much more in common than being from Mexico and Spain. That was a revelation to both of us.

And when I meet Canadians in third countries, I am reminded of a feeling when I met someone from a rival high school when traveling in another state. The differences that seem so important in cheering for different sides during a football game melt away as you leave your hometown, and they are replaced by the shared experience of being at the same game. The future of North America will begin, Ronald Reagan once said, when we stop "thinking of our nearest neighbors as foreigners."

Appendix: Additional Tables and Figures on North America

Table 1: Indicators for North America, EU, and East Asia: 1990–2008

- There are three increasingly integrated regions in the world: the European Union, North America, and East Asia. Together, they account for nearly 80 percent of the world's gross product.
- Of the three regions, North America is the most asymmetric, with one member—the United States—accounting for 85 percent of the GDP and 70 percent of the total trade.

Group or Country	Population (millions)		Land Area (millions of sq.km.)	GDP (billions)		GDP per capita		Total trade (billions)	
	1990	2008	2008	1990	2008	1990	2008	1990	2008
North America	361	443	20.2	$6,603	$16,958	---	---	$ 1,539,655	$ 4,941,980
U.S.	250	304 (69%)	9.2 (46%)	$ 5,757	$1 4,369 (85%)	$ 23,064	$ 47,210	$ 1,141,409	$ 3,456,929 (70%)
Canada	28	33 (7%)	9.1 (45%)	$ 583	$ 1,499 (9%)	$ 20,968	$ 45,003	$ 296,702	$ 875,482 (18%)
Mexico	83	106 (24%)	1.9 (9%)	$ 263	$ 1,090 (6%)	$ 3,157	$ 10,249	$ 101,544	$ 609,569 (12%)
European Union	343	491	4.3	$ 5,940	$18,850	---	---	$ 3,066,830	$ 12,179,900
Germany	79	82 (17%)	0.3 (7%)	$ 1,714	$ 3,656 (19%)	$ 21,584	$ 44,525	$ 776,786	$ 2,631,239 (22%)
U.K.	57	61 (12%)	0.2 (5%)	$ 1,013	$ 2,663 (14%)	$ 17,688	$ 43,361	$ 408,149	$ 1,092,642 (9%)
East Asia	1,301	1,502	9.8	$ 3,637	$10,351	---	---	$ 720,566	$ 4,965,123
China	1,135	1,325 (88%)	9.3 (95%)	$ 357	$ 4,533 (44%)	$ 314	$ 3,422	$ 71,952	$ 2,563,260 (52%)
Japan	124	128 (9%)	0.4 (4%)	$ 3,018	$ 4,887 (47%)	$ 24,432	$ 38,268	$ 648,614	$ 1,544,581 (31%)
South Korea	43	49 (3%)	0.1 (1%)	$ 264	$ 931 (9%)	$ 6,153	$ 19,162	$ 154,065	$ 857,282 (17%)

Note: Italicized percentages represent percent of regional total for 2008. EU figures represent the union's expansion from 12 to 27 members and the reunification of Germany. All dollar figures are in U.S. current dollars.
Source: Population, land area, GDP, GDPpc from World Bank DataBank. 2011 EU GDP and Land Area from CIA *World Factbook*. All trade data is from World Trade Organization, Statistics Database, "Total Merchandise Trade."

Table 2: U.S. Exports of Goods and Services to North America, 1988–2010

- U.S. exports of goods and services to Canada and Mexico have quadrupled from $111 billion in 1988, the start of the U.S.-Canadian Free Trade Agreement, to $485 billion in 2010.
- U.S. exports of services to North America have averaged about 14 percent of total exports with fluctuations. The total would increase significantly by deeper integration.

Year	Exports of Goods and Services to Canada	Service exports to Canada	Exports of Goods and Services to Mexico	Service exports to Mexico	Goods and Service Exports to North America	Service Exports to North America	Services as % of Total U.S. Exports to NA
1988	$ 85,215	$ 10,925	$ 25,531	$ 4,948	$ 110,746	$ 15,873	14.33%
1989	$ 93,415	$ 13,527	$ 31,302	$ 6,638	$ 124,717	$ 20,165	16.17%
1990	$ 99,260	$ 15,901	$ 36,721	$ 8,629	$ 135,981	$ 24,530	18.04%
1991	$ 103,604	$ 17,925	$ 42,804	$ 9,700	$ 146,408	$ 27,625	18.87%
1992	$ 108,626	$ 17,522	$ 50,970	$ 10,561	$ 159,596	$ 28,083	17.60%
1993	$ 118,049	$ 17,347	$ 51,998	$ 10,514	$ 170,047	$ 27,861	16.38%
1994	$ 131,943	$ 17,292	$ 62,046	$ 11,411	$ 193,989	$ 28,703	14.80%
1995	$ 145,440	$ 18,052	$ 54,955	$ 8,783	$ 200,395	$ 26,835	13.39%
1996	$ 153,927	$ 19,640	$ 66,175	$ 9,460	$ 220,102	$ 29,100	13.22%
1997	$ 172,499	$ 20,601	$ 82,094	$ 10,876	$ 254,593	$ 31,477	12.36%
1998	$ 176,306	$ 19,572	$ 90,310	$ 11,687	$ 266,616	$ 31,259	11.72%
1999	$ 189,493	$ 22,780	$ 99,626	$ 12,868	$ 289,119	$ 35,648	12.33%
2000	$ 203,612	$ 24,735	$ 125,534	$ 14,362	$ 329,146	$ 39,097	11.88%
2001	$ 187,775	$ 24,516	$ 116,372	$ 15,191	$ 304,147	$ 39,707	13.06%
2002	$ 185,986	$ 25,071	$ 113,445	$ 16,140	$ 299,431	$ 41,211	13.76%
2003	$ 197,517	$ 27,588	$ 113,529	$ 16,281	$ 311,046	$ 43,869	14.10%
2004	$ 219,786	$ 29,804	$ 128,533	$ 17,927	$ 348,319	$ 47,731	13.70%
2005	$ 245,124	$ 32,932	$ 140,559	$ 20,400	$ 385,683	$ 53,332	13.83%
2006	$ 269,004	$ 38,021	$ 155,387	$ 21,729	$ 424,391	$ 59,750	14.08%
2007	$ 293,110	$ 43,161	$ 159,220	$ 23,408	$ 452,330	$ 66,569	14.72%
2008	$ 308,230	$ 46,359	$ 175,240	$ 24,093	$ 483,470	$ 70,452	14.57%
2009	$ 248,228	$ 42,597	$ 150,619	$ 21,784	$ 398,847	$ 64,381	16.14%
2010	$ 299,046	$ 49,184	$ 186,288	$ 23,042	$ 485,334	$ 72,226	14.88%

In millions of current U.S. dollars
Source: Bureau of Economic Analysis, U.S. International Transactions Account Data, accessed in 2011.

Table 3: U.S. Imports of Goods and Services from North America, 1988–2010

- U.S. imports of goods and services from Mexico and Canada also rose more than four times since 1988.
- U.S. imports of services from Canada are about 40 percent higher than from Mexico.

Year	G&S Imports from Canada	Service imports from Canada	G&S Imports from Mexico	Service imports from Mexico	G&S imports from North America	Service Imports from North America	Services as % of Total U.S. Imports from NA
1988	$93,366	$8,754	$28,461	$5,149	$121,827	$13,903	11.4%
1989	$98,982	$9,038	$33,222	$6,094	$132,204	$15,132	11.4%
1990	$102,743	$9,598	$37,345	$6,838	$140,088	$16,436	11.7%
1991	$103,177	$10,129	$38,667	$7,175	$141,844	$17,304	12.2%
1992	$109,717	$8,819	$43,063	$7,453	$152,780	$16,272	10.7%
1993	$122,457	$9,377	$48,031	$7,600	$170,488	$16,977	10.0%
1994	$141,241	$10,090	$58,124	$8,073	$199,365	$18,163	9.1%
1995	$158,114	$11,198	$70,955	$8,161	$229,069	$19,359	8.5%
1996	$171,109	$12,564	$84,261	$9,129	$255,370	$21,693	8.5%
1997	$184,176	$13,950	$96,741	$10,051	$280,917	$24,001	8.5%
1998	$191,466	$15,294	$105,467	$10,040	$296,933	$25,334	8.5%
1999	$217,722	$16,510	$120,187	$9,573	$337,909	$26,083	7.7%
2000	$251,648	$18,138	$147,931	$10,959	$399,579	$29,097	7.3%
2001	$236,333	$17,689	$143,155	$10,583	$379,488	$28,272	7.5%
2002	$229,939	$18,197	$147,963	$11,830	$377,902	$30,027	7.9%
2003	$244,392	$19,762	$152,072	$12,322	$396,464	$32,084	8.1%
2004	$280,780	$21,054	$172,022	$13,692	$452,802	$34,746	7.7%
2005	$316,887	$22,422	$187,671	$14,185	$504,558	$36,607	7.3%
2006	$330,009	$23,573	$216,540	$14,543	$546,549	$38,116	7.0%
2007	$345,627	$25,367	$229,994	$15,146	$575,621	$40,513	7.0%
2008	$368,133	$25,469	$235,772	$15,436	$603,905	$40,905	6.8%
2009	$250,643	$22,740	$192,932	$13,721	$443,575	$36,461	8.2%
2010	$306,077	$25,336	$246,760	$13,920	$552,837	$39,256	7.10%

In millions of current U.S. dollars
Source: Bureau of Economic Analysis, U.S. International Transactions Account Data, accessed in 2011.

Table 4: U.S. Total Trade of Goods and Services with North America, 1988–2010

- U.S. total trade (exports plus imports of goods and services) with both Canada and Mexico increased from $233 billion in 1988 to $1 trillion in 2010.
- U.S. trade in services to North America climbed from $30 billion in 1988 to $111 billion in 2010, but as a percentage of total trade in North America, it fluctuated between 10 and 15 percent.

Year	G&S Trade Canada	G&S Trade with Mexico	G&S Trade with North America	Service Trade with North America	Services as % of Total U.S. Trade with NA
1988	$178,581	$53,992	$232,573	$29,776	12.8%
1989	$192,397	$64,524	$256,921	$35,297	13.7%
1990	$202,003	$74,066	$276,069	$40,966	14.8%
1991	$206,781	$81,471	$288,252	$44,929	15.6%
1992	$218,343	$94,033	$312,376	$44,355	14.2%
1993	$240,506	$100,029	$340,535	$44,838	13.2%
1994	$273,184	$120,170	$393,354	$46,866	11.9%
1995	$303,554	$125,910	$429,464	$46,194	10.8%
1996	$325,036	$150,436	$475,472	$50,793	10.7%
1997	$356,675	$178,835	$535,510	$55,478	10.4%
1998	$367,772	$195,777	$563,549	$56,593	10.0%
1999	$407,215	$219,813	$627,028	$61,731	9.8%
2000	$455,260	$273,465	$728,725	$68,194	9.4%
2001	$424,108	$259,527	$683,635	$67,979	9.9%
2002	$415,925	$261,408	$677,333	$71,238	10.5%
2003	$441,909	$265,601	$707,510	$75,953	10.7%
2004	$500,566	$300,555	$801,121	$82,477	10.3%
2005	$562,011	$328,230	$890,241	$89,939	10.1%
2006	$599,013	$371,927	$970,940	$97,866	10.1%
2007	$638,737	$389,214	$1,027,951	$107,082	10.4%
2008	$676,363	$411,012	$1,087,375	$111,357	10.2%
2009	$498,871	$343,551	$842,422	$100,842	12.0%
2010	$605,123	$433,048	$1,038, 171	$111,482	10.74%

In millions of current U.S. dollars
Source: Bureau of Economic Analysis, U.S. International Transactions Account Data, accessed in 2011.

Table 5: U.S. Merchandise Trade with North America as a Percentage of Total Trade, 1990–2010

- As a percentage of its exports to the world, U.S. exports to North America climbed from 28 percent in 1990 to 37 percent in 2000 and then fell to 32 percent in 2010. A similar pattern is evident for U.S. total trade with its North American partners.
- This is the main indicator of integration, and it demonstrates the growth of the North American market after NAFTA and then the decline as a result of 9/11 border restrictions and failure by North American leaders to deepen the North American market.

Year	Total US exports to Canada and Mexico	Total US exports to World	US exports to NA as % of US exports	Total US imports from Canada and Mexico	US imports from NA as % of US imports	Total US trade with North America	US-NA trade as % of Global US trade
1990	$111,342	$392,976	28.33%	$121,544	24.54%	$232,886	26.22%
1991	$118,427	$421,730	28.08%	$122,194	25.08%	$240,621	26.48%
1992	$131,186	$448,164	29.27%	$133,841	25.13%	$265,028	27.02%
1993	$142,025	$465,091	30.54%	$151,134	26.03%	$293,159	28.03%
1994	$165,282	$512,626	32.24%	$177,900	26.82%	$343,182	29.19%
1995	$173,518	$584,742	29.67%	$206,470	27.77%	$379,989	28.61%
1996	$191,002	$625,075	30.56%	$230,190	28.94%	$421,192	29.65%
1997	$223,155	$689,182	32.38%	$253,172	29.11%	$476,327	30.56%
1998	$235,376	$682,138	34.51%	$267,885	29.38%	$503,261	31.57%
1999	$253,509	$695,797	36.43%	$308,432	30.10%	$561,941	32.66%
2000	$290,290	$781,918	37.13%	$366,765	30.11%	$657,055	32.85%
2001	$264,721	$729,100	36.31%	$347,606	30.47%	$612,326	32.74%
2002	$258,393	$693,103	37.28%	$343,703	29.59%	$602,096	32.47%
2003	$267,335	$724,771	36.89%	$359,655	28.61%	$626,990	31.64%
2004	$300,611	$814,875	36.89%	$412,261	28.05%	$712,873	31.20%
2005	$332,146	$901,082	36.86%	$460,493	27.52%	$792,639	30.79%
2006	$364,378	$1,025,967	35.52%	$500,691	27.01%	$865,069	30.04%
2007	$384,806	$1,148,199	33.51%	$527,771	26.97%	$912,577	29.39%
2008	$412,370	$1,287,442	32.03%	$555,433	26.40%	$967,803	28.54%
2009	$333,726	$1,056,932	31.57%	$401,448	25.77%	$735,174	28.12%
2010	$411,523	$1,277,503	32.21%	$506,142	26.47%	$917,665	28.77%

In millions of current U.S. dollars
Source: TradeStats Express, U.S. Census Bureau, accessed in 2011.

Table 6: Canadian Merchandise Trade, 1990–2009

- The largest trading relationship between two countries in the world is between the U.S. and Canada. Canada's trade dependence on the U.S. increased from 70 percent of its total trade in 1990 to 79 percent in 2000, but it has since declined to 63 percent in 2010.
- Canada's trade with Mexico expanded 13 times from 1990–2010. By 2009, Canada's third largest source of imports was from Mexico, exceeded only by the U.S. and China, and Mexico was its fifth largest market.

Year	Exports to US	Exports to Mexico	Imports from Mexico	Total Trade w Mexico	Trade w US as % of global	Trade w/ Mexico as % of global
1990	$91,372	$562	$1,499	$2,061	69.5%	0.8%
1991	$91,064	$509	$2,252	$2,760	69.9%	1.1%
1992	$98,630	$673	$2,295	$2,969	71.8%	1.1%
1993	$111,216	$640	$2,876	$3,516	74.5%	1.2%
1994	$128,406	$793	$3,313	$4,106	75.8%	1.3%
1995	$144,370	$846	$3,899	$4,745	75.3%	1.3%
1996	$155,893	$923	$4,426	$5,349	77.0%	1.4%
1997	$167,234	$923	$5,072	$5,994	76.8%	1.4%
1998	$173,256	$989	$5,180	$6,169	78.5%	1.5%
1999	$198,711	$1,085	$6,418	$7,503	79.7%	1.6%
2000	$230,838	$1,370	$8,120	$9,490	78.6%	1.8%
2001	$216,268	$1,779	$7,829	$9,608	77.9%	2.0%
2002	$209,088	$1,541	$8,115	$9,656	77.1%	2.0%
2003	$221,595	$1,578	$8,698	$10,276	75.6%	2.0%
2004	$256,360	$2,379	$10,322	$12,701	74.8%	2.1%
2005	$290,384	$2,778	$12,047	$14,825	73.6%	2.2%
2006	$302,438	$3,858	$14,125	$17,983	71.3%	2.4%
2007	$317,057	$4,616	$15,981	$20,597	69.8%	2.5%
2008	$339,491	$5,485	$16,797	$22,282	68.6%	2.5%
2009	$226,248	$4,208	$14,408	$18,616	66.5%	2.9%
2010	$289,976	$4,863	$21,464	$26,327	62.56%	3.47%

In millions of current U.S. dollars

Sources: Industry Canada, Trade Stats Express, U.S. Census Bureau, accessed in 2011.

Table 7: Mexican Merchandise Trade, 1990–2009

- Mexico's trade dependence on the U.S. also rose from 70 percent of its total trade in 1990 to 72 percent in 2000, but it since declined to 65 percent in 2009.
- Canada has become the second largest market for Mexican exports. Its trade with Canada as a percentage of its global trade nearly doubled from 2.4 percent in 1990 to 4 percent in 2009—still low, but rising rapidly.

Year	Exports to US	Imports from U.S.	Trade w/US as % of global	Trade w/Canada as % of global*
1990	$30.2	$28.4	69.5%	2.4%
1991	$31.1	$33.3	68.2%	2.9%
1992	$35.2	$40.6	68.7%	2.7%
1993	$39.9	$41.6	68.2%	2.9%
1994	$49.5	$50.8	70.2%	2.9%
1995	$62.1	$46.3	70.4%	3.1%
1996	$74.3	$56.8	69.7%	2.8%
1997	$85.9	$71.4	70.4%	2.7%
1998	$94.6	$78.8	70.3%	2.5%
1999	$109.7	$86.9	69.6%	2.7%
2000	$135.9	$111.3	71.5%	2.7%
2001	$131.3	$101.3	70.2%	2.9%
2002	$134.6	$97.5	69.5%	2.9%
2003	$138.1	$97.4	69.2%	3.0%
2004	$155.9	$110.7	68.3%	3.2%
2005	$170.1	$120.2	65.6%	3.3%
2006	$198.3	$133.7	64.7%	3.5%
2007	$210.7	$135.9	61.7%	3.6%
2008	$215.9	$151.2	60.2%	3.6%
2009	$176.5	$129.0	64.8%	4.0%

In millions of current U.S. dollars

*Canada was the second largest market for Mexican exports and the sixth largest origin of imports in 2008. In 1992, Canada was the fourth largest export market and sixth largest source of imports, according to "Anuario Estadístico de los Estados Unidos Mexicanos" published by INEGI, 2009 and 1993.

Source: Trade Stats Express, U.S. Census Bureau; Industry Canada; World Trade Organization.

Table 8: Intra-North American Merchandise Trade, 1990–2009

- The size and growth of trade among the three countries of North America has been staggering—from $468 billion in 1990 to nearly $2 trillion in 2008.
- While North America's intraregional trade as a percent of its global trade peaked in 2000 at 57 percent, and then declined to 50 percent in 2008, the European Union continued to increase from 62 percent in 2000 to 67 percent in 2008, a reflection of the EU's continued commitment to deepen its integration and the indecisiveness of North America.

Year	Intra-NA exports	Total intra-North America trade	Intra-NA exports as % of total NA exports	Intra-NA imports as % of total NA imports	NA intraregional trade as % of global trade	EU intraregional trade as % of global trade
1990	$234,947	$467,833	41.9%	35.49%	43%	65%
1991	$243,381	$484,002	41.1%	36.67%		
1992	$267,996	$533,024	42.6%	36.91%		
1993	$296,675	$589,834	44.8%	37.69%		
1994	$347,288	$690,470	47.0%	38.57%	48%	63%
1995	$384,733	$764,722	44.9%	39.00%		
1996	$426,541	$847,732	46.2%	40.15%		
1997	$482,321	$958,648	47.6%	40.75%		
1998	$509,430	$1,012,691	50.2%	40.85%		
1999	$569,444	$1,131,384	53.2%	40.94%		
2000	$666,544	$1,323,599	54.4%	40.59%	57%	62%
2001	$621,934	$1,234,261	54.2%	40.35%	57%	62%
2002	$611,752	$1,213,849	55.3%	39.17%	57%	62%
2003	$637,266	$1,264,256	54.8%	38.00%	57%	62%
2004	$725,573	$1,438,446	55.0%	37.17%	56%	68%
2005	$807,464	$1,600,103	54.7%	36.31%	56%	67%
2006	$883,052	$1,748,120	53.1%	35.66%	54%	68%
2007	$933,174	$1,845,751	50.7%	35.38%	51%	68%
2008	$990,085	$1,957,888	48.6%	34.85%	50%	67%
2009	$735,174	$1,492,047	45.9%	34.52%		

In millions of current U.S. dollars

Sources: Trade Stats Express, U.S. Census Bureau; World Trade Organization, Selected Regional Trade Agreements; Industry Canada.

Table 9: North American Auto Trade, 1990–2009

- The production and trade in cars among the three countries of North America has been critical to the U.S. auto industry, and auto trade has been the first and most important platform for integrating the three economies. For the U.S., about half of its trade in autos in the world has been with its neighbors, and its exports have exceeded its imports.
- The relative importance of auto trade within North America as a percentage of its total trade in the region has declined even while the value has increased. This is a reflection of the decline of the auto industry and increased diversification of trade.

	U.S. Exports		U.S. Imports		Auto as Percentage of:				
	U.S. auto exports to NA	Total US auto exports	US Auto Imports from NA	Total US auto imports	U.S.-NA Auto Trade as % of Total U.S. Auto Trade	Auto as % of total imports from NA	Auto as % of total exports to NA	US auto exports to NA as % of total auto exports	US auto imports from NA as % of total auto imports
1990	$21,319	$32,254	$29,928	$73,907	48.3%	24.6%	19.1%	66.1%	40.5%
1991	$21,706	$35,113	$30,001	$71,879	48.3%	24.6%	18.3%	61.8%	41.7%
1992	$23,047	$40,362	$33,316	$76,789	48.1%	24.9%	17.6%	57.1%	43.4%
1993	$26,189	$43,485	$39,371	$84,718	51.1%	26.1%	18.4%	60.2%	46.5%
1994	$30,761	$49,379	$44,844	$96,668	51.8%	25.2%	18.6%	62.3%	46.4%
1995	$31,304	$53,110	$50,275	$101,573	52.7%	24.3%	18.0%	58.9%	49.5%
1996	$33,282	$56,179	$54,319	$104,412	54.5%	23.6%	17.4%	59.2%	52.0%
1997	$39,476	$60,923	$58,660	$114,094	56.1%	23.2%	17.7%	64.8%	51.4%
1998	$39,657	$59,295	$61,484	$122,194	55.7%	23.0%	16.8%	66.9%	50.3%
1999	$42,818	$59,029	$76,215	$147,851	57.5%	24.7%	16.9%	72.5%	51.5%
2000	$45,863	$62,500	$82,062	$163,701	56.6%	22.4%	15.8%	73.4%	50.1%
2001	$41,658	$59,132	$76,984	$159,333	54.3%	22.1%	15.7%	70.4%	48.3%
2002	$45,244	$62,764	$78,723	$170,425	53.2%	22.9%	17.5%	72.1%	46.2%
2003	$46,182	$65,567	$78,216	$175,200	51.7%	21.7%	17.3%	70.4%	44.6%
2004	$50,436	$73,918	$85,068	$191,138	51.1%	20.6%	16.8%	68.2%	44.5%
2005	$54,470	$83,687	$88,400	$199,662	50.4%	19.2%	16.4%	65.1%	44.3%
2006	$58,566	$92,349	$94,571	$215,615	49.7%	18.9%	16.1%	63.4%	43.9%
2007	$63,506	$107,213	$94,243	$214,267	49.1%	17.9%	16.5%	59.2%	44.0%
2008	$59,490	$111,698	$79,696	$194,990	45.4%	14.3%	14.4%	53.3%	40.9%
2009	$41,353	$73,602	$58,459	$131,069	48.8%	14.6%	12.4%	56.2%	44.6%

In millions of current U.S. dollars

Source: Customizable database at TradeStats Express, U.S. Census Bureau. Category 87, "Vehicles, except railway or tramway, etc., and parts, etc."

Table 10: Total U.S. Trade with Partners in North America, Asia, and Europe, 1986–2010

- Despite the rapid increase in U.S. trade with China and the continued importance of Europe, no two nations in the world are more important trading partners for the U.S. than Canada and Mexico.
- In 2009, China became the largest source of imports to the U.S., but it ranks third as a market for U.S. goods behind Canada and Mexico. In 2010, the U.S. exports to Mexico were five times more than to Brazil and six times more than to India.

	Total US Trade of Goods and Services (millions of current US$)					
Countries	1986	1993	2000	2007	2009	2010
Canada and Mexico	$179,694	$340,535	$729,299	$1,027,573	$918,655	$1,038,171
Japan and China	$134,172	$234,791	$387,803	$684,046	$727,880	$746,508
Germany and the UK	$91,658	$152,440	$266,138	$411,378	$518,730	$378,915

Source: U.S. Bureau of Economic Analysis, U.S. International Transactions Accounts Data.

Table 11: Relative Importance of Trade for Canada, Mexico, and U.S., 1990–2009

- The table demonstrates the importance of North American trade for all three countries while showing its asymmetric nature.
- One-third to one-half of Canada's GDP and about one-third of Mexico's GDP depend on trade with the United States, but only 4–7 percent of U.S. GDP and one-third of its total trade depend on its neighbors—small in comparison to its neighbors' dependence but the largest trading partners for the U.S.

	Canada					Mexico					U.S.				
	GDP	Total trade w US	Total world trade	Trade w US as % of Total	Trade w US as % of GDP	GDP	Total trade w US	Total world trade	Trade w US as % of Total	Trade w US as % of GDP	US GDP	US trade with NA	Trade w NA as % of US GDP	Total US World Trade	US-NA trade as % of Total US Trade
1990	$583	$174.3	$250.9	69.5%	29.9%	$288	$58.5	$84.3	69.5%	20.3%	$5,757	$233	4.0%	$888.2	26.2%
1995	$590	$271.6	$360.6	75.3%	46.0%	$314	$108.4	$154.0	70.4%	34.5%	$7,342	$380	5.2%	$1,328.3	28.6%
2000	$725	$409.8	$521.4	78.6%	56.5%	$637	$247.3	$345.8	71.5%	38.8%	$9,765	$657	6.7%	$1,999.9	32.9%
2005	$1,133	$502.3	$682.9	73.6%	44.3%	$844	$290.4	$442.4	65.6%	34.4%	$12,364	$793	6.4%	$2,574.5	30.8%
2008	$1,502	$600.6	$875.5	68.6%	40.0%	$1,082	$367.2	$609.6	60.2%	33.9%	$14,097	$968	6.9%	$3,391.1	28.5%
2009	$1,285	$429.6	$645.8	66.5%	33.4%	$1,017	$305.5	$471.2	64.8%	30.0%	$14,430	$735	5.1%	$2,614.8	28.1%

In millions of current U.S. dollars

Sources: TradeStats Express, U.S. Census Bureau; U.N. National Accounts; CIA *World Factbook*.

Table 12: Foreign Direct Investment in and by North America, 1987–2008

- While all three countries have received substantial foreign direct investment (FDI) since NAFTA, they have also become significant sources of FDI as well. U.S. and Canadian FDI abroad increased ten times and Mexican FDI abroad increased 22 times between 1987 and 2008.
- Mexico hoped to receive an infusion of FDI, and that happened as its stock of $13.7 billion in 1987 expanded twenty-one times to $295 billion in 2008. Canada increased its FDI at home by five times to $412 billion, though this is less than it sent abroad, and the U.S. increased its FDI at home by nine times to $2.3 trillion. The fears of Canada and Mexico that the U.S. would buy up their economies proved unfounded as the percentage of FDI owned by the U.S. in Canada and Mexico declined during this period.

United States	1987	1990	1992	2000	2005	2008
Total US FDI Abroad	$326,253	$430,521	$502,063	$1,316,247	$2,051,284	$3,162,021
US FDI in Can	$59,145	$69,508	$68,690	$132,472	$234,831	$227,298
US FDI in Can as % of Total US FDI	18.1%	16.1%	13.7%	10.1%	11.4%	7.2%
US FDI in Can as % of FDI in Can	72.6%	61.6%	63.3%	62.3%	67.1%	55.1%
US FDI in Mexico	$5,434	$10,313	$13,730	$39,352	$71,423	$95,618
US FDI in Mexico as % of Total US FDI	1.7%	2.4%	2.7%	3.0%	3.5%	3.0%
US FDI in Mexico as% of FDI in Mexico	39.6%	46.0%	38.5%	40.5%	34.1%	32.4%
Total US FDI in North America	$64,579	$79,821	$82,420	$171,824	$306,254	$322,916
US FDI in NA as% of US Total FDI	19.8%	18.5%	16.4%	13.1%	14.9%	10.2%
Total FDI in US	$263,394	$394,911	$423,131	$1,256,867	$1,594,488	$2,278,892

Canada	1987	1990	1992	2000	2005	2008
Total FDI Abroad	$57,037	$84,807	$87,870	$237,638	$399,362	$520,399
Can FDI in US	$24,684	$29,544	$37,515	$114,309	$144,033	$221,870
Can FDI in US as % of Can FDI Abroad	43.3%	34.8%	42.7%	48.1%	36.1%	42.6%
Can FDI in US as % of Total FDI in US	9.4%	7.5%	8.9%	9.1%	9.0%	9.7%
Can FDI in Mexico	$190	$211	$355	$2,580	$2,618	$4,275
Total FDI in Can	$81,503	$112,843	$108,503	$212,716	$350,030	$412,268

Mexico	1987	1990	1992	2000	2005	2008
Total FDI Abroad	$2,294	$2,672	$3,496	$8,273	$28,040	$45,389
Mex FDI in US	$180	$575	$1,406	$7,462	$8,653	$7,948
Mex FDI in Can	$11	-$11	$47	$95	$170	$253
Total FDI in Mexico	$13,735	$22,424	$35,680	$97,170	$209,564	$294,680

In millions of current U.S. dollars.

Sources: UNCTAD, *World Investment Report 2006: FDI from Developing and Transition Economies: Implications for Development*; *Inward FDI Stock, by Host Region and Economy, 1980–2006.* Available at http://stats.unctad.org; Bureau of Economic Analysis, *Balance of Payments and Direct Investment Position Data.* Available at http://www.bea.gov. OECD, *International Direct Investment Statistics.* Available at http://miranda.sourceoecd.org. Statistics Canada, Table 376-0051. Available at http://www.statcan.ca.

Table 13: North American FDI in North America and Average Annual Growth Rates, 1987–2008

- The countries of North America have traditionally invested in each other, but NAFTA accelerated the level of investment from an annual average growth rate of 7 percent in the period between 1987–92 to 18 percent during the next eight years. FDI from other sources increased at a still faster rate in the early NAFTA period, demonstrating the attractiveness as the larger market for foreign capital.
- Just as North America peaked in 2000 so did FDI. The average annual growth rate between 2000 and 2008 declined and then leveled off at 11 percent and the gap in growth rates between North American and other FDI closed.

	1987	1990	1992	2000	2005	2008
NA FDI in NA	$89,644	$110,140	$121,743	$296,270	$461,728	$557,262
Total FDI in North America	$358,632	$530,178	$567,314	$1,566,753	$2,154,082	$2,985,841
Total NA outward FDI	$385,584	$518,000	$593,429	$1,562,158	$2,478,686	$3,727,809

***
Average Annual Growth Rate (AAGR)*

	1987–1992	1992–2000	2000–2008
NA FDI in NA	7.16%	17.92%	11.01%
Total FDI in NA	11.64%	22.02%	11.32%

*Average Annual Growth Rate: Total growth in specified period divided by number of years.
In millions of current U.S. dollars

Sources: UNCTAD, *World Investment Report 2006: FDI from Developing and Transition Economies: Implications for Development; Inward FDI stock, by Host Region and Economy, 1980–2006.* Available at http://stats.unctad.org; Bureau of Economic Analysis, *Balance of Payments and Direct Investment Position Data.* Available at http://www.bea.gov. OECD, *International Direct Investment Statistics.* Available at http://miranda.sourceoecd.org. Statistics Canada, *Table 376-0051.* Available at http://www.statcan.ca.

Table 14: Population of Mexico, U.S., and Canada, 1800–2010

- Population and migration have defined the three countries. Mexico's population grew slowly in the nineteenth century, but then it accelerated in the twentieth. In 1800, the U.S. and Mexico had roughly the same population–5.3 million people. A century later, after a tsunami of immigration, the U.S. had a population of 75 million and Mexico had fewer than 14 million.
- Between 1900 and 1950, the U.S. and Mexican population doubled, while Canada increased even more. Then Mexico's population exploded, reaching 112.5 million by 2010 while the U.S. reached 310 million. Canada's grew to 34 million.

Year	Mexico	United States	Canada	North America
1800	5.6	5.3	0.3	11.2
1900	13.6	75.0	5.3	93.9
1950	26.0	150.0	14.0	190.0
1980	67.0	226.0	24.0	317.0
1990	82.0	249.0	27.0	358.0
2010	112.5	310.2	33.8	456.5

Millions of people
Sources: 2010 data from CIA *World Factbook*; 1800–1990 data from Michael R. Haines and Richard H. Steckel, eds., *A Population History of North America* (2000).

Table 15: Mexican-Origin and Hispanic Population in the U.S., 1970–2050

- Since 1970, the United States has absorbed a five-fold increase in the Hispanic population with two-thirds of that from Mexico. Estimates are that the Mexican-American population will double from 31 million to 65.7 million in the next forty years.

	1970	1980	1990	2000	2010	2020	2030	2040	2050
Hispanic	9.6	14.6	22.4	35.3	47.8	59.7	73.0	87.6	102.6
Mexican	6.1	9.3	14.3	22.6	30.6	38.2	46.7	56.1	65.7
Hispanic, non-Mexican	3.5	5.3	8.1	12.7	17.2	21.5	26.3	31.5	36.9

Millions of people
Note: U.S. Census Bureau estimates after 2010.
Source: "Hispanics in the United States," U.S. Census Bureau, Population Division, Ethnicity and Ancestry Branch.

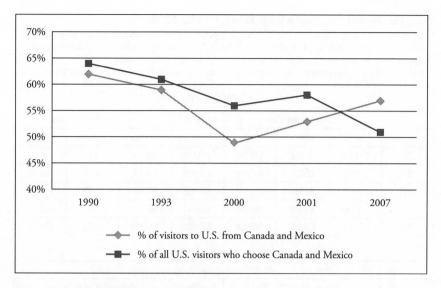

Figure A.1: Tourism in North America, 1990–2007

Sources: U.S. Department of Commerce, Office of Travels and Tourism Industries; Statistics Canada; Banco de México/Secretaría de Turismo.

- North Americans prefer to travel to each other's countries more than to go elsewhere. Between 50 and 65 percent of all visitors to the United States have come from Mexico and Canada and a similar percentage of Americans who travel abroad visit Canada and Mexico.

Table 16: Income Disparity in North America, 1980–2008

- By whatever measure—current dollars or purchasing power parity—the income gap separating Mexico from its northern neighbors has hardly changed since 1980. Mexico's per capita income has remained relatively steady at 28 percent of the North American average (current dollars).
- Canada's per capita income has ranged from 87 percent of the North American average to 120 percent.

	Current U.S. dollars						
	GDPpc (current USD)			NA GDPpc*	GDPpc as % of NA GDPpc		
	Canada	Mexico	U.S.		Canada	Mexico	U.S.
1980	$10,934	$2,876	$12,186	$10,120	108.0%	28.4%	120.4%
1990	$20,968	$3,157	$23,064	$18,308	114.5%	17.2%	126.0%
1993	$19,549	$4,584	$25,409	$20,098	97.3%	22.8%	126.4%
2000	$23,560	$5,935	$34,606	$26,943	87.4%	22.0%	128.4%
2008	$45,070	$10,232	$46,350	$37,597	119.9%	27.2%	123.3%

	Purchasing Power Parity						
	GDPpc (current USD, PPP)			NA GDPpc*	GDPpc as % of NA GDPpc		
	Canada	Mexico	U.S.		Canada	Mexico	U.S.
1980	$11,031	$3,943	$12,186	$10,353	106.6%	38.1%	117.7%
1990	$19,499	$6,179	$23,064	$18,892	103.2%	32.7%	122.1%
1993	$20,579	$6,974	$25,409	$20,735	99.2%	33.6%	122.5%
2000	$28,407	$9,201	$34,606	$28,085	101.1%	32.8%	123.2%
2008	$39,078	$14,570	$46,350	$38,187	102.3%	38.2%	121.4%

*Combined GDP of U.S., Canada, and Mexico, divided by combined population.

Source: World Bank, World Development Indicators & Global Development Finance, accessed in 2011.

Table 17: Income Convergence in the European Union, 1980–2008

- In contrast to North America, the EU invested about $850 billion to narrow the income gap between its richer and poorer members, and the convergence in income is astonishing.
- From 1980–2008, Spain's per capita income as a percentage of the EU average rose from 56 percent to 96 percent; Ireland, from 57 percent to 164 percent (from $6,000 to $60,000), and Greece, from 52 percent to 86 percent.

	GDPpc (current USD)						% of EU average				
	EU avg	Spain	Portugal	Ireland	Greece	Czech Rep	Spain	Portugal	Ireland	Greece	Czech Rep
1980	$10,853	$6,045	$3,221	$6,200	$5,671		55.7%	29.7%	57.1%	52.3%	
1990	$18,920	$13,415	$7,607	$13,636	$9,271	$11,183	70.9%	40.2%	72.1%	49.0%	59.1%
1993	$19,462	$13,009	$9,109	$14,263	$10,005	$10,504	66.8%	46.8%	73.3%	51.4%	54.0%
2000	$21,465	$14,422	$11,016	$25,384	$11,501	$14,993	67.2%	51.3%	118.3%	53.6%	69.8%
2008	$36,871	$35,215	$22,923	$60,460	$31,670	$24,643	95.5%	62.2%	164.0%	85.9%	66.8%

Note: EU average reflects enlargements. 1980 includes Belgium, Denmark, France, Germany, Ireland, Italy, Luxembourg, Netherlands and UK. 1981 adds Greece. 1986 adds Portugal and Spain. 1995 adds Austria, Finland, and Sweden. 2004 adds Czech Republic, Estonia, Cyprus, Latvia, Lithuania, Hungary, Malta, Poland, Slovakia and Slovenia. 2007 adds Romania and Bulgaria.
Source: World Bank, *World Development Indicators & Global Development Finance.*

Table 18: U.S. Government-Funded Research Centers

• The U.S. government supports research centers for every region of the world except North America.

Region /Country	Grants
Asia/Pacific	88
Europe/Russia	66
Latin America	48
Middle East	36
Africa	26
Canada	9
North America	0

Note: The number of centers and grants represents an average per year for the period 2003–2006.

Source: Vassia Gueorguieva, "North American Studies Centers: An Overview," *Norteamérica*, vol. 2, no. 2 (July–December).

Notes

Preface

1. Lou Dobbs, January 25, 2007, CNN transcript and Patrick J. Buchanan, "The NAFTA Superhighway: Coming Soon," *WorldNet Daily*, August 29, 2007.
2. Jerome Corsi is the source of much of their material. He was also the author of books attacking John Kerry (*Unfit for Command*) and Barack Obama (*Obama Nation*). On me, he wrote: "Robert Pastor intends to give away U.S. sovereignty to a newly forming North American Union exactly as he gave away the Panama Canal to Panama during Jimmy Carter's presidency." Jerome Corsi, "Meet Robert Pastor: Father of the North American Union," *Human Events*, July 25, 2006.

Chapter 1

1. Cited by Robert Lindsey, "Reagan Entering Presidency Race, Calls for North American 'Accord,'" *New York Times*, November 14, 1979.
2. For the face on the soccer ball, see *Newsweek*, June 28 & July 5, 2010, p. 10.
3. This incident is recalled in "Obama's War Over Terror," by Peter Baker, *New York Times Magazine*, January 17, 2010.
4. Steven Weber and Janice Gross Stein, "In the Eye of the Storm: The Policy Taker and the Policy Maker," paper prepared for Conference on "North American Futures," University of California, Berkeley, February 2010.
5. Canadian International Council, *Open Canada: A Global Positioning Strategy for a Networked Age* (Ottawa, 2010), p. 18.
6. Clifford Krauss, "Canada Seeks Redress on Food-Labeling Law," *New York Times*, October 13, 2009, p. B3.
7. Data from CIA, *World Factbook, 2010*. Accessed December 2010: https://www.cia.gov/library/publication/the-world-factbook/gov/cia.html
8. Daniel Lederman, William F. Maloney, and Luis Serven, *Lessons from NAFTA for Latin American and the Caribbean* (Washington, D.C.: The World Bank, 2005), p. 2.
9. Dominick Salvatore, "Economic Effects of NAFTA on Mexico," *Global Economy Journal*, Vol. 7, No. 1 (2007), p. 12. Salvatore's article confirms the conclusion of the World Bank on the positive effects of NAFTA on Mexico and also makes a strong case that employment is not the correct criteria to measure the effect of

NAFTA. Rather his analysis focuses on the counter-factual simulation of its effect on intra-NAFTA trade and growth, i.e. how much higher it is with NAFTA than without.

10. Senator Obama blamed NAFTA for one million job losses and declared "entire cities have been devastated" by trade pacts. "I don't think NAFTA has been good for America, and I never have." Senator Clinton called the pact "flawed" and said she had been against it "from the beginning." Pete Engardio, Geri Smith, and Jane Sasseen, "What You Don't Know About NAFTA," *Business Week*, March 28, 2008.

11. Brian Knowlton, "Obama Administration Has No Plans to Reopen Talks on NAFTA," *New York Times*, April 21, 2009, p. B3.

12. U.S. Department of Commerce, Bureau of Labor Statistics, *Current Employment Statistics Survey*. Accessed December 2010: http://data/bls.gov. Alan S. Alexandroff, Gary Clyde Hufbauer, and Krista Lucenti, *Still Amigos: A Fresh Canada-US Approach to Reviving NAFTA* (Toronto, Canada: C.D. Howe Institute, September 2008), See Figure 1 on "U.S. Manufacturing Employment, 1990–2007," p. 3.

13. John Engler, "American Industry Can Stay Ahead of China," *Financial Times*, August 17, 2008.

14. Cable News Network Transcripts, "Lou Dobbs Tonight," September 29, 2006.

15. Jerome R. Corsi, *The Late Great USA: The Coming Merger with Mexico and Canada* (Los Angeles, California: World Ahead Media, 2007), p. 1.

16. See Dan Barry, "Holding Firm Against Plots by Evildoers," *New York Times*, June 26, 2009; and Christopher Hayes, "The NAFTA Superhighway," *The Nation*, August 27, 2007. For a fuller description of the various conspiracy theories, see Heidi Beirich, "The Paranoid Style Redux," and "In the Line of Fire: The Scholar Accused of Being at the Center of a Sinister Plot to Merge Canada, the U.S. and Mexico Speaks Out," *Intelligence Report*, published by the Southern Poverty Law Center, September 2007, pp. 34–43.

17. Samuel P. Huntington, *Who Are We? The Challenges to America's National Identity* (N.Y.: Simon and Schuster, 2004), see especially Chapter 11, p. 221.

18. "State of the Nation Address by Carlos Salinas," November 1, 1991, reprinted in *Foreign Broadcast Information Service*, Latin America, November 13, 1991, p. 14.

19. Author's interview with Carlos Salinas, July 24, 1990 in Mexico City.

20. Huntington, *Who Are We?*, p. xvii.

21. Amy Goldstein and Roberto Suro, "Latinos in America: A Journey in Stages," *Washington Post*, January 16, 2000. This is a summary of a vast survey conducted by the *Post*, the Henry K. Kaiser Foundation, and Harvard University. I address in more detail Huntington's arguments in Robert Pastor, *Toward a North American Community* (Washington, D.C.: Institute for International Economics, 2001), pp. 164–66.

22. Jeb Bush and Robert D. Putnam, "A Better Welcome for Our Immigrants," *Washington Post*, July 3, 2010, p. A19. They cited research by sociologists Claude Fischer and Michael Hout on language acquisition.

23. Jackson Diehl, "The Crisis Next Door," *Washington Post*, July 26, 2010, p. A13; Richard A. Serrano, "U.S. Guns Arm Mexican Drug Cartels," *Los Angeles Times*, August 10, 2008.

24. The length of the borders is calculated by the U.S. Geological Survey. See Janice Cheryl Beaver, "U.S. Borders" (Congressional Research Service, Library of Congress, November 9, 2006).

25. Charles Meier, "Empire without End: Imperial Achievements and Ideologies," *Foreign Affairs* (July/August 2010), p. 159.

26. World Trade Organization, "Regional Trade Agreements Database."; Accessed October 14, 2010: www.wto.org

27. "Preamble to the Treaty of Rome," in *The European Union: Readings on the Theory and Practice of European Integration*, ed. Brent F. Nelsen and Alexander C.G. Stubb, 2nd ed. (Boulder, Co: Lynne Rienner Publishers, 1998), pp. 13–15.

28. That figure is the sum of all the structural, regional, and cohesion funds appropriated from 1961–2010. The dollar figure is simply a nominal, non-inflationary adjusted amount at the exchange rate of $1 USD = .76 €, as of December 9, 2010. Sources: European Union, *Budget, 2007, Final Report, Appendix 2*; and EU, Budget *2009, Annex 2A*.

29. Military spending was for 2008, calculated in 2005 dollars (sipri.org). The gross product and population data is from CIA *World Factbook*, 2009.

30. John N. McDougall, *The Long-Run Determinants of Deep/Political Canada-U.S. Integration* (Canada: Institute for Research and Public Policy, 2003), p. 9.

31. Andrés Rozental, "A Mexican Perspective," in Fen Hampson and Paul Heinbecker, eds., *Canada Among Nations*, 2009–2010 (Montreal and Kingston, Canada: McGill-Queen's University Press, 2010), p. 74.

32. Stephen Blank and Martin Coiteux, *The State of North American Integration* (Waterloo, Ontario: Centre for International Governance Innovation, 2003), pp. 7–9. http://www.portalfornorthamerica.org/sites/files/Blank%20and%20Coiteux_0.pdf

33. Alan Rugman and Chang H. Oh, "Friedman's Follies: Insights on the Globalization/Regionalization Debate," *Business and Politics*, Vol. 10, No. 2 (2008), pp. 6–13.

34. Department of State, *Background Note: Mexico*, May 14, 2010.

35. *Congressional Record, Senate*, 68th Congress, April 18–24, 1924, pp. 6622–33. See also Robert A. Pastor, "U.S. Immigration Policy and Latin America: In Search of the 'Special Relationship,'" *Latin American Research Review*, Vol. 19, No. 3 (1984), p. 40.

36. Jeffrey S. Passel and D'Vera Cohn, "Trends in Unauthorized Immigration: Undocumented Inflow Now Trails Legal Inflow," Pew Hispanic Center Report (Washington, D.C., October 2, 2008), pp. i–iii.

37. U.S, Department of Homeland Security, Office of Immigration Statistics, Performance Analysis System (PAS), G-22.1, 2010.

38. See Carol Wise and Isabel Studer, eds., *Requiem or Revival: The Promise of North American Integration* (Washington, D.C.: Brookings Institution, 2007), Chapter 1. Also see the work of Robert A. Blecker.

39. See http://www.wto.org/english/tratop_e/region_e.htm. Go to "Regional Trade Agreements."

40. John Manley, "Seizing the Initiative: Opportunities for Canada Amid Global Recovery," Montreal, September 21, 2010.

41. Author's interview with Vicente Fox, Washington, D.C., February 7, 2008.

Chapter 2

1. This section borrows from the wonderfully encyclopedic *The Eternal Frontier: An Ecological History of North America and Its People* by Tim Flannery (N.Y.: Grove Press, 2001). For a map of the region before the asteroid struck, see p. 11. See also Francis Moul, *The National Grasslands* (Lincoln: University of Nebraska press, 2006), p. 1.

2. Flannery, p. 86.

3. Flannery, p. 168.

4. See Daniel J. Boorstin, *The Discoverers: A History of Man's Search to Know His World and Himself* (NY: Random House, 1983), pp. 210–17.

5. Estimates of the population in the Americas before Columbus arrived are quite wide-ranging. Alfred Kroeber estimated the population at 8.4 million. Henry Dobyns judged there were 90–112 million people. Russell Thornton puts the number at 75 million. All agree that smallpox and other diseases brought by the Spanish devastated the native population, murdering as much as 95 percent of the natives. For a summary of the debate on the estimates, see Charles C. Mann, *1491: New Revelations of the Americas Before Columbus* (N.Y.: Alfred A. Knopf, 2005), pp. 92–129; Flannery, p. 305. For North America above the Rio Grande, the estimates range from 1 million to 18 million, but Thornton puts the number at 5 million in the present-day United States and 2 million in Canada. See Russell Thornton, "Population History of Native North Americans," in Michael R. Haines and Richard H. Steckel, eds., *A Population History of North America* (Cambridge: Cambridge University Press, 2000), pp. 9–14.

6. Russell Thornton, pp. 9–14.

7. See Flannery, pp. 173–85; and Mann, p. 16.

8. Barry Fell, *America B.C.: Ancient Settlers in the New World* (N.Y.: Pocket Books, 1976).

9. Boorstin, *The Discoverers*, pp. 210–17.

10. Boorstin, pp. 231–23; and Fell, pp. 15–16.

11. These are Columbus's words. "Columbus's Journal of the Third Voyage, May 30–August 31, 1498," cited in Anthony DePalma, *Here: A Biography of the New American Continent* (N.Y.: Public Affairs, 2001), p. 1.

12. Boorstin, pp. 252–23. See John W. Hessler, *The Naming of America*.

13. Cited by Flannery, p. 262.

14. David Brown, "16th Century Mapmaker's Intriguing Knowledge," *The Washington Post*, November 17, 2008.

15. Boorstin, p. 254.

16. Anthony DePalma, *Here: A Biography of the New American Continent*, pp. 2–3.

17. Radha Jhappan and Yasmeen Abu-Laban, "Introduction," in Yasmeen Abu-Laban, Radha Jhappan, and Francois Rocher, eds., *Politics in North America: Redefining Continental Relations* (Peterborough, Ontario: Broadview Press, 2008), p. 12.

18. Sherburne Cook and Woodrow Borah did the estimates. They are cited in a book that reviews the literature on the population of the Americas before the Europeans arrived and the origin of the native peoples. See Charles C. Mann, *1491: New Revelations of the Americas Before Columbus* (NY: Alfred Knopf, 2005), pp. 129–30.

19. The classic story is by William H. Prescott, *The History of the Conquest of Mexico*, abridged and edited by C. Harvey Gardiner (Chicago: University of Chicago Press, 1966). Originally published in 1843.

20. Mann, pp. 129–30.

21. Jack Weatherford, *Native Roots: How the Indians Enriched America* (N.Y.: Fawcett Columbine, 1991).

22. For a good discussion of the many ways in which the word "Indian" has been used to describe a very diverse group of people, who were living in the Americas before the Europeans arrived, and for more contemporary usages, see Michael M. Brescia and John C. Super, *North America: An Introduction* (Toronto: University of Toronto Press, 2009), pp. xiii–xiv, 109–111.

23. Cited in Mann, p. 100.

24. For a good description of the evolution of policies toward the natives in all three countries, see Brescia and Super, *North America: An Introduction*, Chapter VI.

25. Cited in Ralph Barton Perry, "The Declaration of Independence," in *The Declaration of Independence and the Constitution*, edited by Earl Latham (Boston: D.C. Heath and Company, 1956), p. 2.

26. Josefina Zoraida Vazquez estimates that of 24,700 residents of Texas in 1832, most were American and only 3,400 were Mexican. Cited by Jorge Castañeda, *Limits to Friendship: The US and Mexico* (N.Y.: Alfred A. Knopf, 1988), p. 33.

27. Walter McDougall, *Promised Land, Crusader State: The American Encounter with the World Since 1776* (N.Y.: Houghton, Mifflin, 1997).

28. For a review of this history, see Robert A. Pastor, "The United States: Divided by a Revolutionary Vision," in Pastor, ed., *A Century's Journey: How the Great Powers Shape the World* (N.Y.: Basic Books, 1999), pp. 191–238.

29. The governing party evolved and was renamed three times since it was first established in 1929 as the National Revolutionary Party (PNR). In 1938, it became the Mexican Revolutionary Party (PRM), and in 1946, the PRI.

30. See Robert A. Pastor and Jorge G. Castañeda, *Limits to Friendship: The US and Mexico*.

31. See Michael Howlett, Alex Netherton, and M. Ramesh, *The Political Economy of North America: An Introduction*, 2nd ed. (Oxford: Oxford University Press, 1999,); Earl Fry, *Canada's Unity Crisis: Implications for U.S.-Canada Economic Relations* (N.Y.: Twentieth Century Fund, 1992), p. 165. The Maple Leaf became the Canadian national flag in 1965. "O Canada" replaced "God Save the Queen" as its anthem in 1967. The Queen of England remains Canada's head of state,

although the Governor-General, a Canadian appointed by its Parliament, exercises that responsibility. Lipset, p. 43.

32. Seymour Martin Lipset, *Continental Divide: The Values and Institutions of the United States and Canada* (N.Y.: Routledge, 1991), pp. 1, 42.

33. Lipset, pp. 8–9.

34. Keith Spicer, "Canada: Values in Search of a Vision," in Robert L. Earle and John D. Wirth, eds., *Identities in North America: The Search for Community* (Stanford: Stanford University Press, 1995), pp. 16–18.

35. Michael Hart, *Fifty Years of Canadian Statecraft: Canada at the GATT, 1947–1997* (Ottawa, Canada: Centre for Trade Policy and Law, Carleton University, 1998), p. 168.

36. Carlos Salinas de Gortari, *Mexico: The Policy and Priorities of Modernization* (Barcelona, Spain: Plaza and Janes Editores, S.A., 2002), pp. 43–49.

37. Based on the author's conversations with Sandy Berger and Jimmy Carter at the time. Governor Bill Clinton's address was "Expanding Trade and Creating American Jobs," North Carolina State University, October 4, 1992.

Chapter 3

1. Robert A. Pastor and Jorge G. Castañeda, *Limits to Friendship: The U.S. and Mexico* (N.Y.: Alfred A. Knopf, 1988), pp. 37–38.

2. For 2000 and 2002 data: Pew Research Center, *What The World Thinks In 2002: How Global Publics View: Their Lives, Their Countries, The World, America* (2002). For 2003 and 2005 data, see Ekos, *Wave 1—General Public Survey: Canada, the U.S. and Mexico* (2005).

3. On the Mexican views over time, see Alejandro Moreno, "Trust in North America: Why Do Mexicans Distrust Their Continental Neighbors?" *Norteamérica*, Vol. 2, No. 2, July–December 2007, p. 70.

4. Zogby International, "National Survey of Mexicans and Americans," March 2006, p. 8.

5. Chicago Council on Foreign Relations, CIDE, and COMEXEI, *Global Views 2004: Comparing Mexican and American Public Opinion and Foreign Policy* (2004), p. 19. Canada was omitted from the question.

6. For a summary of the surveys up to 2000, see Robert A. Pastor, *Toward A North American Community: Lessons from the Old World for the New* (Washington, D.C.: Institute of International Economics, 2001), pp. 156–57. For the 2004, 2008, and 2010 surveys, see Chicago Council on Foreign Relations, *American Public Opinion and Foreign Policy; Global Views* (2004); and Chicago Council on Global Affairs, *Anxious Americans Seek a New Direction in United States Foreign Policy* (2009) and *Constrained Internationalism: Adapting to New Realities* (2010). The Council changed its name between the first and second report. For an unexplained reason, the last surveys did not include Canada on the thermometer ranking, but a 2005 survey indicated that 76 percent of Americans viewed Canada favorably, and only 9 percent viewed it negatively. Mexico experienced a decline in 2008 and 2010 in "favorability" scores by the U.S. because

of drugs and illegal migration, but that is probably a snapshot during a bad time.

7. Guadalupe Gonzalez and Susan Minushkin, eds., *Mexico and the World, 2006: Public Opinión and Foreign Policy in Mexico* (Mexico City: Centro de Investigacion y Docencia Economicas y Consejo Mexicana de Asuntos Internacionales. 2006). p. 57.

8. Pew Research Center for the People and the Press, *What The World Thinks In 2002: How Global Publics View: Their Lives, Their Countries, The World, America* (2002).

9. Chicago Council on Global Affairs, *Constrained Internationalism: Adapting to New Realities* (2010), pp. 73–74.

10. Seymour Martin Lipset, *Continental Divide: The Values and Institutions of the United States and Canada* (N.Y.: Routledge, 1991); and Samuel P. Huntington, *Who Are We? The Challenges to America's National Identity* (N.Y.: Simon and Schuster, 2004).

11. Miguel Basañez, Ronald Inglehart, and Neil Nevitte, "North American Convergence, Revisited," *Norteamérica*, Vol. 2, No. 2 (July–December 2007), p. 57. See the summary table on page 56 of 19 values, which reflect a convergence from 1990–2006. The convergence is clearest between the U.S. and Canada, but in economic and political values the distance traveled by Mexico toward convergence is impressive.

12. Alejandro Moreno, "Trust in North America: Why Do Mexicans Distrust Their Continental Neighbors?" *Norteamérica*, Vol. 2, No. 2 (July–December 2007), pp. 64, 66.

13. Moreno, pp. 69–71.

14. Innovative Research Group, "Canada and the United States: What Does It Mean to be Good Neighbours—2008 Annual Ottawa Conference Poll," 2008, p. 3. www.innovative research.ca

15. Pew Center, "25-Nation Pew Global Project Attitudes Survey," July 23, 2009.

16. Pew Center for the People and the Press, December 2002.

17. Karl Deutsch, *Political Community and the North Atlantic Area*. For a discussion and update of the concept, see Emanuel Adler and Michael Barnett, eds., *Security Communities* (Cambridge: Cambridge University Press, 1998).

18. Pew Research Center, "Support for Free Trade Recovers Despite Recession," April 28, 2009, and "Public Support for Increased Trade, Except with South Korea and China," November 9, 2010. See http://people-press.org/report/511/free-trade-support-recovers. The gap between positive and negative views is smaller in the Pew study than the one from Ekos. Pew believes that is because their surveys refer specifically to NAFTA and the WTO. Nevertheless, the pattern of support for free trade is the same.

19. Chicago Council on Global Affairs, *Constrained Internationalism: Adapting to New Realities* (2010), p. 29.

20. Chicago Council on Foreign Relations, *American Public Opinion and Foreign Policy* (2004), pp. 46–47.

21. Chicago Council on Global Affairs, *Constrained Internationalism: Adapting to New Realities* (2010), p. 32. For similar results and a more developed argument,

see Kenneth F. Scheve and Matthew J. Slaughter, *Globalization and the Perceptions of American Workers* (Washington, D.C.: Institute for International Economics, 2001).

22. Chicago Council on Foreign Relations, CIDE, and COMEXEI, *Global Views, 2004: Comparing Mexican and American Public Opinion and Foreign Policy* (2004), pp. 25–26.

23. Jack Citrin and Matthew Wright, "E Pluribus Europa," in A. Messina and A. Gould, eds., *The Framing of European Identity* (University of Notre Dame Press, 2011), table 1. When the public was asked in 1987 if they "*never* think of themselves as European" or "*sometimes* think of themselves as European and national," the population in the European Community divided in half—49–48. See Eurobarometer, *Public Opinion in the European Community No. 27* (June 1987). Available at http://ec.europa.eu/public_opinion/archives/eb/eb27/eb27_en.pdf

24. Citrin and Wright, "E Pluribus Europa."

25. In fact, the "dual" identity category is the residual of the question "would you see yourself as a national" Canadian, Mexican, or American. The residual combines the answers to the questions, "do you see yourself as a . . . "continental only," "national and continental," and "continental and national."

26. Robert L. Earle and John D. Wirth, eds., *Identities in North America: The Search for Community* (Stanford: Stanford University Press, 1995), p. 9.

27. Roberto Adrian Fiero Bartlett, "Immigration and Development," introductory remarks at the Congressional Hispanic Institute, May 13, 2009, Washington, D.C.

28. Quoted in Ginger Thompson, "New Requirements on Border ID Stir Worries at Crossings," *New York Times*, May 24, 2009, p. 16.

29. James A. MacDonald, *The North American Idea* (New York: Fleming H. Revell Company, 1917) pp. 69–70. The Cole Lectures of 1917.

30. Zogby poll published in *Newsweek International*, March 27, 2006, p. 24.

31. Ekos, *Wave 1—General Public Survey of Canada, the U.S., and Mexico* (2005), p. 49. This table on "Likelihood of a North American Economic Union" includes data from five separate surveys from May 2000. All are consistent with the 2005 report.

32. Ekos, *Survey of the General Public in Canada—Wave 1: Final Report*, August 24, 2009.

33. Ekos, *Survey of the General Public in Canada*, August 24, 2009, p. 16; and Chicago Council on Foreign relations, CIDE, and COMEXEI, *Global Views, 2004: Comparing Mexican and American Public Opinion and Foreign Policy* (Chicago: Council on Foreign Relations), p. 20.

34. Gallup Poll, "American Views of Mexico," February 16, 2001, February 10, 2003, and February 18, 2004. For American views of Canada, see Pew Research Center for the People and the Press, June 23, 2005.

35. Zogby Poll published in *Newsweek International*, March 27, 2006, p. 20.

Chapter 4

1. Julia Preston, "Inquiry Finds Under-Age Workers at Meat-Processing Plan," *New York Times*, August 6, 2009.

2. A Pew study estimated that nearly half of the 11.1 million undocumented workers in the country in 2009 arrived since 2000, and the annual flow of undocumented workers was 850,000 from 2000–2005. See Jeffrey S. Passel and D'Vera Cohn, "U.S. Unauthorized Immigration Flows Are Down Sharply Since Mid-Decade," Pew Hispanic Center, September 1, 2010.

3. See Robert A. Pastor and Jorge G. Castañeda, *Limits to Friendship: The U.S. and Mexico* (N.Y.: Alfred A. Knopf, 1988), p. 357. Then, Mexican-American leaders promoted assimilation and a "self-conscious sense of American-ness" and distanced themselves both from the Mexican government and the *braceros*.

4. Brescia and Super, p. 137.

5. Brescia and Super, p. 144 on Central American deportations. On the number of Americans in Mexico, see U.S. Department of State, *Background Notes: Mexico*, May 14, 2010.

6. Brescia and Super, p. 136.

7. B. Lindsay Lowell, "Outlook for Labor Mobility," in Armand B. Peschard-Sverdrup, ed., *The Future of North America, 2025: Outlook and Recommendations* (Washington, D.C.: Center for Strategic and International Studies, 2008), p. 135.

8. Lowell, p. 136. For the 12.4 percent from the U.S. (2005), see "Fact Sheet on the Foreign Born, The United States," Migration Policy Institute. http://www. migrationinformation.org/datahub/state.cfm?ID=US

9. Jack Jedwab and Victor Armony, "Hola Canada! Spanish Is Third Most Spoken Language," FOCALPoint, Vol. 8, No. 4 (May 2009), pp. 14–16. *Statistical Portrait of Hispanics in US, 2006* (Washington, D.C.: Pew Center, 2006).

10. Lowell, p. 137; Pew Center, Statistical *Portrait of Hispanics in US, 2006*.

11. For the projections and the statistics, see Lowell, "Outlook for Labor Mobility," pp. 121–53; and Pew Hispanic Center, *Statistical Portrait of Hispanics in US, 2006*.

12. See Pew Center *Portrait of Hispanics in US, 2006*, table 5; and Lowell, p. 136.

13. Woodrow Wilson International Center for Scholars Mexico Institute, *The United States and Mexico: Towards A Strategic Partnership*, (Washington, D.C., January 2009), see the table on p. 43.

14. German Marshall Fund, *Transatlantic Trends: Immigration* (Washington, D.C., 2008) See http://www.transatlantictrends.org/trends.

15. Ruy Teixeira, "What Does the Public Want on Immigration?" The Century Foundation, April 5, 2006.

16. Zogby Poll in *Newsweek International*, March 27, 2006.

17. Ekos, *Wave 1: Surveys of the General Public in Canada and the United States: Part of the Re-thinking North America Study* (Ottawa: Ekos, December 2006).

18. Cited in Pastor and Castaeñda, *Limits to Friendship*, p. 357.

19. Joseph Contreras, *In the Shadow of the Giant: The Americanization of Modern Mexico* (New Brunswick, N.J.: Rutgers University Press, 2009).

20. For a summary of these steps, see John Fonte, *Dual Allegiance: A Challenge to Immigration Reform and Patriotic Assimilation* (Washington, D.C.: Center for Immigration Studies, November 2005). Fonte is critical of the Mexican approach and argues that "dual nationality" is a threat to the integrity of the United States.

21. Joseph Contreras, *In the Shadow of the Giant*.

22. Interview with Dr. Remedios Gomez-Arnau, San Diego, October 6, 2008.
23. Alducin y Asociados, "Emigracion de Mexico a Estados Unidos y Monto de las Remesas." (Mexico, D.F., May 2003), p. 17. The national sample was 5,065.
24. Christopher Sands e-mail to Robert Pastor, July 21, 2010.
25. Rakesh Kochhar, "Survey of Mexican Migrants: The Economic Transition to America." (Washington, D.C.: Pew Hispanic Center, December 6, 2005.)
26. *Immigration and America's Future: A New Chapter: Report of the Independent Task Force*, Co-Chaired by Spencer Abraham and Lee H. Hamilton (Washington, D.C.: Migration Policy Institute, 2006), p. 13.
27. International Labour Organization, *Key Indicators of the Labour Market Programme*, 5th edition (September 2007): available at http://www.ilo/pubic/english/employment/strat/kilm/index.htm
28. John Burstein, *U.S.-Mexico Agricultural Trade and Rural Poverty in Mexico, Report from a Task Force of the Woodrow Wilson Center's Mexico Institute* (Washington, D.C., April 13, 2007), pp. 1–13.
29. TradeStats Express, *Product Profiles of U.S. Merchandise Trade with Mexico*, July 21, 2010.
30. Interview with Alicia Bon Martin, Nogales, Mexico, February 14, 2008 and February 16, 2009.
31. Edgar Aragon, Anne Fouquet, and Marcia Campos, *The Emergence of Successful Export Activities in Mexico: Three Case Studies* (Washington, D.C.: Inter-American Development Bank, February 2009), pp. 1–48. This case study was supplemented by Wikipedia's entries on avocados.
32. Leonardo Martinez-Diaz, "Latin America: Coming of Age," *World Policy Journal* (2008), p. 224.
33. UNCTAD, *World Investment Report 2006*. Bureau of Economic Analysis, *Balance of Payments and Direct Investment Position Data: U.S. Direct Investment Abroad.* OECD, *International Direct Investment Statistics*. Statistics Canada, Table 376–0051: International Investment Position. Available at http://www.statcan.ca.
34. Julie Schmir, "Canadians' Home-Buying Power Weakens in USA," *USA Today*, November 7, 2008.
35. Pankaj Ghemawat, *Redefining Global Strategy: Crossing Borders in a World Where Differences Still Matter* (Boston: Harvard Business School, 2007), pp. 34–35. Thomas L. Friedman, *The World Is Flat: A Brief History of the 21st Century* (N.Y.: Farrar, Straus and Giroux, 2006).
36. Alan Rugman and Chang H. Oh, "Friedman's Follies: Insights on the Globalization/Regionalization Debate," *Business and Politics*, Vol. 10, No. 2 (2008), pp. 6–13. The other companies did not have geographically based data available.
37. Pankaj Chemawat, "The Globalization of CEMEX." (Boston, Mass.: Harvard Business School, November 29, 2004.)
38. Andrea Mandel-Campbell, *Why Mexicans Don't Drink Molson: Rescuing Canadian Business From the Suds of Global Obscurity* (Vancouver and Toronto: Douglas and McIntyre, 2007), pp. 2–5.
39. Interview with Tony Vortola, Manager of Jeld-Wen, Nogales, Mexico, February 15, 2008.

40. Tina Peng, "Ultimate Outsourcing: Now Mexican Medicine. American companies are building hospitals south of the border to serve refugees from an ailing health-care system," *Newsweek Web Exclusive*, November 19, 2008.

41. Stephen Blank used this figure from Martinrea in a learning module on North American Business.

42. James M. Rubenstein and Thomas Klier, "Restructuring of the Auto Industry: Geographic Implications of Outsourcing," paper presented to Industry Studies Association, May 28–29, 2009, pp. 12, 14. Data on trade is from Trade Stats Express database.

43. Michael Kergin and Birgit Matthiesen, *A New Bridge for Old Allies* (Canadian International Council, Border Issues Report, November 2008), p. 1. www.canadianinternationalcouncil.org

44. Ian Austen, "To the North, Grumbling Over Trade," *New York Times*, August 8, 2009.

45. Joseph M. Dukert, "North American Energy: At Long Last, One Continent." Washington, D.C.: Center for Strategic and International Studies, Occasional Contributions, October 2005, No. 2, pp. 2, 5, 6.

46. Jad Mouawad, "Report Weighs Fallout of Canada's Oil Sands," *New York Times*, May 18, 2009.

47. Rossana Fuentes Berain, *Oil in Mexico: Pozo de Pasiones: The Energy Reform Debate in Mexico* (Washington, D.C.: Woodrow Wilson Center, 2008), p. 4.

48. Meeting with Mexican Secretary of Energy Georgina Kessel, Washington, D.C., April 6, 2009.

49. Author's interview with Victor Clark Alfaro, a Mexican human rights advocate, who monitors the human and drug trafficking issues. Tijuana, Mexico, October 4, 2008.

50. U.S. Department of Justice National Drug Intelligence Center, *National Drug Threat Assessment, 2010*, Product 2010-Q0317–001, pp. 19–20, 36.

51. Department of Homeland Security, *United States-Mexico Bi-National Criminal Proceeds Study*, June 2010. They also estimated that they only seize about 1 percent of that. The U.S. Department of Justice National Drug Intelligence Center, *National Drug Threat Assessment, 2010*, estimated proceeds at $17.2 billion, citing a previous NDIC estimate between 2003–04, p. 47.

52. Randal C. Archibold and Andrew Becker, "Border Agents, Lured by the Other Side," *New York Times*, May 27, 2008.

53. See Vanda Felbab-Brown, *The Violent Drug Market in Mexico and Lessons from Colombia* (Washington, D.C.: Brookings Policy Paper, No. March 12, 2009); and Clare Ribando Seelke, *Mexico-U.S. Relations: Issues for Congress* (Washington, D.C.: Congressional Research Service, Library of Congress, September 2, 2010), p. 6. For the numbers and geographical concentration of the murders through 2010, see Viridiana Rios and David Shirk, *Drug Violence in Mexico: Data and Analysis Through 2010* (San Diego: Transborder Institute, 2011). See Randall C. Archibold, "Mexican Leader's Crime Effort Fails to Advance," *New York Times*, December 17, 2010.

54. The Mexican Embassy placed the violence in context. In March 2009, the rate of violent deaths in Mexico was 10.4 per 100,000 persons, which was 25 percent less than in 1990, 2.5 times lower than in Brazil, 3.6 times lower than in Guatemala, and equivalent to the United States in the early 1990s. More than half the violence occurred in eleven towns (out of 2,492), and one-fifth in a single city, Ciudad Juarez. The government arrested 60,000 organized crime figures, seized 33,454 firearms; confiscated $230 million in cash, 77 tons of cocaine, 445 tons of marijuana, and 584 kilos of heroin. Embassy of Mexico, *Mexico and the Fight Against Drug-Trafficking and Organized Crime: Setting the Record Straight* (Washington, D.C., March 2009).

55. The U.S. Joint Forces Command issued a report on January 14, 2009 that stated: "In terms of worst-case scenarios for the Joint Force and indeed the world, two large and important states bear consideration for a rapid and sudden collapse: Pakistan and Mexico." U.S. Department of Defense Joint Forces Command, *Joint Operating Environment* (Norfolk, Va.: January 14, 2009). For an excellent critique, see Luis Rubio, "Mexico: A Failed State?" (University of Miami, Center for Hemispheric Policy, February 12, 2009).

56. Paul Richter, "Obama Rejects Clinton Comment on Mexico," *Los Angeles Times*, September 10, 2010.

57. Nick Miroff and William Booth, "Mexican Drug Cartels Bring Violence With Them In Move to Central America," *Washington Post*, July 27, 2010, p. 1. The data comes from the UN, FBI, and Mexican sources.

58. U.S. Department of Justice National Drug Intelligence Center, *National Drug Threat Assessment, 2010*, pp. 9–12.

59. Sam Dillon, "Kidnapping in Mexico Sends Shivers Across the Border," *New York Times*, January 4, 2009.

60. Charlie Savage, "Hundreds Held in Drug Raids in 16 States," *New York Times*, June 10, 2010.

61. David Shirk, "Strengthening Mexican State Capacity," Discussion paper for Council on Foreign Relations, July 12, 2010, p. 4.

62. Colby Goodman and Michel Marizco, *U.S. Firearms Trafficking to Mexico: New Data and Insights Illuminate Key Trends and Challenges* (Woodrow Wilson International Center for Scholars Mexico Institute, and University of San Diego Trans-Border Institute, August 2010), pp. 5, 14.

63. Government of Canada, Policy Research Initiative, "Canada-US Relations and the Emergence of Cross-Border Regions," 2006. www.policyresearch.gc.ca

64. Paul Krugman, *Geography and Trade* (Cambridge: MIT Press, 1991).

65. Stephen M. Clarkson, *Does North America Exist? Governing the Continent After NAFTA and 9/11* (Toronto: University of Toronto Press, 2008).

Chapter 5

1. Edward Alden, *The Closing of the American Border: Terrorism, Immigration, and Social Security Since 9/11* (NY: Harper Collins, 2008), pp. 18–21. For this case and similar ones.

2. Data provided by Vincent Bond, Office of Public Affairs, Department of Homeland Security, San Ysidro, California, October 8, 2008. The data covers the fiscal years from 2002–2007. During that time, 29–38 million people entered the United States in cars, and another 7–9 million as pedestrians.

3. Stated in a meeting in early 2005 for the Council on Foreign Relations Task Force on the Future of North America, of which he and I were both co-vice chairs.

4. Edward Alden, *The Closing of the American Border*, p. 42.

5. Thomas H. Kean and Lee H. Hamilton, Co-Chairs, *The National Commission on Terrorist Attacks Upon the United States: The 9/11 Report* (N.Y.: St. Martin Paperbacks, 2004), p. 466.

6. Edward Alden, *The Closing of American Border*, pp. 41–48.

7. That phrase came from a "shared border agreement" negotiated between the U.S. and Canada in 1996. See Department of Foreign Affairs and International Trade, "Canada-U.S. Accord on Our Shared Border" (Ottawa, 1996).

8. I am grateful to David Shirk of the University of San Diego and Rick Van Shoik of Arizona State University for their observations on the effect of the new south-bound strategy of the U.S. Author's conversation, September 29, 2010, Washington, D.C.

9. Doris Meissner and James W. Ziglar, "Why the U.S. Had to Challenge Arizona on Immigration," *Washington Post*, July 22, 2010, p. A19. The authors point out the discrepancy between the visas and the large number of unauthorized migrants, and they suggest more flexibility on determining the numbers of visas to take account changes in the labor market.

10. Jeffrey S. Passel and D'Vera Cohn, "U.S. Unauthorized Immigration Flows Are Down Sharply Since Mid-Decade," Pew Research Center, September 1, 2010, pp. 1–3.

11. Presentation by Raul Benitez-Manaut at the National Defense University Workshop, "Changing Strategic Dynamics in the Caribbean Basin," August 6, 2009; and conversation with author.

12. Tom Ridge, *The Test of Our Times: America Under Siege . . . And How We Can Be Safe Again* (N.Y.: St. Martins Press, 2009). Ridge wrote that Secretary of Defense Donald Rumsfeld "pointed out the need to keep terrorism alive as an issue throughout his tenure as secretary. Terrorism was a legitimate issue, and references to it benefited the administration politically." (p. 234) Ridge also described a conference call on the eve of the election when Rumsfeld and Ashcroft argued to raise the threat level. Ridge said there was no justification for doing so and thought to himself: "Is this about security or politics? Post-election analysis demonstrated a significant increase in the president's approval rating in the days after the raising of the threat level." (pp. 236–37)

13. Michael Hoefer, Nancy Rytina, and Bryan C. Baker, "Estimates of the Unauthorized Immigrant Population Residing in the United States: January 2007," Department of Homeland Security, Office of Immigration Statistics, September 2008; "Remarks by Homeland Security Secretary Michael Chertoff on the State of Immigration," October 23, 2008. http://www.dhs.gov/xnews/speeches/sp_1224803933474.shtm; Jeffrey S. Passel and D'Vera Cohn, "Unauthorized Population: National and State Trends," Pew Research Center, January 2011.

14. For the increase in numbers of personnel under Bush, see "Remarks by Homeland Security Secretary Michael Chertoff on the State of Immigration," October 23, 2008. For the update under Obama, see Peter Schrag, "Why Strengthening the U.S.-Mexican Border Leads to More Illegal Immigration," *Washington Post*, July 18, 2010, p. B4.

15. See Department of Homeland Security, Office of Inspector General, "Review of CPB Actions Taken to Intercept Suspected Terrorists at US Ports of Entry," OIG-06–43, June 2006.

16. NEXUS—(May 2010); Fact sheet: http://www.cbp.gov/linkhandler/cgov/ newsroom/ fact_sheets/travel/nexus/nexus_fact.ctt/nexus_fact.pdf; SENTRI (September 2008), Fact sheet: http://www.cbp.gov/linkhandler/cgov/newsroom/ fact_sheets/travel/sentri/sentri_fact.ctt/sentri_fact.pdf

17. Interview with Ms. Louis Yako, Langley, British Columbia, Canada, June 4, 2008. She provided details on the costs of complying with 12 different requirements, including C-TPAT Training: $9,000; FAST Cards: $15,000; Customs Brokers/ Docs, Trade Act, FDA Prior Notice: $400,000; Border crossing fees + Annual Decal Costs + APHIS Fees: $250,000; ACE Declaration Costs + ACE EDI Costs: $150,000; and additional Conveyance & Trailer Inspection: $160,000.

18. The Canadian Chamber of Commerce, *Finding the Balance: Reducing Border Costs While Strengthening Security*, February 2008, p. 7.

19. Susan I. Bradbury and Daniel Turbeville III, "Are Enhanced Trade and Enhanced Security Mutually Exclusive?" *American Review of Canadian Studies*, vol. 38, 3 (November 2009), pp. 331–32.

20. The Canadian Chamber of Commerce, *Finding the Balance: Reducing Border Costs While Strengthening Security*, February 2008, p. 11.

21. Department of Foreign Affairs and International Trade, *NAFTA@10: A Preliminary Report*, October 2003, pp. 55–57. http://www.international.gc.ca/economist-economiste/analysis-analyse/research-recherche/10_pre.aspx?lang=eng#prin

22. Cited by Juan Carlos Villa, *Transaction Costs in the Transportation Sector and Infrastructure in North America: Exploring Harmonization of Standards* (Washington, D.C.: Center for North American Studies at American University and UN Economic Commission for Latin America, April 2007), p. 30.

23. Dr. Hart Hodges, "Explaining the Decline in Border Crossings Since 1990," Research Note, February 2, 2006, Western Washington University Border Policy Research Institute. See http://www.wwu.edu/depts/bpri/files/2006_Feb_ Research_Notes_HodgesNote_pub.pdf

24. Steven Globerman and Paul Storer, *The Impacts of 9/11 on Canada-US Trade* (Bellingham, Washington: Border Policy Research Institute of Western Washington University, July 2006) pp. 1–11. Michael Burt of the Conference Board wrote that he did "not find evidence of a significant shift in trade volumes since 9/11" or "that tighter security measures after 9/11 had a significant impact" on trade, but he drew that conclusion because trade grew. Globerman and Storer projected the rate of growth without 9/11 and demonstrated that it was less than would have been the case, so the two studies were not inconsistent. The Conference Board of Canada,

Tighter Border Security and Its Effect on Canadian Exports, report by Michael Burt (Canada, 2007), p. 13.

25. A summary of this study and several others can be found in HDR, *Imperial Valley-Mexicali Economic Delay Study: Final Report*, November 19, 2007, pp. 22–28.

26. John C. Taylor, Douglas Robideaux, and George C. Jackson, *The U.S.-Canada Border: Cost Impacts, Causes, and Short to Long-Term Management Options*, for the Michigan Department of Transportation, the U.S. Department of Transportation, and the New York State Department of Transportation, May 21, 2003, p. 2.

27. The average U.S. tariff rate on Mexican imports before NAFTA came into effect was 2 percent. See Daniel F. Lederman, William F. Maloney, and Luis Serven, *Lessons from NAFTA for Latin America and the Caribbean* (Washington, D.C.: World Bank and Stanford University Press, 2005), p. 3.

28. North America Steel Trade Committee (NASTC), "The Border Story—A North American Steel Industry Perspective," February 2008, pp. 5–6. See: http://www.nastc.org/border_story_feb_2008.pdf

29. The report was done in July 2005 by the Coalition for Secure and Trade-Efficient Borders. See Paul Viera, "Border: A Mess in Business," *National Post*, July 26, 2005.

30. El Colegio de la Frontera Norte, *U.S.-Mexico Ports of Entry: A Capacity Analysis and Recommendations for Increased Efficiency: Executive Summary* (Tijuana, Baja California, December 19, 2007).

31. Ibid., p. 13. The financial losses totaled $7.5 billion and the remainder reflects estimated costs to the environment.

32. U.S. Government Accountability Office, *Border Security: CBP Lacks the Data Needed to Assess the FAST Program at U.S. Northern Border Ports* (Washington, D.C.: GAO-10-694, July 2010), pp. 13, 40.

33. See http://www.cbsa-astc.gc/general/times/menu-e.html

34. The Conference Board of Canada, *Reaching a Tipping Point? Effects of Post-9/11 Border Security on Canada's Trade and Investment* (Danielle Goldfarb), 2007, p. 5. Also, "Is Just-in-Case Replacing Just-in-time? How Cross-Border Trading Behavior Has Changed Since 9/11." June 2007.

35. Karlyn Bowman and Frank Graves, "One Issue, Two Voices: Threat Perceptions in the United States and Canada," Woodrow Wilson International Center for Scholars, Issue October 4, 2005, see graph on p. 11. Also for Mexican, Canadian, and American threat perceptions, see Ekos, *Wave 1; General Public Survey in Canada, the U.S., and Mexico* (2005), tables on pp. 16–25.

36. Innovative Research Group, Inc., *2008 Annual Ottawa Conference Poll: Canada and the United States: What Does It Mean to be Good Neighbours*, Toronto, Canada, Fall 2008, p. 6.

37. For the definition and analysis of cabotage in North America, see Christine Drennen, "Trucking Services Under NAFTA," in Alan M. Rugman, ed., *North American Economic and Financial Integration* (Berkeley: Elsevier, Inc., 2004), pp. 265, 281.

38. Todd Drennan, "Where the Action's At: The U.S.-Mexican Border," U.S. Department of Agriculture. FAS online. www.fas.usda.gov/info/agexporter/1999/wherethe.html

39. Embassy of Mexico in Washington, "U.S.-Mexico Cross-Border Trucking Demonstration Program: Fact Sheet," October 2007.

40. Cited by Juan Carlos Villa, *Transaction Costs in the Transportation Sector and Infrastructure in North America: Exploring Harmonization of Standards* (Washington, D.C.: Center for North American Studies at American University and UN Economic Commission for Latin America, April 2007), p. 32.

41. Justin Carretta, "Cross-Border Program Extended Two Years," *Fleet Owner*, August 5, 2008. This article noted that the American Trucking Association, Caterpillar, and the National Association of Manufacturers were among sixty-nine organizations that supported the program.

42. "U.S. Truck Decision Hurts 26,000 Jobs," www.latinbusinesschronicle.com, April 8, 2009; "Restore and Expand Mexico Truck Program," by James M. Roberts, www.latinbusinesschronicle.com, March 24, 2009.

43. "Statement from the Mexican Embassy," Washington, D.C., August 16, 2010.

44. Val Meredith, *Trade Corridors Report: A Report to the Canada-US Inter-Parliamentary Group* (Ottawa: House of Commons, May 2000), p. 7.

45. "Northeast Blackout of 2003," Wikipedia.

46. Eric Kelderman, "The State of the Union-Crumbling," *The State of the States Report, 2008*, pp. 40–44, www.stateline.org. The U.S. ranked 6th in the World Economic Forum's score on quality of infrastructure; Canada was 8th, and Mexico was 64th of 125 countries.

47. Raul Rodriguez Barocio, Director Gerente de NADBank, *"NADBank: Desarrollo de Infraestructura básica en la Frontera Norte,"* 13 de Enero 2005, p. 15.

48. Marcelo Guigale, Olivier Lafourcade, and Ninh H. Nguyen, eds., *Mexico: A Comprehensive Development Agenda for the New Era* (Washington, D.C.: World Bank, 2001), pp. 2, 10–11, 357–76.

49. Western Provincial Transportation Ministers Council, Western Canada Transportation Infrastructure Strategy for an Economic Network, March 2005, cited by Stephen Blank, Graham Parsons, Juan Carlos Villa, "Freight Transportation Infrastructure Policies in Canada, Mexico, and the U.S.: An Overview and Analysis," Working Paper No. 5, Arizona State University North American Center for Transborder Studies, March 2008, pp. 8–9.

50. "Message to the Nation from the President of Mexico," Felipe Calderon Hinojosa, on his first State of the Nation Report, September 2, 2007, p. 15. Secretario de Communicaciones y Transportes, *National Program of Infrastructure, 2007–12*.

51. Blank, et. al., "Freight Transportation Infrastructure Policies," pp. 12–18.

52. Guy Stanley, "Review of Recent Reports on North American Transportation Infrastructure," Arizona State University North American Center for Transborder Studies, Working Paper No. September 3, 2007, p. 3.

53. David Randolph, "Preparing for the Future Mexican Land Bridge to the United States," Arizona State University North American Center for Transborder Studies, Working Paper No. July 6, 2008.

54. Cited in "Despite Growing Opposition, Homeland Security Stands by its Border Fence," *New York Times*, May 21, 2009, p. A20.

55. Michael Hart, *Trading Up: The Prospect of Greater Regulatory Convergence in North America* (Washington, D.C.: Center for North American Studies at American University and UN Economic Commission for Latin America and the Caribbean, April 2007), p. 8. Hart's work has informed the discussion on regulatory issues in this chapter.

56. Alex Jameson Appiah, *Applied General Equilibrium Model of North American Integration with Rules of Origin*, Doctoral Dissertation for Simon Fraser University, November 1999. Gary Clyde Hufbauer and Jeffrey J. Schott, *NAFTA Revisited: Achievements and Challenges* (Washington, D.C.: Institute for International Economics, 2005), pp. 24, 474–763.

57. Danielle Goldfarb, *The Road to a Canada-U.S. Customs Union: Step-by-Step or in a Single Bound?* (Toronto: C.D. Howe Institute, No. 184, June 2003), pp. 2, 8–13.

58. Olivier Cadot, Jaime de Melo, Antoni Estevadeordal, Akiko Suwa-Eisenmann, and Bolormaa Tumurchudur, *Assessing the Effect of NAFTA's Rules of Origin* (Washington, D.C.: World Bank, 2002). Mexican exports to the United States were $236 billion in 2008.

59. Alex Jameson Appiah, *Applied General Equilibrium Analysis of North American Integration with Rules of Origin*, Ph.D. thesis at Simon Fraser University, 1999.

60. Hart, *Trading Up*, pp. 9–11. On the number of U.S. rules, see James L. Gattuso, "The Rulemaking Process and Unitary Executive Theory," testimony before the House Judiciary Committee, May 6, 2008.

61. NAFTA Land Transportation Standards Subcommittee, Working Group 2, "Harmonization of Vehicle Weight and Dimension Regulations with the NAFTA Partnership," October 1972, photocopy, p. 2. For a table identifying the differences, see Juan Carlos Villa, *Transaction Costs in the Transportation Sector and Infrastructure in North America: Exploring Harmonization of Standards*. Washington, D.C.: Center for North American Studies, American University, August 2007, p. 25.

62. World Trade Organization, *The Importance of Regulatory Cooperation for Improving Governments' Ability to Fulfill Legitimate Policy Objectives while Facilitating Trade, The North American Experience*, Document G/TBT/W/317, June 15, 2009.

63. Michael Hart, *Trading Up: The Prospect of Greater Regulatory Convergence in North America* (Washington, D.C.: Center for North American Studies at American University and UN Economic Commission for Latin America and the Caribbean, April 2007), p. 16.

64. Jeff Davis, "The SPP's Death Knell Has Sounded," *Embassy Magazine* (Canada), August 26, 2009.

65. White House, "Joint Statement by North American Leaders," Guadalajara, August 2009.

66. Data on autos from U.S. Department of Commerce, Office of Trade and Industry Information, U.S. Census Bureau, Trade Statistics Express Database. tse.export.gov. Mexico's auto industry was not hurt as badly as Canada's because it is tied to the more efficient auto industry that shifted to the south of the United States.

The data on the decline of Mexico can be found in an excellent essay on Mexico's economic crisis by Sidney Weintraub, "Mexico's Periodic Bad Times," Center for Strategic and International Studies, No. 115, August 2009.

67. These petitions were introduced in Arizona, Georgia, Montana, and six other southern, western, and plains states, using a model that was developed by the John Birch Society, which published a special edition, "The North American Union Edition," in their journal, *The New American* (October 15, 2007). For a more informed conservative critique on the sovereignty issue, see John Fonte, "Dual Allegiance: A Challenge to Immigration Reform and Patriotic Assimilation," Washington, D.C.: Center for Immigration Studies, November 2005. Fonte writes that greater economic integration and "dual citizenship" is leading ineluctably toward "a weakening of American constitutional sovereignty."

Chapter 6

1. Vicente Fox, interview with the author, February 6, 2008, Washington, D.C.
2. Gary Hufbauer, "CN Trade Relations Forums: The New Obama Administration and the Democratic Congress." (Edmonton, Alberta: Western Centre for Economic Research, University of Alberta, December 11, 2008), p. 4.
3. Robert A. Pastor, ed., "Symposium: Democracy and elections in North America: What Can We learn From Our Neighbors?" published in *Election Law Journal* (2004).
4. Author's interview with Michael Ignatieff, Ottawa, Canada, June 14, 2007.
5. For development of this thesis, see Robert A. Pastor, "The United States: Divided by a Revolutionary Vision," in Pastor, ed., *A Century's Journey*.
6. Comments by Jim Kolbe and Raul Rodriguez at the Conference at the Wilson Center for International Scholars, Washington, D.C., June 2, 2008.
7. Interview with Andres Rozental, April 28, 2009.
8. OECD, http://www.oecd.org/dataoecd/48/34/42459170.pdf; http://www.acdi-cida.gc.ca/mexico; www.acdicida.goc.ca/cida.gc.ca/INET/IMAGES.NSF/vLUImages/stats/$file/CIDA_STATS_REPORT_ON_ODA%202006–07-E.pdf, pp 41.
9. See John Manley and Gordon Giffin, "A Table for Two, Not Three: Canada and the U.S. Share a Special Long-Standing Relationship That Doesn't Include Mexico," *Globe and Mail* (Ottawa), May 5, 2009.
10. Interview with Thomas D'Aquino, Ottawa, October 27, 2008.
11. Palin first applied for a passport in July 2007 in order to visit the Alaska National Guard in Kuwait. Michael Cooper and Elizabeth Bumiller, "McCain Chooses Palin as Running Mate," *New York Times*, August 29, 2008.
12. E-mail from Kim Richard Nossal, September 11, 2008.
13. Stephen Clarkson, *Does North America Exist? Governing the Continent After NAFTA and 9/11* (Toronto: University of Toronto Press, 2008), p. 43.
14. Lee Richardson, Chair, Standing Committee on International Trade of Canada's House of Commons, *Report: An Examination of Selected U.S.-Canada Border Issues*, June 2009.

15. Allan Gottlieb, *"I'll Be with You in a Minute, Mr. Ambassador": The Education of a Canadian Diplomat in Washington* (Toronto: University of Toronto Press, 1991).

16. Victor Landa, "Latinos in Congress, by the Numbers" http://newstaco.com/2011/01/10/latins-in-congess-by-the-numbers/

17. For this section, see Gerardo Esquivel and Fausto Hernandez-Trillo, "How Can Reforms Help Deliver Growth in Mexico?" in Liliana Rojas-Suarez, ed., *Growing Pains in Latin America* (Washington, D.C.: Center for Global Development, 2009), pp. 192–235; Eduardo Zepeda, Timothy A. Wise, and Kevin P. Gallagher, *Rethinking Trade Policy for Development: Lessons from Mexico Under NAFTA* (Washington, D.C.: Carnegie Endowment for International Peace, 2009); and Robert A. Blecker and Gerardo Esquivel, "NAFTA, Trade, and Development," *CESifo Forum, Vol.* 4 (2010), pp. 17–30.

18. Blecker and Esquivel, "NAFTA, Trade, and Development," p. 18.

19. Richardo Hausman, Eilio Lozoya Austin, and Irene Mia, eds., *The Mexico Competitiveness Report, 2009* (World Economic Forum and Harvard University, 2009), p. 12.

20. Author's Interview with John Dickson, Tempe, Arizona, February 13, 2008.

21. I am indebted to former Secretary of State Madeleine Albright for proposing the idea of using the vice president as the principle vehicle for coordination.

22. Author's interview with Ms. Roberta Jacobson, Deputy Assistant Secretary of State for North American Affairs, March 13, 2010.

23. See Chapter 3, Figure 3.8. Ekos, *Survey of Americans; US Wave of the Security Monitor, 2006–7* (July 2007).

24. Richard M. Stana, Director, Homeland Security and Justice Issues, U.S. Government Accountability Office, "Various Issues Led to the Termination of the U.S.-Canada Shared Border Management Pilot Project," GAO-08-1038R, September 4, 2008.

Chapter 7

1. For much more detail on the development challenge and the proposal for a North American Investment Fund, see Robert A. Pastor, "The Solution to North America's Triple Problem: The Case for a North American Investment Fund," *Norteamerica*, Vol. 2, No. 2 (July–December 2007), pp. 185–207, and for more on the European case, see Robert Pastor, ed., *The Paramount Challenge for North America: Closing the Development Gap*, a report for the North American Development Bank (Washington, D.C.: Center for North American Studies at American University, March 14, 2005). [www.american.edu/sis/cnas]

2. Robert A. Pastor, "The Solution to North America's Triple Problem," p. 192.

3. European Union, *EU Budget, 2008: Financial Report* (Luxembourg: Publication Office of the European Union, 2009), pp. 85–89.

4. World Bank, *World Development Indicators & Global Development Finance.* Accessed in October 2010.

5. Sherman Robinson, Samuel Morley, and Carolina Diaz-Bonilla, "Mexico's Development Strategy: What It Takes to Close the Gap," in Robert A. Pastor, ed., *The Paramount Challenge for North America.*

6. Marcelo Guigale, Olivier Lafourcade, and Vinh H. Nguyen, eds., *Mexico: A Comprehensive Development Agenda for the New Era* (Washington, D.C.: World Bank, 2001), pp. 2, 10–11, 357–76.

7. The North American Transportation Competitiveness Research Council, chaired by Stephen Blank and Barry Prentice, and sponsored by Arizona State University's North American Center for Transborder Studies has produced the best research on the problems, needs, and proposals in this area.

8. Maria Luisa O'Connell, "Border Infrastructure and Resources," 2008. See: http://thebta.org/content/wp-content/uploads/2008/10/mlobir21presentation.pdf

9. Blank and Prentice, p. 9.

10. Earl H. Fry, "Canada's Economic Relations with the United States," *Policy Options* (April 2009), p. 35.

11. Danielle Goldfarb, *The Road to a Canada-U.S. Customs Union: Step-by-Step or in a Single Bound?* (Toronto: C.D. Howe Institute, No. 184, June 2003), pp. 2, 8–13; Alex Jameson Appiah, *Applied General Equilibrium Analysis of North American Integration with Rules of Origin*, Ph.D. thesis at Simon Fraser University, 1999.

12. Hufbauer and Schott propose a new NAFTA provision that would remove rules-of-origin provisions when 90 percent of all three countries' tariff levels fall within 1 percent of the average. This would encourage the reduction of tariffs to the lowest levels. To make this politically feasible, they propose exemptions for certain agricultural products (dairy, field crops, cattle) and some specialized industrial products and textile and apparel. A "snap-back" provision could deter violations of the agreement. Hufbauer and Schott, pp. 475–76.

13. Several Canadians have studied the challenge of negotiating a customs union, and their reports are quite useful. See Bill Dymond and Michael Hart, *Policy Implications of a Canada-U.S. Customs Union* (Ottawa: The Centre for Trade Policy and Law, June 2005); Axel Huelsemeyer, *Toward Deeper North American Integration: A Customs Union?* (Orono, Maine: University of Maine Canadian-American Center, October 2004); and Danielle Goldfarb, *The Road to a Canada-U.S. Customs Union*.

14. Michael Hart, *Trading Up: the Prospect of Greater Regulatory Convergence in North America* (Washington, D.C.: Center for North American Studies at American University and UN Economic Commission for Latin America and the Caribbean, April 2007), p. 17.

15. Hart, *Trading Up*, p. 13.

16. I am grateful to Luis de la Calle for developing this proposal for Mexico and for Jennifer Jeffs for suggesting that it would also work for Canada.

17. U.S. Government Accountability Office, *Merida Initiative* (GAO-10-837, July 2010), pp. 6, 22, 14.

18. *Drugs and Democracy: Toward a Paradigm Shift, Statement by the Latin American Commission on Drugs and Democracy*, 2009. See www.drugsanddemocracy.org

19. Gary Fields, "White House Czar Calls for End to 'War on Drugs,'" *Wall Street Journal*, May 14, 2009.

20. Tim Weiner and Ginger Thompson, "U.S. Guns Smuggled into Mexico Feed Drug War," *New York Times*, May 19, 2001, p. A3.

21. U.S. Government Accountability Office, *Firearms Trafficking: US Efforts to Combat Arms Trafficking to Mexico Face Planning and Coordination Challenges*, GAO-09-709, June 2009.

22. Colby Goodman and Michel Marizco, *U.S. Firearms Trafficking to Mexico: New Data and Insights Illuminate Key Trends and Challenges* (Woodrow Wilson International Center for Scholars Mexico Institute and University of San Diego Trans-Border Institute, August 2010), p. 15. David Ignatius, "The U.S. Gun Lobby Holds Mexico Hostage," *Washington Post*, August 1, 2010.

23. Jonathan Kent, "The IBETs and Integrated Border Management Between Canada and the United States," *SITREP: The Journal of the Royal Canadian Military Institute*, 68, 2 (March–April 2008), pp. 5–10.

24. U.S. and Canadian officials inspect containers in several third country ports but not in the three countries of North America.

25. Many of these recommendations are adapted from the Council on Foreign Relations, *Building a North American Community*, Independent Task Force Report No. 53, 2005. I was co-chair of the Task Force and helped draft the report. See pp. 8–9. [Hereafter CFR, North America (2005)]

26. See Tova Andrea Wang, "The Debate over a North American Security Perimeter," (Washington, D.C.: The Century Foundation Homeland Security Project, n.d.).

27. Ekos, *Rethinking North America, November 2006 Surveys of the General Public in Canada and the United States*.

28. Cited in CFR, North America (2005), p. 11.

29. Centro de Investigacion y Docencia Economicas (CIDE), *Mexico, The Americas, and the World* (Mexico City, December 2008), pp. 57–58.

30. John M. Broder, "From a Theory to a Consensus on Emissions," *New York Times*, May 17, 2009.

31. For a description of the potential for North American cooperation in non-carbon energy technologies, see Duncan Wood, *Environment, Development, and Growth: U.S.-Mexican Cooperation in Renewable Energies* (Washington, D.C.: Woodrow Wilson International Center for Scholars, Mexico Institute, May 2000).

32. I am indebted to Maria Isabel Studer for her insights and knowledge on the subject. See also Jeffrey J. Schott and Meera Fickling, "Setting the NAFTA Agenda on Climate Change," Peterson Institute for International Economics, No. PB09-18, Policy Brief, August 2009.

33. Brian Knowlton, "Obama Administration Has No Plans to Reopen Talks on NAFTA," *New York Times*, April 21, 2009.

34. Of the eight legally binding ILO conventions, the U.S. has ratified only two: one on the abolition of forced labor and one on the elimination of the "worst forms" of child labor. The reason is that many labor laws are made by states, and the Senate has been reluctant for reasons of federalism to ratify such international agreements. See "Global Trade, Jobs, and Labor Standards," Center for Global Development, 2004, p. 4.

35. Steve Charnowitz, "The Labor Dimension of the Emerging Free Trade Area of the Americas," in Philip Alston, ed., *Labor Rights as Human Rights* (Oxford,

England: Oxford University Press, 2005), pp. 155–56. Charnowitz is critical of NAFTA's weakness on labor issues but also writes: "Using a labor treaty to achieve common national objectives on labor would seem to be a more straightforward path than using a trade treaty." (p. 169)

36. I am indebted to Jennifer Jeffs for these suggestions to promote the North American Idea by promoting music, film, and sports events.

37. Rebecca Slocum, "Rethinking Hazardous Waste Under NAFTA," Center for International Policy, The Americas Program, August 10, 2009. See http://americas.irc-online.org

38. See White House Office of the Press Secretary, "Joint Statement by North American Leaders," Guadalajara, Mexico, August 10, 2009. www.whitehouse.gov. For other suggestions, see Robert A. Pastor, "Mexico Summit Must Be More than Photo-Op," The Miami Herald, August 9, 2009; and Greg Anderson and Christopher Sands, "The Summit Pandemic: Do Leaders meet too much, and should North American-centered meetings be the first to go?" The Edmonton Journal, August 9, 2009.

39. CFR, North America (2005), p. 31.

40. Joseph A. McKinney, Created from NAFTA: The Structure, Function, and Significance of the Treaty's Related Institutions (Armonk, N.Y.: M. E. Sharpe, 2000), p. 25.

41. These proposals were offered by Raul Rodriguez, previous president of the NADBank, and were incorporated in the CFR, North America (2005), pp. 14–15.

42. Louis Belanger, "NAFTA: An Unsustainable Institutional Design," in Gordon Mace, Jean-Philippe Therien, and Paul Haslam, eds., Governing the Americas: Assessing Multilateral Institutions (Boulder, Colorado: Lynne Rienner, 2007), p. 205.

43. Elliot J. Feldman, "NAFTA Chapters 11, 19, and 20: Time to Start Over," address to the Canada-United States Law Institute, Case Western Reserve University, 2009 Annual Conference, p. 2.

44. Hufbauer and Schott, NAFTA Revisited, p. 477.

45. Stephen Clarkson, Does North America Exist? Governing the Continent after 9/11 (Toronto and Washington, D.C.: University of Toronto Press and Woodrow Wilson Center Press, 2009), pp. 455, 471.

46. Office of Management and Budget, Historical Budget Tables of the U.S. Government (Fiscal Year 2011), Table 4.1, "Outlays by Agency," pp. 82–83.

47. Dana Priest and William M. Arkin, "A Hidden World, Growing Beyond Control," Washington Post, July 19, 2010, p. 1.

48. U.N Economic Commission for Latin America and the Caribbean, Preliminary Overview of the Economies of Latin America and the Caribbean, 2010 (N.Y.: United Nations, December 2010), Chapter on Mexico, pp. 1–3. For U.S. exports to Mexico, see Table 2, Appendix, and for exports to China and India, see Trade Stats Express, National Trade Data, "Top 25 US Trading Partners, 2009" This does not include services. US export of services to Mexico in 2009 was $22 billion, substantially higher than to China.

49. For a detailed summary and analysis of the estimates of the cost of both wars by the Congressional Budget Office and other institutions, see Amy Belasco, *The Cost of Iraq, Afghanistan, and Other Global War on Terror Operations Since 9/11* (Washington, D.C.: Congressional Research Service, September 2, 2010).

50. Cited in Ethan Bronner, "Amos Oz, Approaching 70, Sees Israel With a Bird's Eye View," *New York Times*, April 13, 2009, pp. C1, 6.

Bibliography on North America

There is an extensive literature on U.S.-Mexican and on U.S.-Canadian relations, but only recently have we seen the emergence and growth of scholarship on the whole of North America. Rather than include references to the two bilateral relationships, let me refer the reader to the bibliographic essays in W. Dirk Raat and Michael M. Brescia's *Mexico and the United States: Ambivalent Vistas*, 4th ed. (Athens, GA: The University of Georgia Press, 2010) and John Thompson and Stephen J. Randall's *Canada and the United States: Ambivalent Allies*, 4th ed. (Athens, GA: The University of Georgia Press, 2008).

On North America, the list below will allow the reader to recognize both the breadth and depth of the new scholarship, but permit me to highlight several of the authors. On the idea of North America, Anthony DePalma's *Here: A Biography of the New American Continent* and Joel Garreau's *Nine Nations of North America* are innovative ways to rethink the continent. On the economic integration of North America, see the work of Gary Hufbauer and Jeffrey Schott and Sidney Weintraub; on trade and regulations, Michael Hart; on the borders, see Edward Alden, Peter Andreas, and Daniel Drache; and on energy, see Isidro Morales.

Abu-Laban, Yasmeen, Radha Jhappan, and François Rocher, eds. *Politics in North America: Redefining Continental Relations* (New York: Boardview Press, 2008).

Alden, Edward. *The Closing of the American Border: Terrorism, Immigration, and Security Since 9/11* (New York: Harper Collins, 2008).

Andreas, Peter, and Thomas J. Biersteker, eds. *The Rebordering of North America: Integration and Exclusion in a New Security Context* (New York: Routledge, 2003).

Appel Molot, Maureen, ed. *Driving Continentally: National Policies and the North American Auto Industry* (Ottawa: Carleton University Press, 1993).

Ayres, Jeffrey M. K, and Laura MacDonald, eds. *Contentious Politics in North America: National Protest and Transnational Collaboration Under Continental Integration* (Basingstoke, UK: Palgrave Macmillan, 2009).

Barlow, Maude, and Bruce Campbell. *Take Back the Nation 2: Meeting the Threat of NAFTA* (Toronto: Key Porter Books, 1993).

Barry, Donald, Mark O. Dickerson, and James D. Gaisford, eds. *Toward a North American Community? Canada, the United States, and Mexico. The Political Economy of Global Interdependence* (Boulder, CO: Westview Press, 1995).

Bayes, Jane H, et. al. *Women, Democracy and Globalization in North America* (Basingstoke, UK: Palgrave Macmillan, 2006).

Bonser, Charles F., ed., *Toward a North American Common Market: Problems and Prospects for a New Economic Community* (Boulder, CO: Westview Press, 1991).

Brescia, Michael M, and John C. Super. *North America: An Introduction* (Toronto: University of Toronto Press, 2009).

Brunelle, Dorval, John N. McDougall, and Jennifer M. Welsh. *The Long-Run Determinants of Deep/Political Canada-U.S. Integration and North American Citizenship* (Montreal: Institute for Research on Public Policy, 2004).

Brunet-Jailly, Emmanuel. *Borderlands: Comparing Border Security in North America and Europe* (Ottawa: University of Ottawa Press, 2007).

Capano, Giliberto and Michael Howlett, eds. *Policy Change in Europe and North America: Policy Drivers and Policy Dynamics* (London: Routledge, 2009).

Chambers, Edward J, and Peter H. Smith, eds. *NAFTA in the New Millennium* (La Jolla, CA: Center for U.S.-Mexican Studies, University of California, San Diego, 2002).

Clarkson, Stephen. *Does North America Exist? Governing the Continent After NAFTA and 9/11* (Toronto: University of Toronto Press and Woodrow Wilson Center, 2008).

Conant, Melvin. *The Long Polar Watch: Canada and the Defense of North America* (New York: Published for the Council on Foreign Relations by Harper, 1962).

Council on Foreign Relations, Canadian Council of Chief Executives, and Consejo Mexicano de Asuntos Internacionales. *Building a North American Community: Report of an Independent Task Force No. 53* (New York: Council on Foreign Relations, 2005).

Corsi, Jerome R. *The Late Great U.S.A: NAFTA, the North American Union, and the Threat of a Coming Merger with Mexico and Canada* (New York: Threshold Editions, 2009).

Courchene, Thomas J. *FTA at 15, NAFTA at 10: A Canadian Perspective on North American Integration* (Montreal: Institute for Research on Public Policy, 2004).

DePalma, Anthony. *Here: A Biography of the New American Continent* (New York: PublicAffairs, 2001).

Diez, Jordi, ed. *Canadian and Mexican Security in the New North America: Challenges and Prospects* (Montreal: McGill-Queen's University Press, 2006).

Doran, Charles F. and Alvin Paul Drischler, eds. *A New North America: Cooperation and Enhanced Interdependence* (Westport, CT: Praeger, 1996).

Drache, Daniel, ed. *Big Picture Realities: Canada and Mexico at the Crossroads* (Waterloo, Ontario: Wilfred Laurier University Press, 2008).

———. *Borders Matter: Homeland Security and the Search for North America* (Halifax, NS: Fernwood, 2004).

Earle, Robert L. and John D. Wirth, eds. *Identities in North America: The Search for Community* (Stanford, CA: Stanford University Press, 1995).

Fergusson, Michelle L., ed. *Economic, Political, and Social Issues of North America* (Hauppauge, NY: Nova Science Publishers, 2010).

Flannery, Tim F. *The Eternal Frontier: An Ecological History of North America and Its Peoples* (New York: Atlantic Monthly Press, 2001).

Garreau, Joel. *The Nine Nations of North America* (Boston: Houghton Mifflin, 1981).

Grayson, George W. *The North American Free Trade Agreement: Regional Community and the New World Order* (Lanham, MD: University Press of America, 1995).

Grinspun, Ricardo and Maxwell A. Cameron, eds. *The Political Economy of North American Free Trade* (New York: St. Martin's Press, 1993).

Haines, Michael R. and Richard H. Steckel, eds. *A Population History of North America* (Cambridge, UK: Cambridge University Press, 2000).

Hakim, Peter, and Robert E. Litan, eds. *The Future of North American Integration: Beyond NAFTA* (Washington, D.C.: Brookings Institution Press, 2002).

Hart, Michael. *A North American Free Trade Agreement: The Strategic Implications for Canada* (Ottawa: Centre for Trade Policy and Law, 1990).

Helleiner, Eric. *Towards North American Monetary Union?: The Politics and History of Canada's Exchange Rate Regime* (Montreal: McGill-Queen's University Press, 2006).

Hoberg, George, ed. *Capacity for Choice: Canada in a New North America* (Toronto: University of Toronto Press, 2001).

Huelsemeyer, Axel. *Toward Deeper North American Integration: A Customs Union?* (Orono, ME: Canadian-American Center, University of Maine, 2004).

Hufbauer, Gary C. and Jeffrey J. Schott. *NAFTA Revisited: Achievements and Challenges* (Washington, D.C.: Institute for International Economics, 2005).

Hussain, Imtiaz, ed. *Community, Diffusion, and North American Expansiveness: The Political Economy of Flux* (Mexico City, D.F.: Universidad Iberoamericana, 2008).

Inglehart, Ronald, Neil Nevitte, and Miguel Basañez. *North American Trajectory: Trade, Politics and Values* (New York: Aldyne de Gruyter, 1996).

Jackson, Robert J., Gregory S. Mahler, Holly Teeters-Reynolds, and Carl C. Hodge. *North American Politics: Canada, USA, and Mexico in a Comparative Perspective* (Toronto: Pearson Education, 2004).

Lustig, Nora, Barry Bosworth, and Robert Z. Lawrence, eds. *North American Free Trade: Assessing the Impact* (Washington, D.C.: Brookings Institution, 1992).

MacDonald, James A. *The North American Idea* (New York: F.H. Revell Company, 1917).

Mace, Gordon, ed. *Regionalism and the State: NAFTA and Foreign Policy Convergence* (Aldershot, UK: Ashgate, 2007).

Markell, David L., and John H. Knox, eds. *Greening NAFTA: The North American Commission for Environmental Cooperation* (Stanford, CA: Stanford Law and Politics, 2003).

Martin, Philip. *Bordering on Control: Combating Irregular Migration in North America and Europe* (Geneva, Switzerland: International Organization for Migration, 2003).

Mayer, Frederick W. *Interpreting NAFTA: The Science and Art of Political Analysis* (New York: Columbia University Press, 1998).

McKinney, Joseph A. *Created from NAFTA: The Structure, Function, and Significance of the Treaty's Related Institutions* (London: M.E. Sharpe, 2000).

Mitchell, Robert D. and Paul A. Groves, eds. *North America: The Historical Geography of a Changing Continent* (Totowa, NJ: Rowman & Littlefield, 1987).

Morales, Isidro. *Post-NAFTA North America: Reshaping the Economic and Political Governance of a Changing Region* (New York: Palgrave Macmillan, 2008).

Nevaer, Louis E.V. *NAFTA's Second Decade: Assessing Opportunities in the Mexican and Canadian Markets* (Mason, OH: Thomson South-Western, 2004).

Oropeza Garcia, Arturo, ed. *America del Norte En el Siglo XXI* (Mexico City, D.F.: Universidad Autonoma de Mexico/Instituto de Investigaciones Juridicas, 2010).

Pastor, Robert A., ed. *The Paramount Challenge for North America: Closing the Development Gap*, a report for the North American Development Bank (Washington, D.C.: Center for North American Studies at American University, March 14, 2005).

———, ed. "Democracy and Elections in North America: What Can We Learn From Our Neighbors?" Special Issue of *Election Law Journal* (2004).

———. *Toward a North American Community: Lessons from the Old World for the New* (Washington, D.C.: Institute for International Economics, 2001).

———. *The Controversial Pivot: The U.S. Congress and North America* (Washington, D.C.: Brookings Institution Press, 1998). Co-edited with Rafael Fernandez de Castro.

Peschard-Sverdrup, Armand, ed. *The Future of North America, 2025: Outlook and Recommendations* (Washington, D.C.: Center for Strategic and International Studies, 2008).

Rugman, Alan M., ed. *North American Economic and Financial Intetegration* (New York: Elsevier, 2004).

Rosenberg, Jerry Martin. *The New American Community: A Response to the European and Asian Economic Challenge* (New York: Praeger, 1992).

———. *Encyclopedia of the North American Free Trade Agreement, the New American Community, and Latin-American Trade* (Westport, CT: Greenwood Press, 1995).

Schwanen, Daniel. *Deeper, Broader: A Roadmap for a Treaty of North America* (Montreal: Institute for Research on Public Policy, 2004).

Studer, Isabel. *Ford and the Global Strategies of Multinationals: The North American Auto Industry* (New York: Routledge, 2002).

Studer, Isabel and Carol Wise, eds. *Requiem or Revival: The Promise of North American Integration* (Washington, D.C.: Brookings Institution, 2007).

Thomas, Kenneth P. *Competing for Capital: Europe and North America in a Global Era* (Washington, D.C.: Georgetown University Press, 2000).

Vaughan, Scott. *Thinking North American Environmental Management* (Montreal: Institute for Research on Public Policy, 2004).

Ware, Alan, ed. *Democracy and North America* (London: Frank Cass, 1996).

Weintraub, Sidney, ed. *NAFTA's Impact on North America: The First Decade* (Washington, D.C.: Center for Strategic and International Studies, 2004).

Weintraub, Sidney and Christopher Sands, eds. *The North American Auto Industry Under NAFTA* (Washington, D.C.: Center for Strategic and International Studies, 1998).

Index

Page numbers in italics refer to figures and tables.

NAFTA and, 7, 8
national identity, 67
North America
as designer of modern set of institutions
for, 158, 166
nationalist groups against, 76
reluctant to North American idea, 73
strategy toward, 151, 152–153
North American Development Bank and,
195
population
1800–2010, *217t*
projection, 89
provinces' efforts to construct
continentalism, 109
public opinion (*See* Canadians)
refusal to join a trilateral smart border
agreement, 152
regulations, 135
and term North American, 69
trade
merchandise, 1990–2009, *208t*
with Mexico, 18
relative importance, 1990–2009, *213t*
with U.S., 10, 18
U.S. and
adapting American legislation, 146
asymmetry of relation, 6, 150
border agreement, 126
dependence on U.S. market, 138
effect of 9/11 border closure, 115
effect of 2008 financial crisis, 174
importance for the U.S., 6
influence on U.S., 85
"special relationship," 153
uncertainty in relationship with U.S.,
49
Canada Command, 183
Canada-U.S. Free Trade Agreement (1988), 8
Canadian-American Border Trade Alliance
(Lewiston, ME), 110
Canadian Automated Commercial
Information (ACI), 122
Canadian Border Services Agency, 175
Canadian Chamber of Commerce, 122
Canadian International Council, 4
Canadians
on integrated policies, *74f*
on NAFTA, 63

need to distinguish themselves from
Americans, 62
on right to be in the U.S., 93
stereotypes of, 57
support for trilateral free trade
agreements, *63f*
view of Mexico, 60
view of U.S., 59, 62
Canadian-U.S. Inter-Parliamentary Group,
130
carbon emissions, 187, 195
Cardenas, Lázaro, 47, 52
Caribbean, North America and, 184
Carleton University, 194
Carrey, Jim, 85
Carter, Jimmy, 55, 161
Castañeda, Jorge G.
on asymmetry of U.S. and Mexico, 47
Limits to Friendship, 59
and "smart border" agreement, 152
C.D. Howe Institute, 134
CEC. *See* North American Commission for
Environmental Cooperation
Cellucci, Paul, 114
CEMEX, 99–100
Center on U.S.-Mexican Studies, 110
Centers for Disease Control, 3
Centers for North American Studies, 190
Central America, North America and, 184
Champlain, Samuel de, 40
Charnowitz, Steve, 244n35
Chertoff, Michael, 120
Chicago Council on Foreign Relations,
228n6
2004 survey on NAFTA, 64
Chicago Council on Global Affairs, 60,
228n6
Chicago Council on World Affairs, 64–65
China
competition from and slow-down of
NAFTA integration, 26
exports to North America, 132
U.S. trade with, 9, 19
Chretien, Jean
and "cohesion fund," 28
Fox and, 143
refusal to join the North America
Development Bank, 152
at Summit of the Americas, 23